Bread for the Journey

Bread for the Journey

Notes to Those Preparing for Ministry

Thomas W. Currie

Thomas W. Currie

November 27, 2015

RESOURCE *Publications* · Eugene, Oregon

BREAD FOR THE JOURNEY
Notes to Those Preparing for Ministry

Resource Publications
An Imprint of Wipf and Stock Publishers
199 W. 8th Ave., Suite 3
Eugene, OR 97401

www.wipfandstock.com

ISBN 13: 978-1-4982-3185-5

Manufactured in the U.S.A.   08/31/2015

To the students, faculty, staff, and friends who helped bring the
Charlotte campus of Union Presbyterian Seminary into being,
and with whom it was a privilege to serve.

Contents

Acknowledgements

In writing these weekly notes over 13 years, I was aided by my colleague in the dean's office, Mrs. Terry Johns, who not only kept my schedule and posted helpful reminders to me, but also who collected these notes and made sure they were preserved in one place. For this and many other reasons, I need to acknowledge my indebtedness to her.

There are others I would mention as well. Our faculty and staff would meet regularly on Wednesday mornings for devotionals. Since many of these notes were written on Wednesday afternoons, the witness of those morning devotionals often loomed large in my thinking and writing. I would like to thank my faculty colleagues, Richard Boyce, who is the current dean, and Pamela Mitchell-Legg, Rodney Sadler, and Sue Setzer, as well as staff colleagues, David Mayo, our librarian, Susan Hickok, Nadine Ellsworth-Moran, Susan Griner, Lisa McLennan, Anne Rankowitz, and student participants, Thomas Agbemenou and Kevin Davis.

From the very beginning I received unflagging support from Louis Weeks, who as President of the seminary, invited me to serve as dean, and from Brian Blount, the current President, who was and continues to be a source of encouragement not only to me but to all who are engaged in theological education.

In 2014, the board of trustees granted me a sabbatical during which I was able to put these notes in some form of coherent order. I want to thank them for that extraordinary gift. I spent part of the sabbatical at Westminster College in Cambridge, England, where I was made to feel most welcome by the Principal, Neil Thorogood, and the staff, particularly Syd Harper and her administrative colleagues. My wife and I are deeply indebted to Westminster College for the hospitality we received there, and I particularly want to thank the minister of St. Columba's United Reformed Church, Nigel Uden, for his pastoral care to us during this time and for the preaching and worship that congregation shared with us.

Upon our return, we moved temporarily to Shreveport, Louisiana, where my son, Chris, is pastor of First Presbyterian Church. I want to thank him for providing his father some space to finish this book. In particular, I want to thank Ann Dodson, the church librarian, who was helpful in tracking down certain sources for me.

Introduction

In 2001, the board of what was then Union-PSCE (and now, Union Pres-byterian Seminary), located in Richmond, Virginia, voted to call me to serve as the dean of a proposed extension campus in Charlotte, N. Caro-lina. For 25 years I had been a parish minister of two congregations in Texas, serving each for 12 and a half years. This new campus in Charlotte was intended to serve second-career students, new immigrant popula-tions, and the strong African-American Presbyterian constituency in North and South Carolina. Dr. Billy O. Wireman, who was then presi-dent of Queens University of Charlotte, graciously enabled this fledgling enterprise to nest on that university's lovely Selwyn Avenue campus.

Classes began in February of 2002, and continued on the Queens campus until the fall of 2012, at which time the seminary moved into a new building of its own on land leased from Sharon Presbyterian Church.

Because most of our students were working in full-time or part-time positions and were themselves scattered over a wide swath of North and South Carolina (one or two from Georgia and Tennessee), commut-ing to school at nights or on weekends, the seminary worked hard from the very beginning to put in place ways that a *community* of learning and faithfulness might be established that would contribute to their forma-tion as pastors and teachers. Regular worship, weekly table fellowship, admission by cohort, small group tutoring sessions, and strong adminis-trative support from colleagues in Richmond and Charlotte helped build a vital sense of community that in some ways was more formative and visceral than that known in residential settings.

One of the most important ways the seminary sought to build and maintain a "life together" was through weekly notes from the dean ad-dressed primarily to the students. Many of these notes sought to encour-age those who were undertaking the hard work of preparing for ministry. Often these notes reflected on the even more challenging work of ministry itself, pointing out the peculiar joys and burdens hidden in that form of Christian discipleship. Many of these notes share insights from others who have traveled this way, some of whom articulate the journey poetically, while others describe this path in more strictly theological terms. Sometimes note is taken of specific events within the life of the seminary itself (e.g., a death of a student) or some local or national event (e.g., the Iraq War, school shootings, etc.), or events in the life of the church (e.g., a denominational split or church council decision) in an effort to provide a theological context for reflection. More often, the beginning and ending of terms provided occasions for self-examination, asking again and again what we thought we were doing in studying and preparing for ministry. Some of these notes deal with certain disciplines of the faith like prayer, reading, worship, and learning, - sanctifying gifts that strengthen disciples for this journey. Sometimes the notes are simpler, expressing unapologetically the joy of being alive in God's creation and being called into God's service.

The purpose of these notes from the dean was not simply communication or building community or offering words of encouragement or exhortation. Rather, these notes sought to offer a vision of Christian discipleship that would inspire, and even make one glad that God had called one to walk this particular path. Does that seem too pious or idealistic or happy? Perhaps it does, especially if such inspiration overlooks or ignores the messiness of ministry and the challenges of bearing faithful witness to Jesus Christ today. But neither ministry nor theological education, however rigorously undertaken, is a dreary thing. The task is overwhelming and there is plenty of reason to be discouraged, especially when we look at our own resources. Still, in the witness of both Israel and the church there bursts out, unaccountably, the praise of God and the joy of being called into this work. The psalmist is not reluctant to confess just such joy in being glad to come into the house of the Lord. Jesus is not afraid to speak of a joy that cannot be taken away from those who follow him. Paul sings in, among other places, prison. "Why this juice and joy?" as the poet asks. Indeed. That is the underlying question behind all these notes, the question I hoped our students would engage. Unless one sees the vision and can rejoice in it, theological education and the ministry it seeks to support become exceedingly boring things. The God of Jesus Christ, however, is not boring, and neither is theological education that seeks to serve this God by preparing women and men for ministry. It is the intent of these notes to bear witness to this eternally rich and ever surprising God who calls us all to rejoice and be glad in his service.

Although these notes were written over a period of 13 years, I have not arranged them chronologically but rather according to certain themes or categories. Some of these categories, like ministry itself, overlap. I have also included a homily for entering students in 2010, and a sermon preached before Charlotte Presbytery toward the end of my service at the seminary.

The original audience for these notes was a group of students who were preparing for ministry at Union Presbyterian Seminary's Charlotte campus. The work of ministry possesses its own idiom and seeks to foster its own set of skills and virtues. But since this work is carried out on behalf of the whole church and for the sake of its mission, there is no part of it or its preparation that can be divorced from the joys and challenges of Christian discipleship. That is why these notes may be of interest to pilgrims who are not studying for the ordained ministry but who are facing the same joys and challenges in seeking to live the Christian life. In making these notes available to a wider audience, the dean who first wrote them hopes they will strengthen any who venture on to this path. To employ a theological term often scorned today but worth recovering, these notes seek to serve as an element of sanctification in the lives of those who follow Jesus Christ.

Chapter 1: Beginnings

January 3, 2007

The New Year begins with prayer. One of the forms of prayer which the church has used over time is called a "collect," or more simply, "prayer for the day." Such a prayer is usually a short acknowledgement of God's grace combined with a direct and specific appeal for God's help. One of the collects suggested for New Year's Day reads as follows: "Eternal God, who has brought thy servants to the beginning of another year: Pardon, we humbly beseech thee, our transgressions in the past, and graciously abide with us all the days of our life; through Jesus Christ our Lord. Amen."[1]

We notice right away the "thees" and "thous," the fact that we haven't "beseeched" anyone for some time or used the word "abide" except in a hymn. Still, I invite you to look again at this prayer and what it is asking. It begins by remembering that it is the Lord God who has brought us to this day. We are not here by accident, and certainly not by virtue of our own achievements. No, we are here because the gracious Lord God "has brought thy servants to the beginning of another year." And like most collects, this little prayer contains a blunt and direct demand, basing such not on the urgency or virtues of those praying but on the acknowledged character of that One who graciously invites such claims. "Pardon," the prayer asks. At the beginning of the new year, "pardon us." The new year can only begin with God's grace, and because of that, we are bold and right to pray, at the beginning, "pardon." It is out of God's own gracious forgiveness that we are enabled to begin at all. And the aim of this little prayer is very clear: that God would "graciously abide with us all the days of our life." This is not a prayer for riches or straight "A's" or an untroubled semester but simply a prayer that God "would graciously abide with

---

1. *Proposed Book of Common Prayer, 1928, Church of England, Collect for the New Year.*

us"—than which there is no greater gift, no higher delight—"all the days
of our life."

The prayer concludes with the simple acknowledgement that as the
beginning of this new year belongs to God, so are our endings entrusted
to him. A helpful word to begin a new year and a new term together.

September 4, 2007

Recently I was asked to lead a Bible study on the book of Acts. Theologians are sometimes accused of straying rather far from the biblical text
so this was a good opportunity for me to dig deeply into scripture itself.
One of the treasures I dug up was the discovery of the difference between
"they" and "them" and "we" and "us."

The main character in the book of Acts is the Holy Spirit, who, empowers the early church to flourish and grow in faith through the witness
of various apostles, martyrs, saints, and heroes of the faith. Mostly it is a
story about "them": Peter, Stephen, Phillip, and Paul. But at Acts 16:10
the story shifts. In describing one of the Apostle Paul's journeys, Luke
writes: "When he had seen the vision, we immediately tried to cross over
to Macedonia, being convinced that God had called us to proclaim the
good news to them." A big change. Up until this point, the narrative had
been a story about "they" and "them." But somewhere along the way, that
story became a story about "we" and "us".

I think that this kind of shift is true for every seminarian. For some
time our faith has been a story about "them": our parents, teachers,
pastors, friends, heroes and heroines, near and more distant neighbors
whose witness has been as compelling as it has been somewhat detached.
But at some point in following "their" story, even when we have followed
it only from afar or with more or less growing interest, at some point
we have come to see "their" story as including "us." Not that the story is
about "us" anymore than it is about "them," but that their story engages
"us" in its narrative, sweeping "us" along a river from whose bank we had
formerly been only spectators.

I am thinking particularly of our first-year students, who may have
thought about seminary for a long time or may be only just now dipping
their toes into the water, but who are sensing that the pronouns have begun to change, the winds have shifted, the direction has become less general and more vocational, even specific. The strange thing about all of this

is that when the story becomes "our" story, the landscape becomes more interesting, the path, even in all its difficulty, more clear, the questions more compelling, sharp, and even possessing a curious delight. I don't know about Luke, but I do know that beginning seminary, as scary as such a prospect may seem to some, may also provide an occasion for joy, a rejoicing that is happy to be getting underway, leaving the handwringing and self-analysis behind, and hitting the road. It is a long road with its own challenges, but on this road are "good companions" with whom to walk, and best of all, *the good companion*, who, in breaking bread with us, puts an end to our being a "they" or "them" and enables us to become, in his company, a "we" and an "us."

January 2, 2008

When my wife and I lived in Scotland, we discovered that the Scots reserved most of their winter holiday partying for New Year's, not Christmas. Which is not to say that they did not celebrate Christmas (and even more these days) but only to note that by culture and formation they marked the passing of the old year and the coming of the new with special enthusiasm. It was a Scot (Robert Burns), after all, who gave us the song, "Auld Lang Syne." In any case, "Hogmanay" is what they called the new year celebration, an occasion for much whooping and hollering, imbibing and celebrating that can last most of the night. One of the traditions connected with this event was called, "first-footing," which consisted of being the first to visit friends and neighbors in their homes in the early hours of New Year's Day, that is, any time after 12 midnight. I don't think I could do "first-footing" now but I was younger then and could stay up later. I enjoyed the tradition of being welcomed into a home as one of the first visitors of the "year."

The new year (and the new term!) ought to be welcomed with such generosity, even when the future seems at best uncertain. And the reason for this really has nothing to do with hospitality *per se*, but everything to do with hope.

There are plenty of reasons not to welcome the new year: wars, terrorism, economic dislocations, racial and ethnic conflict, failing health and the ravages of disease, just to name a few. In addition, for a student beginning yet another school term, the mountain to be climbed can look especially daunting. It is tempting to view the beginning of the term as a kind of chore to be completed, a task that can be done, but hardly a gift from God's own hand. Some may even call this kind of resignation "a mature outlook" or even "wisdom."

I have a friend who is dying of ALS, who recently sent me an email. He will not likely see the beginning of 2009. In his note to me he quoted some poetry and asked me some questions dealing with the doctrine of the Trinity and worship, a theme that has occupied his D.Min. studies. Now, I wonder about all of that. What right does he have to be so focused? He did not whine or complain, nor did he seek to appear noble or long-suffering. Rather, he was never more himself, and in the face of his own daily weakening and dying, he was passionately engaged in the praise and service of God. What gives one such blessed "un-self-consciousness," such robust hope? After all, what does my friend have to hope for? He will be dead within the year. Yet he wants to know what faithful worship of the triune God looks like.

The gift of the new year and the new term is that the "first-footing" belongs not to us, but to the God who enters our lives and takes up residence there even in the darkest times. That is why we can welcome the future so gladly, because it too belongs to the God who comes to meet us in our time and who is drawing us into his life "each newborn day." Simply to praise, to offer doxology, strikes me more and more as what both theology and ministry are about. I do not mean that having faith is to lose judgment or to ignore the pain and suffering that are so near. My friend can see all of that quite clearly. But it takes hope and even joy to embrace such judgment and pain and suffering, and not despair of such things or write the world off as a bad job, or worse, become "wise" in our resignation. My friend with his questions was not seeking the wisdom of resignation. Rather, he reminded me of nothing more than a lily. Jesus said something about lilies of the field that neither toil nor spin, and which, like grass, are quite vulnerable to the vicissitudes of time. Yet they simply praise and are beautiful in their praising. We could do worse as we begin this term and new year together.

September 3, 2008

As I write this note a group of entering students is being oriented by our faculty and staff, with the help of some "veteran" students. Getting oriented to seminary is the first of many steps these new students will take together. But in truth, getting oriented is a daily struggle and much larger than any seminary. Augustine described the plight of fallen human beings as one of being "disoriented," that is, of living disordered lives. Our tendency, he maintained, was to love things and use God, when in fact, we are called to love God and use things. To be oriented, or rather, to become re-oriented, is to find our loves rightly ordered in their true orientation toward God. As the Shaker song asserts: "When true simplicity is gained, to bow and to bend we shan't be ashamed, to turn, turn, will be our delight, till by turning, turning we come round right." That is the aim, the hope of all our orientations, that we will be oriented toward our true center so that in all our various turnings, we come round right.

January 7, 2009

In late December, 1944, Dietrich Bonhoeffer wrote a note to his mother in which he thanked her for being "there for me and the whole family" during such a difficult time. At the end of the letter, he expressed the hope that in the coming year, "we may have the joy of being together."[2] It would be beyond presumptuous to compare the troubles of 2008–09 with Bonhoeffer's situation, but as we begin this new year, I believe his words and his life continue to give strength to our own witness in our own day and time.

As we enter 2009, a year full of expectation and hope, but also a year not without its clouds and fears, we do well to hear again Bonhoeffer's words of gratitude, not as words of optimism about the future—after all, scarcely four months after he wrote these words, he was executed—but as words of hope.

Hope is not a carefully calculated assessment of our future prospects but an anchor rooted in the reality of Christ's resurrection. That anchor holds amidst the storms that assail us, even the scary ones that seem dark and frightening. And it is that anchor that makes each new day, even the ones we fear as we begin a new term, a gift.

September 8, 2009

In one of his poems, John Donne writes these words about the nature of ministry:

2. Bonhoeffer, *Letters and Papers from Prison*, 548–550.

What function is so noble, as to be
Ambassador to God and destiny?
To open life, to give kingdoms to more
Than kings give dignities; to keep heaven's door?
Mary's prerogative was to bear Christ, so
'Tis preachers to convey him, for they do
As angels out of clouds, from pulpits speak . . .
How brave are those, who with their engines, can
Bring man to heaven, and heaven again to man.[3]

Well, you say, that is just so much metaphysical poetry, and perhaps not all that theologically perceptive. After all, in the Reformed tradition, ministers are hardly thought of as "angels," nor do they, of themselves, lift up anyone to heaven or bring heaven down to anyone. True. But, like Mary and all faithful disciples, they do "convey" Christ in bearing their own witness, and to that extent, their function is not to be despised. Donne is right that ministry is a noble task, and one whose work should be praised and celebrated, not for the angelic virtues of the minister, but for the beauty and importance of the task.

Karl Barth, in talking about students of theology, writes: "[No] one should study merely in order to pass an examination, to become a pastor, or in order to gain an academic degree. When properly understood, an examination is a friendly conversation of older students of theology with younger ones, concerning certain themes in which they share a common interest . . . . Only by his qualification as a learner can [a person] show himself to become a teacher. Whoever studies theology does so because to study it is (quite apart from any personal aims of the student) necessary, good, and beautiful in relationship to the service to which he has been called."[4]

So we begin, not just with the study of various disciplines, but with the journey of a lifetime, bravely, perhaps also foolishly, entering into a conversation that has been going on long before we dare to enter it. This conversation, I think you will find, can be both daunting and delightful, and will, in any case, stretch us and strengthen us to "convey" a gift more precious than gold. I look forward to beginning with you.

---

3. Donne, *"To Mr. Tillman After He Had Taken Orders" The Complete Poems of John Donne*, 115.

4. Barth, *Evangelical Theology*, 172.

September 7, 2011

In those same lectures which he delivered in America, Barth noted that theological study is not a passing phase of life. The "theologian, if he [or she] was in fact a *studiosus theologiae*, remains so even to his death. (Schleiermacher, it is reported, even in his old age, prefixed his signature at times with the usual German designation '*stud.theol.*')"[5] That is how Barth viewed his own vocation, I believe, and represents, he thought, the most that can be said of anyone who sets out on this course of study. At the end of our life's work, though we may be in a very different place than where we were at the beginning, we will still be students of theology, disciples seeking to follow their Teacher.

Barth was not a particularly modest man or theologian but he knew that in following Jesus Christ one never ceases to be a learner. One always has to ask. And one must never be ashamed of asking or of being a student. Indeed, as Barth's statement implies, one matures and grows in this course of study, precisely to the extent that one learns to ask, struggling with answers that question us and our questions more deeply. To become a student of theology is to learn not to be embarrassed by one's poverty. We are all beggars here.

My favorite time of the day is about 6 a.m. when I set out for my morning run. Really it is more like a jog or a run-walk. I am not a runner and have never been enthusiastic about exercise, but I do like to wake up early and go for a 2.5 mile jog through my neighborhood. The hard part is getting started. Especially, since in our neighborhood there is a steep hill at the very beginning. On cold or inclement days, I find it very hard to get going. But once I do, the going is good and when it's over, I enjoy so much walking back through my neighborhood, "cooling down" while seeing the sun streaming through the trees. The world in that moment seems a beautiful place. It's the getting started that is hard. Like learning to ask questions that may reveal how little I know. Being ashamed of our poverty is something we need to get over. It's time to start running, to start asking, to rejoice in being invited to a great conversation.

5. *Ibid.*, 172.

Chapter 2: Life Together

September 29, 2004

This past week I have had the opportunity to talk with several of you and have become aware yet again, how much we depend on each other for encouragement along the way. I think one can bear a good deal if one senses that one is not alone. For instance, it is somehow encouraging to discover that Hebrew looks weird to other people besides yourself, or that you are not alone in thinking that Augustine's journey of faith can seem at times utterly bizarre, or that reading Calvin or Barth is not without its frustrations and times of bafflement. The way is long and there are many competing obligations and claims that must be addressed. Life has a way of crashing in, most especially when we have finally got everything planned and settled.

Recently, my wife and I went to see the movie *Vanity Fair*, starring Reese Witherspoon. In the movie (and even more in Thackeray's novel), the world is portrayed as a place full of schemes and shrewdness, where those who are wise as serpents regularly triumph over those who are innocent as doves. However, the title comes from a very different book, a book which, not unlike Augustine's *Confessions*, has to do with an individual's journey of faith. John Bunyan's *Pilgrim's Progress* is where "Vanity Fair" makes its first appearance, and there it is not so much about "getting ahead" in a glamorous world as it is about the despair of living in a world where everything is for sale. "Christian" and "Faithful" are beaten in "Vanity Fair" and "Faithful" even dies. The way is hard. Yet the journey, in all of its hardship and struggle, is strangely more satisfying than the endless diversions of "Vanity Fair."

I don't mean by this that those who study here are more virtuous than other people or better than those who hustle for mere money. In my opinion, there is nothing "mere" about money at all. But I do think that studying to become a teacher or pastor in the church is a marvelously liberating gift, precisely in the focus and stringent demands it places on one's life. Thursday nights or Friday nights or all day Saturdays have to be planned around, prepared for, aimed at, all of which describes a course of walking in company together toward a specific destination, living a focused, or rather a "called" life. Such a journey is not characterized by the diversions of "Vanity Fair," but it gives what "Vanity Fair" cannot offer, and what the modern world often holds in contempt: a called life, that is, a life set toward a particular direction. The gift of being directed in accordance with a particular voice is what the faith calls freedom. "Christian" discovered in the company of "Faithful" that we are not made for endless diversions. Endless diversions are finally soul destroying, imprisoning us in comfortable isolation. There are few greater gifts than finding that one is living, in the company of others, a "called" life.

February 16, 2005

When my wife and I lived in Scotland, the announcements given during worship were called, "Intimations," a word which carried with it not only the sense of "announcement" or "making known," but also the sense of speaking to familiar friends of things affecting the whole community. There is a tenderness about "Intimations." Many of these notes I am writing to you contain "intimations" like that, i.e., the description of and concerns with our common life.

The other night when Dr. Wireman spoke to us, I watched little groups of students form after the evening meal, some to talk about what he said, others to cram for Hebrew, others simply enjoying each other's company. Viewing all of that made me realize how much I have come to depend on this community—as scattered and fragmented and weary as we are. I am grateful for these "intimations" which, strangely, give me joy and hope.

January 31, 2007

Our life together, such as it is, is one of the most important things about our fledgling seminary. These words from Dietrich Bonhoeffer's book, *Life Together*, apply therefore also to us, I think: "If we do not give thanks daily for the Christian community in which we have been placed, even where there are no great experiences, no noticeable riches, but much weakness, difficulty, and little faith— and if, on the contrary, we only keep complaining to God that everything is so miserable and insignificant, and does not at all live up to our expectations—then we hinder God from letting our community grow according to the measure and riches that are there for us all in Jesus Christ."[1] Those words are underlined in my copy of *Life Together*. Perhaps I need to hear them more than you. Still they are worth remembering and I commend them to your attention.

October 3, 2007

Before Dietrich Bonhoeffer returned to Germany in 1939, he wrote a little article summarizing his impression of American Protestantism. The article was entitled, "Protestantism Without Reformation." In that article Bonhoeffer expressed skepticism concerning what Americans called "freedom of religion," seeing in the multiple denominations that worship God in their own way, not an example of freedom so much as a flight from the church's confessional nature and its true unity in Christ. He thought that American Protestants were no longer scandalized by their inability to confess and live together and so they celebrated their disunity by calling it "freedom." Bonhoeffer was particularly suspicious of a freedom celebrated by largely white congregations that somehow did not implicate them in the life and worship of largely African American churches. In opposition to what he thought was a false notion of freedom, Bonhoeffer spoke of the "freedom of the Word of God,"[2] a freedom that cuts against the claims we so often idolize, and draws us instead into a peace we have not made, a life together that comes to us as a gift, a baptism in which we find ourselves placed beside those we have not chosen.

This Saturday I have been asked to preach for Coastal Carolina Presbytery. The presbytery asked me to exhort the assembled saints "to pull together." All of which has caused me to think how easy it is and how much better we are at pulling apart. In preparing for this sermon, I was struck with how much of scripture has to do with our "pulling apart": Cain vs. Abel; Jacob vs. Esau; Joseph and his brothers; Saul vs. David. If you want to read a sad story, read 1 Kings 12 and the story of Israel's

---

1. Bonhoeffer, *Life Together*, 37.

2. Bonhoeffer, *"Protestantism Without Reformation"* in *A Testament to Freedom*, 524.

split from Judah. "To your tents, O Israel! Look now to your own house, O David." (1 Kgs 12:16)

In one version or another, that slogan has described the "freedom" which has characterized so much of American Protestantism, and particularly our own denomination (i.e., PCUSA). We are free to . . . split, a freedom that is indistinguishable from divorce or "pursuing my own happiness," or even worshipping the god I choose and find useful. What is more difficult is to worship the God who has chosen us in Jesus Christ, and has done so quite without our permission. In the divine economy of this God's choosing, freedom is manifest in "bearing, believing, and hoping all things." It endures. It is free from that kind of self-absorption that insists on having its own way. It is the freedom Charles Wesley sings about, the gift of being "lost in wonder, love, and praise." This freedom, Paul writes, does not come from our splitting apart but from God's free decision to stick us to Jesus Christ, and in him to each other. That basic unity is what is real, not our splits. Our splitting reflects not our freedom but our enthrallment to death, the last enemy whose intention it is to split us from God and from each other. But, Paul writes that Christ is "our peace," and he has made us one, reconciling us "in one body through the cross." (Eph 2:14–16)

Our real problem is not our much feared and whined about propensity to split apart. No, our problem is that deep down where it really matters, we are already one in Christ. We cannot escape that Christological fact, try as we might. We were baptized into it, and so we have to deal and learn to deal with those whom Christ has given us to love. In Christ, we are stuck with each other. And the amazing thing is that those with whom we are stuck are given to us as gifts—not enemies to be avoided, not objects to be overcome, but gifts. The whole joy of the gospel comes from this very fact: our unity in Christ keeps surprising us with such unwanted, unexpected, and unlikely gifts. Choosing your own god, and even more choosing your own kind, is finally boring as it is deadly. Our freedom in Christ is much more surprising and adventuresome and disturbing than that. And it is also more beautiful.

February 11, 2009

I have always been fascinated by martyrs. I am sure that part of the reason has to do with their courage, and the inevitable question as to whether or not I would be able to face up to such a fate. It is a silly question, asked only by those who have the luxury to consider such eventualities. I suspect that most martyrs of the faith did not worry over much about their martyrdom. Dietrich Bonhoeffer, reportedly, walked to the gallows naked, having prayed, and committed himself to the Lord whom he had sought to serve. Other martyrs had even less time to consider their situation. One thinks of Dr. Martin Luther King, Jr. or Oscar Romero. And, as my mother would be quick to remind me, most martyrs do not have such dramatic and well-publicized ends: the single Mom who raises her children, brings them to church, gets them educated and launched; the pastor who spends his whole life in small, unpromising settings and does so without remorse or regret, happy in the service of God; the woman dying of breast cancer, digging in her garden, planting flowers she will never see and enjoying that day's sunshine. These are martyrs too and quite unromantic ones.

Our suspicion of martyrdom (e.g., "I don't want to be a martyr!" Or, "Don't play the martyr act on me!) is meant to indicate that we can see through the religious language so often used to disguise baser motives. Thinking that we can see through all of that hypocritical piety, we easily convince ourselves that there are no real motives for living faithfully or dying well. Martyrs, however, remind us otherwise, which is why we find them so disturbing.

From the beginning, the Christian faith has made it clear that following Jesus Christ can get you killed, either slowly or sometimes quite suddenly. The strange thing is that when people hear that, it sounds like martyrs must be brave if rather sad people, tragic figures, really, like heroes dying for some lost cause. What is more difficult to convey, however, is the martyr's . . . .what? Good cheer? Confidence? Equanimity? Clarity of mind? Joy?

This morning at devotionals I read the story of Polycarp's death (+155 A.D.). Polycarp was 86 years old when he was burned to death by his Roman persecutors. Given a chance to denounce his Lord and save his life, Polycarp replied to his tormentors, simply, "Eighty-six years I have served him and he never did me any wrong. How can I blaspheme my King who saved me?"[3] Reading Polycarp's story has always put a smile on my face, not because I think I could do something like that or that

---

3. *"The Martyrdom of Saint Polycarp,"* in *Early Church Fathers,* 152.

something like that would be easy, but because there is a hint in his words of a friendly insouciance, a kind of careless dismissal of the threat.

In 1996, Father Christian de Cherge, a French monk living in Algeria, was kidnapped by Islamic terrorists and along with his fellow monks, beheaded. (You can read more about this in the book, *The Monks of Tibhirine* (St. Martin's 2003), a story that has also received cinematic treatment in the movie, *Of Gods and Men*.) In a note to his family, he asked them to pray for the troubled country of Algeria and for the gracious people who lived there. He did not want to become a martyr, and particularly he did not want his Algerian captors to be implicated in his death. His last words were addressed to the one who was poised to behead him. He wrote: "And you also, the friend of my final moment, who would not be aware of what you are doing. Yes, for you also I wish this "thank you"—and this adieu—to commend you to the God whose face I see in yours. And may we find each other, 'happy good thieves' in Paradise, if it please God, the Father of us both. Amen."[4]

Do you hear the same ridiculous note in this testimony, that executioner and executed might both be found to be "happy good thieves" whom Jesus might surprise with his unaccountable grace? As if the moment were but a moment and the drama more encompassing and more mysterious than we can know.

Martyrs should not make us feel guilty or subvert our own witness, however small. I think they are given to us as gifts, in part to bring to vivid life what is at stake in this business of the faith, but also to encourage us, even to make us smile, as old Polycarp's story makes me smile. They also serve to remind us that the Christian life is a life together, a life where others give strength, a life where martyrs make us want to do things we would otherwise never venture.

Maybe that is why we are so quick to disclaim any sense of martyrdom. Their freedom actually scares us. Maybe we should pray to be so free.

March 11, 2009

It's odd how generations just miss one another sometimes. Some of you would know or at least recognize the name, "Sara Little," but others might not recognize that name at all. She had been retired from her work as a

4. Father Christian de Cherge, *"Last Testimony,"* in *First Things*, August/September *1996*, 21.

teacher some time before this seminary in Charlotte got going. She had taught on the Richmond campus of Union Theological Seminary and before that, across the street at Presbyterian School of Christian Education. In any case, hers was a name to be reckoned with. I suspect she was one of the first women to be awarded a PhD from Yale in Christian Education, and I know she was one of the first women to teach at Union in Richmond. She was first in a lot of categories. Her many books had established her reputation as a scholar (above all, her book on teaching, entitled, *To Set One's Heart*, (Westminster John Knox, 1983)). Her reputation in the classroom was legendary.

When I arrived in Charlotte in 2001, I knew her by name and reputation only, though if I had attended PSCE or Union, I daresay I would have had a much more vivid impression. At her memorial service yesterday, I heard a former student and colleague of hers talk about what a gift it was—a scary gift at times—to be in the classroom with Sara Little. I also listened to one of her pastors speak about how intimidated he was to find her in his "New Members Class" at Sharon Presbyterian Church. My purpose here is not to praise Sara Little but simply to note that toward the end of her life when she was quite retired, she helped the seminary get started here by giving a lecture on Christian Education. She was old then and not active, but willing, nevertheless, to give us a little push.

Sara was buried in the cemetery at Amity Presbyterian Church, in a part of town where she grew up. When Sara was a child the church was in a rural part of Mecklenburg County, but now the city has swallowed it up and the church finds itself in a transitional neighborhood. Sara was raised on a red clay cotton farm on the edge of Charlotte, attended Queens College, Presbyterian School of Christian Education, and Yale University. She was in many ways a product of the Presbyterian Church and the culture it fostered in this area, a culture of learning and service and hard work and stubborn hope.

As her remains were returned to the soil, I thought about the long journey she had taken from home, the many lives she had touched, but also of the church that was capable of producing such saints. Times have changed. Where there was once a cotton farm with cows grazing in the meadows, now there are deteriorating neighborhoods, gang graffiti, and unceasing traffic. The challenges before us in our day are fearsome indeed and will demand everything and more of us in response. Still, in the early afternoon of a lovely spring day, I stood beside the cemetery and watched as the church's day school children were enjoying their morning recess.

Black and white and Hispanic, 4 and 5 year-olds kicking a large ball around the yard, laughing and rough-housing together in the glorious sunshine. None of them knew Sara Little, but all were playing in the fields of the Kingdom, where the gospel that enabled Sara to set her own heart was making space for them to grow and to flourish. They too will have a long road to travel, a harder one, perhaps, than Sara's. Still we should not forget the words of the psalmist, "One generation shall laud your works to another . . . ." (Ps 145:4) Sometimes we forget that. In the case of Sara Little, I am glad we did not.

May 8, 2009

One of the many things that Dietrich Bonhoeffer wrote that continues to nourish me is the following: " . . . that a person in the arms of his wife should long for the hereafter is, to put it mildly, tasteless and in any case not God's will."[5] Resting in the arms of one's wife ought to be enough for a man, one might think, but often it is not. We want more. To change the metaphor, it ought to be enough for the church as the "Bride of Christ" to rest in the arms of her Bridegroom, but again, so often we want something more than Jesus. What we are looking for is something more spectacular, exotic, even ecstatic, perhaps even a kind of divine gnosis that will clinch every argument and explain away every mystery.

Recently I attended worship at a so-called mega-church here in Charlotte. It has advertised itself as "Not your grandparents church!" And it promised to provide an "elevated" form of Christian experience. What are we to make of such a claim? I suppose that this claim is better than "Slough of Despond" church or "The Darkside Congregation" but it seems to me that either way the claim is about my expectations for myself. To be "elevated" here is to desire something more than the presence of Christ and being content in his service.

Not too long ago I was talking to a gifted pastor here in Charlotte Presbytery. He told me that he was looking forward to offering a new Bible study for his people on Wednesday night. He had worked hard on it and felt as if he really had something good to present. But he was distressed when the vast majority of his congregants signed up for the "line-dancing" course that was being offered at the same time in the fellowship hall. He laughed when he told me this story, admitting that line-dancing

5. Bonhoeffer, *Letters and Papers from Prison*, 228.

may actually have been a more attractive option than what he was offering, but still I could tell he felt a bit like a jilted lover.

We live in a culture that is in love with the transcendent, a celebrity culture that looks down on the ordinary. We crave excitement. Recently my wife and I went to the movies and 7 of the 8 previews portrayed nothing but car crashes, explosions, and various iterations of the end of the world. Like a drug addict, we need bigger and bigger hits, and soon cannot even see the gifts of the ordinary, the life together that sustains life.

Simone Weil has noted that evil is often depicted as glamorous while good is portrayed as boring. On the movie screen, a car crash looks exciting. But, she points out, in real life a car crash is not exciting but painful, disturbing, and wearisome. Similarly, the boring goodness so easily dismissed in a drama, is in ordinary life a delightful thing, a gift, endlessly creative.[6]

We are in Christ's arms, and while we often long to be elsewhere, he somehow holds on to us, and in ways that continue to astonish, gives us himself through the ordinary, daily, enduring, often unexciting and at times too exciting gift of life in him. It would be in the height of bad taste to want to be elsewhere.

May 13, 2009

This morning at staff meeting, Susan Griner reminded us of some salient demographic facts. Hispanics currently represent 12.5% of our population in the United States; African-Americans represent 12.1% and Asian-Americans 3.6% There are more Jews living in America than in Israel, more Cubans in Miami than in any city except Havana, more Poles in Chicago than in any city except Warsaw, more Armenians in Los Angeles than in any city in the world. By the middle of this century a majority of Americans will be non-European.

What to make of all of this? First of all, I suspect these numbers are pretty accurate. Secondly, these numbers reflect my own experience and perceptions. Thirdly, what strikes me about these numbers is not their political or even cultural significance—I see them neither as a threat nor a cause for triumphalism—but their significance for the faith. Many of these groups (e.g., Poles, Armenians, Hispanics) have deep roots in Roman Catholic and Orthodox traditions. African-American worship has

---

6. Weil, *Gravity and Grace*, 62–63.

not only provided the spiritual resources to overcome years of oppression but has also shaped how the whole church has heard the gospel in a new way.

My very little point is this: though these changes may well take Presbyterians of European descent way out of our comfort zone, and though we may well find ourselves in a distinct minority (which, by the way, is not always a bad place for Christians of whatever stripe to find themselves), there is every reason to be hopeful about a future church that will be richer in its expressions of faith, more knowledgeable of the many traditions that contribute to the faith, and more open to ways in which the faith can bear witness in the future.

Some of the traditions Susan mentioned (e.g., Armenians, African-Americans, and others) have much to teach us about what it means to be in a minority *and* to confess the faith gladly.

Will there be a place for the Reformed witness in all of this? I believe there will be, though it may look very different from our world today. The Reformed tradition teaches us that the church is always in need of being reformed, and this not because we constantly have better ideas on how to improve it, but because we are a church that seeks to follow Jesus Christ, and therefore are a church that is saved not by its perfection but by his grace. Whatever else salvation will look like in the future, it will be a salvation that will draw us into the lives of those whom we have not chosen but without whom Jesus will simply not be our Savior. There truly is no salvation apart from *his* church! And this is so not because the church is the exclusionary condition but because Christ does not save us apart from others with whom he has stuck us. We are, by his grace and often to our chagrin, connected. Whatever demographic shape the future takes, Jesus Christ will be at the center, which is why we have nothing to fear about the future of the church, though, no doubt, we will have much to learn.

March 24, 2010

Last Wednesday night I was invited to speak to a class that meets at South Mecklenburg Presbyterian Church. Matt Brown is the pastor there and Kim Lee, one of our students, serves on the staff. "South Meck" is a relatively new church located in the far southern reaches of Charlotte, housed in a lovely new building in the middle of suburbia. The people were warm and welcoming and made me feel right at home. What struck me about those who were there was their passion for living the Christian life faithfully amidst all the messiness of early 21st century American suburbia, and the variety of places and traditions from which these very different voices emerged. I would venture to say that most who were gathered there were not from traditional, Presbyterian backgrounds. Some were. But most were from some other tradition or even none: Catholic, Baptist, unchurched, even hostile to the church. Yet God had, in ways more mysterious than we usually note, brought them together and made them a part of the body of Christ.

As I listened to them talk, I sensed for the first time in a long time the miracle that is the church. It is so easy to forget that miracle or overlook it, but a Wednesday night gathering of this sort brings it vividly to life. They were hungry for the gospel of Jesus Christ. They may be hesitant to express that hunger, and their hunger may well be disguised underneath other names or claims, but they are wanting to be fed and are seeking to live a life that is faithful to the gospel that has claimed them.

When I was a pastor, I used to be more amazed than I am now that folk came to church. We often complain at how paltry and small our field of labor is, or how unresponsive others are to what we think important, but the fact is that people still hear the gospel gladly. They come. They worship. They will even come to hear you preach. That may seem like a small or obvious thing, but it is not. It is a miracle.

June 9, 2010

Since my youth, I have been a baseball fan. Growing up, my team was the Brooklyn Dodgers. After they moved to California, I lost interest in them, but before they left, well, Jackie Robinson and Branch Rickey were my heroes, as they still are. The "boys of summer" were my team and I can still recount for you the starting lineup of the early 50's. My father and I would watch the "Game of the Week" which came on Saturday afternoons with Dizzy Dean, sponsored by Falstaff beer. In 1955 the Dodgers won their one and only World Series as Brooklyn's team, beating the hated Yankees in 7 games. I was in the 5th grade then and got in trouble with one of my teachers because I whooped out loud when I heard the final score. The next year, 1956, the Dodgers and Yankees played in the World Series again but this time the Yankees won with a pitcher named

Don Larsen hurling a perfect game. In my opinion Larsen was a medio-cre pitcher who got lucky in one game against a really great pitcher, Sal Maglie. Still, a perfect game, 27 up and 27 down, impressed.

Last week an unheralded pitcher for the Detroit Tigers, Armando Galarraga, pitched an almost perfect game against the Cleveland Indians. 26 up and 26 down. The 27th batter, Jason Donald, hit a dribbler between first and second, and Galarraga ran over to cover the bag, getting there just in time to receive a throw to make the final out. Only the umpire, Jim Joyce, called Donald safe. Unbelievable!

There has been a great deal written since then about the "lessons" both umpire and pitcher have provided the rest of us in their responses to this "injustice." Galarraga's immediate reaction, that is, his unconsidered, uncalculated response, was to look up to heaven, smile in bafflement, and put his hands on his head. He did not jump up and down or go after the umpire (as I would have done) with veins bulging and expletives fly-ing. Rather he seemed curiously chagrined by it all, smiling in bafflement and incomprehension. Then he went back to the mound and got the 28th batter out.

Later the umpire apologized to Galarraga and admitted he had been wrong and had blown the call. All of this may seem trivial, but it does stand in marked contrast to the way our culture practices outrage in oth-er areas of life. The oil spill in the gulf offers abundant evidence from the world of business and politics that the reservoir of good will is distress-ingly shallow and unlike the oil business itself, does not require that one drill very deeply before hitting a gusher of incoherent rage. But why point the finger at businessmen and politicians when the church itself seems to offer such a sad spectacle of "passionate intensity." We find it so hard to extend mercy to others. I am more convinced than ever that especially in church debates "winning" and "losing" are massively inappropriate terms to describe the mind of Christ.

Love, I suspect, "wins" few debates, and more often, "suffereth wrong," often bearing with defeats that turn out to be more victorious than any victory won by votes. What was so striking about Galarraga and Joyce was that in the midst of "injustice" and its aftermath, neither lost his humanity. How did that happen?

In a not entirely unrelated column, Michael Gerson wrote the following concerning politicians who stray from their marital commit-ment: "Moral conservatives need to admit that political character is more complex than marital fidelity . . . . 'The sins of the flesh are bad,' said

C.S. Lewis, 'but they are the least bad of all sins. All the worst pleasures are purely spiritual: the pleasure of putting other people in the wrong, of bossing and patronizing and back-biting, the pleasures of power and hatred . . . .' Yet moral liberals have something to learn as well. The failure of human beings to meet their own ideals does not disprove or discredit those ideals. The fact that some are cowards does not make courage a myth. The fact that some are faithless does not make fidelity a joke. All moral standards create the possibility of hypocrisy. But I would rather live among those who recognize standards and fail to meet them than among those who mock all standards as lies . . . . This recognition should lead toward the most underrated of the moral virtues: mercy."[7]

Mercy. Could it be that mercy is what keeps our humanity intact, keeps us from reducing ourselves and others to "winners" and "losers"? Does mercy tell us something true about ourselves, not as a form of politeness but as something that is theologically true? We seek forgiveness, Calvin reminds us, not in the hope of securing a merciful God, much less to appease an angry deity. Rather, God is merciful. And because God is merciful, we can dare to approach "the throne of grace" with confidence, knowing that we will find mercy there. And having found such mercy, we can afford to be extravagant in sharing it with others.

As our denomination begins another "marching season" of church debates, one hopes for mercy.

September 21, 2010

Yesterday I was in a meeting with area pastors to discuss Eugene Peterson's book, *Practice Resurrection* (Eerdmans, 2010). Peterson will be here next month to give a set of lectures. The book is an extended reflection on the letter to the Ephesians and accordingly, our discussion centered on the nature and mission of the church. One of the recurring points of discussion among the pastors had to do with the extent to which the church is under obligation to pay attention to the cultural context in which the gospel is proclaimed, as over against the extent to which the church is called to keep faith with the claims of gospel itself. This is not a new debate. Its lineaments have been traced by H. Richard Niebuhr (*Christ and Culture*, Torchbooks, 1975), among others, and more recently, by Stanley Hauerwas and William Willimon (*Resident Aliens*, Abingdon, 2014).

7. Gerson, *Washington Post*, June 4, 2010.

After the discussion, I reflected further on the matter. So many of the agendas which seek to make the church and its message more intelligible have little to say concerning what I would call the "soul" of the church. One of the pastors remarked that it seemed to him that Peterson was interested in what he called "deep church," that is, the church not merely as a cultural phenomenon but something with a life of its own, possessing its own strange identity.

I do not think that pastor was arguing for returning to the glorious days of yesteryear, when the church was stronger, more numerous, and more visibly important to the culture. For one thing, those days were not all that glorious. However, the culture we are seeking to address today is a culture that is, ostensibly, not much interested in the mystery of the gospel's word of grace, and which is, to speak the truth, often asking other kinds of questions. Some of these questions have to do with the effectiveness of the church as a consumer item which can do something for "me" or the extent to which the church is an agency of change that will accomplish some generally regarded good or the way in which the church can serve as an instrument for cultural or political persuasion. Pastors are sometimes encouraged to judge their effectiveness in responding to these questions, and by the resulting increase in the number of members their congregations can record or the impact they can make on their communities. These are not unimportant indices of pastoral leadership. The Gospel of Luke-Acts seems very interested in precisely these kinds of criteria, noting the numbers by which the early church grew and the way in which the church's influence was spread over the Mediterranean world.

Yet as I listened to the discussion and occasionally bit my tongue, I wondered what it would look like if our determination to be relevant succeeded, and the church became a more effective institution led by excellent managers and therapists who could provide the necessary religious commodities that consumers of our culture would like. Having done so, would we have lost our souls, forgotten how to speak the strange language of grace, where so much growth is underground (Cf. John 12:24: " . . . .unless a grain of wheat falls into the earth and dies, it remains just a single grain; but if it dies, it bears much fruit . . . .") and where what is measurable is often what is of least importance? I know that arguing in this way can be an effective way of dodging hard realities and giving into laziness or sentimentality. There is more than one kind of "cheap grace." But I also know that we are dealing here with mysteries of the gospel that beggar description and simply cannot be reduced to "measurable objectives" or the trivialities of body count.

So what do I want? I hope that our seminary trains pastors who are at least uncomfortable with the culture's rush to measure things, who are not afraid of being measured but who know the church will be judged not by the culture's standards or its own, but by the God whose judgment is both more severe and more gracious than we can conceive. I believe that the word of the gospel always finds its own hearers and gathers them together in community. It may not be the community we would have chosen or even would want. It may not look like us or be what we are used to, but it will not be one we have programmed or targeted or managed, but one the Holy Spirit insists on giving us. The church, Will Willimon reminds us, unlike a seminary or university, does not get to have an admissions department. We have to worship and work with whomever Jesus drags to church that day.[8] My hope is simply that we train students to love and to serve that ridiculous church. I think if we do that, we will find that the church will become both more transformative and a more interesting place to be, such that even the culture will grow curious about such a strange body in its midst.

February 1, 2012

In 1919 William Butler Yeats published his poem, *The Second Coming*, whose sentiments have almost become a cliche today. He was writing in the aftermath of World War I, yet the poem articulates what many of us are feeling in the church today: a sense that the centrifugal forces that are pulling us apart are more powerful than the glue that holds us together. "Turning and turning in the widening gyre, the falcon cannot hear the falconer; Things fall apart; the centre cannot hold . . . ."

The other much-quoted line in the poem expresses what seems all too true in our culture and religious wars of the day: "The best lack all conviction, while the worst are full of passionate intensity." I suppose that line could apply to many of the political campaigns that are surrounding us at the moment, but they might also apply to the politics of the church, describing a poor choice between a wise and wearied indifference on the one hand, and the passions of entrepreneurial intensity on the other.

---

8. Willimon, *Currie Lecture on Salvation*, Austin Seminary, 2008.

It seems strange that largely affluent, comfortable, unthreatened American Presbyterians have found it so easy to pull apart, so hard to stay together, so exciting to construct a new denomination, so tiresome to bear with each other in the old one. I wonder why we are so angry today, why resentment provides such powerful rhetorical fuel for our arguments and divisions. Resentment adds by dividing; it increases by subtracting. And it is very powerful.

So what is the opposite of resentment? And how do we find that stuff? How do we find the grace to bear with each other? The church, Calvin reminds us, exists where the gospel is proclaimed and the "visible word" of the sacrament bears to us Christ himself. Word and sacrament do not bear to us instruments of social policy or denominational purity. They bear to us Jesus Christ, whose life among us is a social policy, whose Passion liberates us from our worst and most earnest passions. As Paul writes, "He himself is before all things, and in him all things hold together. He is head of the body, the church . . . ." (Col 1:17, 18) *In him all things hold together*. Which means, I take it, that resentment dies as we are drawn to him. His cross bleeds our anger away.

The most prophetic word that can be said today has to do with what it means to be the church. We know how to serve this or that political end; we know how to engage with this or that righteous cause. What we do not know is what it means that "in him all things hold together." We would rather grow weary with our resentments and divisions, angrily and no doubt passionately inventing a more spiritual body. Splits happen, we tell ourselves. Divorces are sadly prevalent. That's the way it is.

I don't know the solution, much less the best ecclesial strategy. I do know that there is absolutely no point in trying to justify ourselves. There is enough sin around for everyone. And self-justification, no matter how righteous, is finally boring and tedious work. And if, in fact "in him all things hold together," then we are surely liberated from such tedium and called instead to rejoice in his word of hope. Such liberation deprives our many divisions of the honor of taking them quite as seriously as they demand. In any case, the only appropriate song that answers to our separations and resentments is doxological in nature, a song sung not defiantly or ironically but happily and truly in the knowledge that not even we, with all our "passionate intensity," can tear apart what Christ has joined together.

February 15, 2012

This past week our seminary has been enriched by the presence of Dr. Darrell Guder. His lectures on the missional church have reminded me of another great missional churchman, Lesslie Newbigin. Many of our students have read Newbigin's book, *The Gospel in a Pluralist Society*. In that book, there is a chapter entitled, "The Logic of Election," in which Newbigin exegetes Romans 9–11 to show that the God of Jesus Christ always saves by electing the "wrong people."[9] For example, God employs the Jews to save the Gentiles, a scandalous thing to do, particularly since the Jews, in Paul's judgment, have rejected the gospel. But, he insists, the promises of God are irrevocable, and Israel remains God's people. Their rejection of the gospel only makes room for the Gentiles to come in. Conversely, the inclusion of the Gentiles is meant to make Israel jealous, and though a hardening has come upon Israel, it will only last until the full number of Gentiles has come in. But when that happens, to quote Paul, "all Israel will be saved." (Rom 11:26a)

Newbigin's point is that the Gentiles weren't particularly looking for the Jews to save them, and the Jews weren't particularly looking to be saved by the Gentiles, the last people from whom they would expect help to come.

If all of this seems a bit contrived to you, think of all the places in scripture where people are saved by the wrong person. The man who fell among thieves is not saved by his fellow countrymen or co-religionists but by the wrong guy, a Samaritan. Joseph's brothers are saved from starvation by the wrong guy, the guy they had considered murdering and in fact had sold into slavery. The mighty warrior Naaman is healed by paying attention to a little Jewish slave girl, hardly the right person. Jonah considers himself the wrong guy for this job and eventually sulks because the wrong people repent. The "apostle to the Gentiles" is the Jew, Saul, who was bent on persecuting the church, holding the garments while others stoned a follower of the Way. He became Paul who appeared to many as absolutely the wrong guy for this job. God's people are saved by the wrong guy because they are saved by the Wrong Guy. There was no room for this guy in the inn. Foxes have holes and birds of the air nests, but this guy has no place to lay his head. This guy was a prophet lacking honor in his own country. He came to his own and his own knew him

9. Newbigin, *The Gospel in a Pluralist Society*, 80–88.

not. This guy eventually is judged to be so wrong that he is placed on a garbage dump between two other outcasts to be killed.

We are all saved by the Wrong Guy—there is no other way. The point? Well, our church is so quick to divide in part because we find it painful, even impossible to put up with the wrong people—whether they be of the left or the right. We prefer to be with the right guys and gals, people like us. Which is why it is so hard for us to hear the gospel, why its gracious logic upsets our more conventional type, why it often leaves us standing outside the party, harrumphing, while our Father and others are celebrating with the wrong guy who just came home.

What connects us to the other wrong guys is not tolerance or a sense of diversity or our own virtues. What connects us to other wrong guys is the Wrong Guy himself. In him "all things hold together," says Paul (Col 1:17). In him. The divine comedy is just that, a comedy. What we fear, what we have so quickly separated, God insists on being joined together, surprising us with the wrong people who become the very means of our salvation. God is sneaky that way, but then what would you expect of One who sticks us to the wrong people by sticking us to the Wrong Guy?

October 3, 2012

A quote from Dietrich Bonhoeffer: "Those who love their dream of a Christian community more than the Christian community itself become destroyers of that Christian community even though their personal intentions may be ever so honest, earnest, and sacrificial."[10]

Yesterday, I was having a conversation with a friend, during the course of which I was struck by what seemed to me to be the crucial issue facing the church today. There are so many issues one might mention: hunger and poverty, war and peace, ethnic and racial conflict, internal anger and bitter divisions, economic hardship and limited resources. My friend was justifiably upset with the weakness of the church's response to many of these issues, and even angrier about the quality of life exhibited in the church itself.

It is so easy to grow bitter about the church. Richard John Neuhaus has written about sheep who all too easily become wolves. And he has noted further that for ministers just starting out, congregational life can provide a real shock in terms of the virulence of sheer nastiness that

10. Bonhoeffer, *Life Together*, 36.

Christians can deal out to each other. "It is a special sort of nastiness," he writes, "perhaps because proximity to the sacred multiplies the force of the demonic. Envy, resentment, and unalloyed hatred can make their appearance in any association, but they seem so ghastly in the church because they so flagrantly contradict the stated purpose of the association."[11]

So the temptation is to imagine a better church, one that is more attractive, successful, even nicer. And there is nothing wrong with that. We should all long for a church to which people cannot wait to enter, for worship services that are filled to overflowing, for benevolent budgets that expand to include the whole world, for programs that transform lives, communities, even cities. The hard part is living with our disappointment that people don't always love what we do, or support what is obviously worthy of their best passions, or accept our vision of what the church can be and do. Then is when it becomes difficult to love the church. Then is when it becomes easy to write people off. Then is when we are tempted to look for an exit. But then is also when the crucial question presses upon us: Can we love the church?

Or do we love our dreams of the church more?

I have recently been reading an account of the German church struggle and despite the occasional heroism displayed by various individuals, the witness there was, frankly, disappointing. I wonder if we would have done any better. And I think of those whose task it was to try to rebuild the church in Germany after World War II. How hard it must have been to summon a gospel witness amidst the ruins and manifest failure of the church itself.

But maybe it was no harder than what we face today, where our affluence and abundance of choices so easily trivialize the faith. Maybe our preoccupation with our own decline is more of a symptom of our desire for self-preservation than it is of anything else.

The truth is we are not promised increasing number of pulpits in an ever-growing denomination of successful people. There is very little of that in scripture. Rather there is only (!) manna; only loaves and fishes; only waiting and not knowing and bearing witness and being raised again from the dead. John Calvin insists that the church lives only as it is raised from the dead again and again. Can we love such a church? It seems so paltry at times, so unfashionable, so awkward. Are we really called to love that mess?

---

11. Neuhaus, *Freedom for Ministry*, 120.

A final note: recently I represented our seminary at the inaugural event at another seminary nearby. I was struck by the service, which contained two sermons! There was a good deal of celebration of the success that had already been attained. Success upon success. No stumbles, no failures, no questions, no wilderness, no exile, no losses. Where was the struggle, I wondered.

Perhaps we are blessed to be living with a church that struggles so obviously. It is a gift to be preserved from some kinds of "success." The hardness, the difficulty, the limits are probably closer to the "narrow way" the church has ever been called to walk. And as affluent and comfortable as we are, we have much to learn still. Only in America might we think that being the church is meant to be one successful thing after another. The crucial issue of our day, as it is of any day, is whether the church will be the church, whether it will, with its words and actions, its life and possessions, bear witness to Jesus Christ. Can we love the Body whose body is always a mess, and is always at its best when struggling? Or would we rather have something neater, cleaner, nicer, more spiritual, something that carries less theological baggage? There is only one reason to love a church that is so messy and troubled. The head of the church seems to do so.

January 31, 2013

We often think of tradition as confining. We learn early on to celebrate "non-conformity" even as we buy the same kind of shoes and shirts. But musicians and bricklayers, I would guess, might tell us that real non-conformity lies on the other side of mastering a particular tradition. One cannot attempt to improvise until one has mastered the instrument or craft and is comfortable enough in that mastery to think imaginative thoughts in another vein. Otherwise, what one is doing is merely cheap and silly and self-absorbed.

The life shaped by Christian discipleship is none of those things. Wallace Alston, in his essay, "The Education of a Pastor-Theologian," suggests that it is in fact our tradition, particularly in preparing students for ministry, that actually liberates. He notes that in the Reformed tradition, the "ordered life" is a rather different thing from the "driven life" (and by extension, "the purpose-driven life"), just as it also differs from the "scattered" life or the "un-called" life. What is an "ordered life"? Alston calls it a life "lived in the confession of the power of the living God to make

sense of human living and dying." He cites John Greenleaf Whittier's lyrics: "Drop thy still dews of quietness, till all our strivings cease; Take from
our souls the strain and stress, and let our *ordered lives* confess the beauty
of thy peace."[12]

In a similar vein Karl Barth refers to the "ordered life" when he
writes that it is the Holy Day, Sunday, that signals true human freedom.[13]
By ordering our lives the Sabbath liberates us from both the drivenness
of our self-justifying busyness and the lassitude of our self-justifying
despair.

Alston is bold to suggest what I think to be profoundly true, and
that is that no small part of the work of ministry is the task of tradition-
ing. He points out how many sermons today seem to be "first-generation"
sermons, all about the experience of the preacher, as if the text had never
been commented upon by saints from previous ages whose wisdom
might be garnered and made fruitful for today and from whose acquaintance contemporary worshippers might benefit.

There is much that is tired and cliche-like in the term, "the Reformed
tradition," and it is true that worshipping at the idol of such a formative
way of being Christian is still worshipping an idol. But again, as Alston
notes, the point of mastering or better being mastered by a particular
tradition is to be able to bear witness to the essential unity of the church.
Our little traditions serve no other purpose than to provide us an entry
into the church's long and broad conversation with scripture's witness.

So what? Well, so this: there are a number of groups, including various constituencies within our own church and seminary that are trying in
earnest to discern God's plan for the future for both. That future is hard to
see for a variety of reasons, not least the various vested interests we might
want to preserve. But one thing seems clear to me: trying to discern the
future of the church without paying attention to the tradition that has
passed the gospel on to us is worse than foolish, and will produce only a
stunted and silly, and finally boring something, a something that, unlike
the church of Jesus Christ, will be deeply captive to its own trivialities.
Traditionalism is not the answer. But the tradition to which we belong
is not our enemy. Rather, it is a gift that can liberate us to see beyond it.

12. Alston, *The Power to Comprehend with All the Saints*, 68.
13. Barth, *Church Dogmatics* III/4, 67.

February 6, 2013

Yesterday I received an email from a friend with whom I studied in seminary. What occasioned his note to me was the struggle he and his wife
were having in their attempts to help the church where they worship.
They were in anguish because their pastor wanted to take the congregation out of the denomination, and they, and others, wanted to try to stay.
There was a lot of hurt and anger in this note. But in truth, the anguish
my friend was feeling about this congregational split is only part of the
hurt. Like any divorce there are at least two sides (if not more) and plenty
of presenting issues and underlying causes. What my friend was feeling,
however, was not just anguish over the split (and anger at his pastor), but
a deeper loneliness, a feeling that the church had forgotten how to be a
"life together." Instead, what many seemed to want was a purity of some
kind, a righteousness that would be self-evident. They seemed to want
their youth back, the time when the congregation was young and vigor-
ous and important. They wanted to be young again, and were suspicious
of the old, who were such obvious failures.

One can make too much of the church. Our Reformed forebears
sacrificed a lot in protest against the church making an idol out of itself
or thinking that it was as important as the One to whom it was called to
witness. But I sometimes think that the struggles we are going through
to be the church are deeper and more important than mere ecclesiastical
squabbles. We are adding to the loneliness of American life with our splits.

Here at the seminary, we say we want to "form leaders and transform the church," but I wonder if we know how to be the church that we
want to transform. Well, maybe we shouldn't worry about all of this. As
a friend reminds me, the church will last exactly as long as God has need
of it. According to the Revelation of St. John the Divine, there will be no
temple in the heavenly city ("for its temple is the Lord God Almighty and
the Lamb." Rev 21:22). And in truth, our denomination, our seminary
even, has no special claim on God's will and God is certainly under no
obligation to make life safe and secure for us.

Still, I think God does will us to live a "life together" in Jesus Christ.
Which means that the church has no more important task today than
to gather, worship, serve, and share in whatever life together the Holy
Spirit grants to our congregations. Being the church today seems to me
to be the most counter-cultural act we could undertake, countering our

loneliness and isolation and anger and despair, with the gospel of him who "welcomes sinners and eats with them."(Luke 15:2)

February 20, 2013

I sometimes wonder if affluence and Christianity can really get along very well. God, Philip Jenkins has said, seems to do much better south of the equator.

Recently I interviewed a potential student, a recent immigrant, who, with his wife and children, had to flee their native Burma and go first to Malaysia, and then to America. He was a pastor in Burma, among the Chin people. When he fled the country, he worked with the UN High Commission on Refugees, helping to care for the 50,000 or so Burmese in the camps in Malaysia. I asked him about that work. He replied: "I woke up in the morning and visited those in prison first at 6 a.m. Then I went to the detention centers to welcome new refugees. Then I went to the camps to visit various folk, and finally to the hospitals to care for the sick and dying." At one point he was hired by an NGO, eventually being recognized by the UN for his pastoral care for those in need.

"What is your ministry goal?" I asked him. "I want to plant new churches," he replied. He is currently pastoring a flock of 140 Burmese here in Charlotte. He has applied for U.S. citizenship, but he eventually wants to return to Burma to help start new congregations.

The man is poor; he is living in his third or fourth country after fleeing his own. English must be his fifth or sixth language. And he wants to start new churches . . . .

I have been reading Anne Applebaum's new book, *Iron Curtain: the Crushing of Eastern Europe, 1945–1956* (Anchor, 2013). She is an excellent reporter whose account of those years makes for unbearably sad reading. She focuses on three countries: Poland, E. Germany, and Hungary. When you read what these people endured during World War II, first from the Nazis and then from the Soviets, you wonder that any of them are able to hope or plan or envision any kind of positive future.

Among the most crushed were explicitly Christian groups, especially youth groups but also seminaries and pastors. When I read what they went through, and what various minorities went through, I am ashamed of ever complaining about the plight of the American church or the miseries of our own denomination. We haven't got troubles. Yes, there are splits and disappointments and anger, but most of these wounds are self-inflicted and mimic an affluent culture rather than contradicting it.

I remember once hearing Tom Gillespie speak when he was president of Princeton Theological Seminary. He and his wife, who was of German extraction, were visiting her family's home town in what was then E. Germany. On Sunday, they went to church, where there might have been 10 people in worship. Gillespie, like a typical American, asked the pastor how many members there were that worshipped in that congregation. "On a good day, like Easter," the pastor replied, "we might have 18." 18. Gillespie wondered to himself if he would have the courage to pastor for 20 years, as this pastor had, a flock which, on a good day, might number 18 souls.

So what? Well, so this: maybe we should quit worrying about demographics, strategies for resuming our place of prominence in the culture, the resentments we must struggle against. Maybe we should simply pray to God for courage to bear witness in our day. That is hard enough.

May 22, 2013

Earlier this month I led a travel seminar to various sites in Europe associated with the Reformed witness. One of the places we visited was a little town in southeastern France called Le Chambon sur Ligne. This is a small town, I would guess of no more than 2,000 souls today. It has a city hall and a defunct railroad station and a small city park near the center of town. But it also has a French Reformed Church (a "temple" as it is called), whose pastor, André Trocmé, and congregation, saved the lives of over 3500 Jewish children during World War II.

Near the church, on a stone wall opposite the sanctuary, the state of Israel has placed a commemorative plaque honoring these "righteous Gentiles." The church itself is simple and quite unadorned. The current pastor, a German native, met us and allowed us to sit in the sanctuary, to see the pulpit, and to hear him tell something of his work in this little, ordinary, small town congregation. To hear him speak, to sit in that sanctuary, to walk down the street to the gate of the church manse (called, "the presbytery"), on the door of which Jewish refugees knocked asking for help, was to sense that one was walking on holy ground.

But here is what struck me. The only adornment on the church building was an inscription over the door. It said, simply, (in French):

"Love one another." There could be no more threadbare Christian sentiment than what is expressed in that phrase. But given what happened in
that community and through that congregation besieged by collabora-
tors, Nazis, and others, the words, "Love one another" seemed to sum up
the audacity and beauty and power of the gospel as no other words could.

One other note: I cannot emphasize enough the ordinariness of
this little church. It was not a cathedral, not anywhere near the centers
of power, probably not the pulpit that every young, aspiring pastor was
seeking. It was quite ordinary. Yet just so the gospel was enacted there in
a powerful way. Could that be the way the gospel happens here too? In
Great Falls, Norwood, Mt. Gilead, Waxhaw, Marion, Mansfield, Hillsville,
Roanoke Rapids, Weir Shoals, Union Presbyterian Seminary, Charlotte?
The gospel is strange that way. It keeps showing up in the most ordinary
of places.

October 23, 2013

Yesterday I attended a meeting of Charlotte Presbytery. There is, as I have
discovered, no rubric in *Robert's Rules of Order* for a howl of lament, but
yesterday I wish there had been.

Four congregations voted to leave the denomination and yesterday
Charlotte Presbytery gave them permission to do so. The congregations
had fulfilled "all righteousness" in securing the requisite percentage of
voters to leave, granting them the ability to exit and take their property
with them, so there was no debate about that. Indeed, there was little
debate about anything. Rather, this was going to be an apparently "ami-
cable" divorce—no expressions of grief, no howl of lament, no expression
of hurt or anger or regret, simply a quiet prayer at the end asking God's
blessing on those departing and on those remaining. A pastor of one
of the departing congregations even thanked the presbytery for understanding, and expressed delight that he could now see us in the grocery
store without worrying about any "awkward moments."

Well, I hope there are some awkward moments. He and the rest of
us deserve more than a few, if for no other reason than to bear witness to
our mutual shame.

I understand there is an agreed upon protocol for splitting up,
which in this case was followed to the letter. I understand that no one
wants a court fight. I understand that the time for a reconciling word to

be spoken had come and gone, and there were no more words to be said except, "Farewell."

But the occasion deserved more than that. It deserved some hot angry tears that we have come to such a place with each other; it deserved a voice wailing that we are so much better at hurting each other and separating from each other than we are at coming together in Christ's service and at his table. It deserved a voice that could acknowledge the death in our midst and could grieve the loss of saints whose leaving will render those of us who remain (as well as those who leave) lonelier, less interesting, and more broken than before.

There were one or two brave souls who voted against this divorce. Bless them. I don't think their vote was really aimed at those who were leaving. And I don't think their vote was a vote for hiring attorneys to defend the inevitable lawsuit that would result. I think their vote was a witness that what these congregations were asking and what the presbytery was blessing was quite impossible, and indeed, impossibly unfaithful. The vote was quite impossible because as much as these congregations wanted to leave, and as contented as the rest of us might be for them to leave, a vote really cannot destroy what unites us in Christ. Nothing, we are told, can separate us from the love of Christ; not even a presbytery vote dismissing congregations to separate bodies. And to pretend that we can do so or even acquiesce in such a request is to tell a theological lie.

I know denominations are poor excuses for representing the body of Christ, but as weak and poor as they are, they represent, to some extent, the energy and commitment the church must invest in the hard work of bearing with one another in the body. Otherwise, why would we take ordination vows promising to do that? Smaller, purer, fragments of the church appear to have an advantage here. They do not have to muster such energy or commitment. Leaving liberates them from that chore.

It is hard to be the church. When has it not been? We would all like some easier way. But our wealth, our vaunted "religious freedom," our own considerably refined and cultivated resentments all encourage us to listen to our own "inner voices" rather than the voices of brothers and sisters in Christ. My howl of grief is not a howl of anger at those who have left. I do not blame them for leaving. There have been many times when that option has appealed to me too. Nor do I think my denomination, the PCUSA, is exempt from guilt here. A divorce is never the fault of one side only. And the PCUSA, in my judgment, has done many stupid and thoughtless and even unfaithful things in the past several years. But when has the church not done many stupid, thoughtless, and unfaithful things? Our ability to avoid such is not what keeps us united. Rather, it is Christ who holds on to his stupid, thoughtless, and unfaithful brothers and sisters that keeps us whole and makes of us a church. And it is that reality that made me want to howl at a meeting where that reality was not even acknowledged or called upon or celebrated through our tears.

March 12, 2014

Sometimes I think we come closer to genuine faithfulness not when we busy ourselves with urgent or even important matters, but rather, when we cultivate the power to ignore distractions. I confess that I find this very hard to do.

For example, when I am working on a lecture or a sermon, something will pop into my brain and I will feel as if I have to check my email right now to see if there is something to which I must respond. Simone Weil famously said, "Absolutely unmixed attention is prayer."[14] She notes further that that kind of prayerful attention is "so full that the 'I' disappears."[15] My prayer life, unfortunately, is not that full; there is still plenty of 'I' intruding, which may explain why checking my email is such a powerful temptation.

But I wonder if this problem is confined to my personal habits. I wonder, for example, if our church should not cultivate a certain indifference, or better, freedom, that would allow us to say from time to time: "We don't know about that right now; we have no word from the Lord at the moment; we are going to have to struggle together a bit longer on that topic."

Perhaps you think this is a cop out, another way of justifying not doing anything. "Not to decide," a slogan from the days of protest in the 1960's had it, "is to decide." And it is true that far too often the church has stood by silently, when we should have spoken out. Why was the German church so silent during the Nazi era, or why were white Protestant pastors so late in seeing and proclaiming the gospel's message for people, white and black, in the American South? Scripture knows of this failure as well: "Among the clans of Reuben there were great searchings of heart. Gilead stayed beyond the Jordan; and Dan, why did he abide with the

14. Weil, *Gravity and Grace*, 106.

15. *Ibid.*, 107.

ships?" (Judg 5:16f.) Indeed. God's people have often missed making the critical confession when it has most been needed. I get that.

But I wonder if every issue is equally critical or equally as clear. I wonder if confessing the faith in the face of every concern that arises does not trivialize and diminish our witness. I wonder if we are so afraid of being found with Reuben and Dan that we readily address matters not out of faith but out of fear of potential embarrassment if we do not. Our words cover ourselves but do not bring much light or healing to the issue at hand.

There is something admirable, I think, about the monastic commitment to a rule of faith that allows the order's life and worship to determine the shape of their particular witness. In the book, *The Monks of Tibhirine*, the distractions of the world of terror collide with the rule of stability of a Benedictine monastery in N. Africa. Interestingly, the presenting issue for the monks is not how to address the problem of terrorism, much less, articulating a theological response to it. The question they face is whether to stay or to go. As simple, and as difficult as that. In the event, the monks stay. The distractions of terror do not distract them from their mission of prayer and work, *ora et labora*. They focus their attention on God and on their life together, both as monks and as members of a community in Algeria to whom they minister. Their decision to stay cost them their lives. Christian witness will do that—not it seems to me, by getting on the right side of every issue, but by bearing witness, attentively, faithfully, joyfully wherever God has placed us.

We may debate about what that looks like—well and good—but we will only truly get lost if we lose our focus, our *attention*, on the One who has called us into the life of Jesus Christ. But for that, we will need the help of the Holy Spirit, for otherwise we will get lost in the 'I' that so eagerly distracts and has so many other agendas for us.

Chapter 3: Time and Preparation

September 16, 2002

There never is enough time. C.S. Lewis was an Augustinian in that he believed that all human beings were made for God and that our hearts are restless until they find their rest in God. Lewis offered some unusual proofs that we are made for God. For example, he points out that we are always shocked by the passage of time. We shouldn't be. Time, after all, is the sea we swim in. But when, after some time, we see a little child that has grown to adulthood, we are astonished. "How he's grown!" we exclaim, as if such growth were a novelty. But what did we expect? That the child would remain forever small? Why is it that growth stuns us so? Unless, Lewis argued, unless we were made for something beyond time, something like eternity.[1]

Whatever you make of Lewis' argument, it is the witness of scripture that the God of Israel and of Jesus Christ has time for us. "My times," the psalmist claims, "are in your hand," (Ps 31:15) a verse that appears in the same psalm Jesus quotes from the cross ("Into your hand, I commit my spirit." Ps 31: 5). God has our time, and even more, has time for us. What greater gift is there than to have time for another? What worse thing can we do than to tell someone that we have no time for him or her? And what else is eternal life than to have, finally, enough time?

October 29, 2007

One of Eugene Peterson's early books dealing with ministry was entitled, *A Long Obedience in the Same Direction* (IVP Books, 2000), an accurate description, he thought, of the nature of this calling. His point was that the work of ministry—study, prayer, preaching, pastoral care, teaching,

---

1. Lewis, *Reflections on the Psalms,* 138.

bearing witness in a particular community—is part of a long, long journey of faith, "a long obedience in the same direction."

The notion that discipleship takes time contradicts one of our culture's most cherished illusions, namely, that good things are "instant" and
"quick" and "consumable." The work of ministry is none of those things.
And neither is the work of preparing to become ministers, which is why
what we are doing here is so counter-cultural. Growth takes time and is
not always smooth.

One might think that those of us who have been shaped by the Reformed tradition would know this better than some, given our emphasis
on sanctification and growth in grace. But we do not, largely because we
like our providential paths to be straightforward, well-organized, and
planned. Forty years in the wilderness getting from Egypt to the Promised Land does not strike us as the most effective way to prepare for ministry. Following an itinerant rabbi throughout Galilee for three years and
then heading toward certain trouble in the big city again does not appear
to be the most fruitful way to go about preparation for discipleship.

We are offended by the mystery of a gospel that resists our efforts
to render it more obvious and straightforward, just as the disciples were
offended by Jesus who so often did things they did not understand. "A
long obedience in the same direction" means there will be a lot of not
knowing, struggling forward amidst the fog of many questions, dealing
with the messiness of things not easily or quickly sorted out. This is hard,
especially when one has a theology paper to write or a take-home New
Testament exegesis to prepare, not to mention a job to do, a spouse to
love, a home to make, children to nurture.

Yes, it is hard. But it is not just hard. There are pleasures in doing
something hard that pleasure knows not of. One of the failings of our tradition is that in talking about "the long obedience in the same direction,"
we have rarely mentioned the joy that accompanies this journey. Calvin
wrote eloquently about self-denial, but not so much about the joy of being called to this work and being strengthened by others through our life
in Christ. "The pay begins in this life," one of the church's saints has said.[2]
And indeed it does, but it never comes easily or cheaply. Discipleship,
ministry, preparing for this work takes time, which is not a limitation
but a gift.

2. Theresa of Avila, *Meditations on the Song of Songs,* 246.

March 25, 2009

This past winter I read Alan Jacobs' book, *Original Sin, A Cultural History*. Jacobs has written extensively on matters theological and literary. In this book he notes the following in a footnote:

> For centuries theologians and leaders of the church had affirmed that the key date in human history was March 25, on which date occurred the Fall itself; the angel Gabriel's Annunciation to Mary, which heralded the birth of the One who would undo the effects of the Fall; and the Crucifixion, which defeated the forces of evil, which had been unleashed upon the world by Adam's sin. It was with these events in mind that Dionysius Exiguus, the sixth-century monk and calendar-maker, determined that the year itself should begin on March 25, which it did throughout Europe for a very long time. It was England's official New Year's Day until 1752, though by that time January 1 had been celebrated by most English people for hundreds of years.[3]

Interesting. I had never realized that March 25 was such an important date. I do remember reading John Donne's poem, "Upon the Annunciation and the Passion Falling Upon One Day (March 25, 1608)". There he wrote:

> All this, and all between, this day hath shown,
> Th'abridgement of Christ's story, which makes one
> (As in plaine maps, the furthest west is east)
> Of the angel's *Ave*, and *Consummatum est*.[4]

Which suggests that this is the day that comprehends all days—fall and redemption, annunciation and passion, our beginning and our end. I know that we no longer celebrate March 25th as New Year's Day, and in truth, I am not advocating that we return to that calendar, but I am struck at how people of old saw in the narrative of Christ's life the meaning of their own days and lives, and how our more recent calendars, geared to so many more pressing dates—academic, commercial, national, etc.—lack both the richness and joy of this way of numbering our days. Jacobs notes at the end of this extended footnote a curious reference to March 25th in more recent literature. He writes: "J.R.R. Tolkien, knowing this history very well, made a point of placing the destruction of the Ring and the

---

3. Jacobs, *Original Sin*, 43.
4. Donne, *The Complete Poems*, 328.

overthrow of Sauron on March 25."[5] That Good Friday and Christmas and New Year could be so deeply connected fills me with strange delight, a sense that even if our calendars have become much more up-to-date, the story that comprehends our story knows a deeper way of counting and a more joyful way of hoping.

5. Jacobs, *Original Sin,* 43.

Chapter 4: Ministry and Joy

October 2, 2002

In the class I am teaching this fall we are reading *The Journals of Father Alexander Schmemann* (St. Vladimir's, 2000), and I have been struck once again with his references to "joy" as a theological term. He does not think "joy" is to be interpreted as "happiness" or "feeling good" or "simple euphoria." Rather, he thinks the word contains some deeper meaning, something that combines settled confidence with gratitude and hope. Since "joy" has not always characterized the way the gospel has been mediated to me, and since so much of the modern world seems to be engaged in "joyless" pursuits, I thought I might simply offer you some quotes from Schmemann's book as a gift this week.

> The source of false religion is the inability to rejoice, or, rather, the refusal of joy, whereas joy is absolutely essential because it is without doubt the fruit of God's presence. One cannot know that God exists and not rejoice. Only in relation to joy are the fear of God and humility correct, genuine, fruitful. Outside of joy, they become demonic, the deepest distortion of any religious experience. A religion of fear. Religion of pseudo-humility. Religion of guilt: They are all temptations, traps,—very strong indeed, not only in the world, but inside the church. Somehow "religious" people often look on joy with suspicion."[1]

> I think God will forgive everything except lack of joy; when we forget that God created the world and saved it. Joy is not one of the "components" of Christianity, it's the *tonality* of Christianity that penetrates everything—faith and vision. Where there is no joy, Christianity becomes fear and therefore torture. We know about the fallen state of the world only because we know about its glorious creation and its salvation by Christ. The knowledge

1. Schmemann, *The Journals*, 129.

of the fallen world does not kill joy, which emanates from the world, always constantly, as a bright sorrow . . . . This world is having fun; nevertheless it is joyless because joy (different from what is called "fun") can only be from God, only from on high—not only joy of salvation, but salvation as joy. To think—every Sunday we have a banquet with Christ, at His table, in His Kingdom; then we sink into our problems, into fear and suffering. God saved the world through joy: " . . . you will have pain but your pain will turn into joy . . . ." (John 16:21 "When a woman is in travail, she has sorrow, because her hour has come; but when she is delivered of the child, she no longer remembers the anguish, for joy that a child is born into the world."[2])

. . . for if a man would see what I call joy, or if a man would simply love Christ—just a little, would come to Him, nothing else would be needed. If not, nothing will help. All begins with a *miracle*, not with conversations. I feel tired of the noise and petty intrigues that surround the church, of the absence of breathing space, of silence, of rhythm, of all that is present in the Gospel. Maybe that is why I love an empty church, where the Church speaks through silence. I love it before the service and after the service. I love everything that usually seems to be 'in between' (to walk on a sunny morning to work, to look at a sunset, to quietly sit a while), that which may not be important, but which alone, it seems to me, is that chink through which a mysterious ray of light shines. Only in those instances do I feel alive, turned to God; only in them is there the beating of a completely 'other' life."[3]

April 16, 2003

A month or so ago, we read Karl Barth's *Dogmatics in Outline* (Harper Torchbooks, 1959), an exposition of the Apostles' Creed. In commenting on "The third day, he rose again from the dead," Barth writes:

> If you have heard the Easter message, you can no longer run around with a tragic face and lead the humorless existence of a man who has no hope. One thing still holds, and only this one thing is really serious, that Jesus is the Victor. A seriousness that would look back past this, like Lot's wife, is not Christian seriousness. It may be burning behind—and truly it is burning—but

2. *Ibid.,* 137.
3. *Ibid.,* 193.

we have to look not at it, but at the other fact, that we are invited
and summoned to take seriously the victory of God's glory in
this man Jesus and to be joyful in him. Then we may live in
thankfulness and not in fear.[4]

So rejoice in this Easter season, not in ignorance or denial of all the
world's miseries, but in the knowledge that as miserable as all of these no
doubt are, they are not capable of doing what they want to do, that is, to
separate us from the love of Christ. Jesus is Victor! That is the reason to
be glad and rejoice in this day

November 6, 2003

Yesterday at staff meeting I read some words from Father Schmemann,
which I would like to share with you. A leader in the Orthodox Church,
Father Schmemann was often called upon to settle church squabbles
and debates. This entry is dated Monday, April 10, 1978, and it expresses
some of Father Schmemann's weariness with turf battles in the church.
He writes:

I feel no desire to fight, only a desire to leave (to get away) as far
as possible. Not out of cowardice, but out of conviction that it
is impossible to even hint at what would be the goal of such a
fight. To hint at the joy (of the Gospel)—mysterious, never loud;
at the beauty and humility—secret, never showy; at the goodness, never extolling itself. 'Come to me . . . .and I will give you
peace.'—How can this be reconciled with a never ending, thun-
derous, 'we declare, we demand . . .' [While] standing on Second
Ave. changing a tire in the garage, I contemplated people on the
street who were going home from work with shopping bags; and
earlier, a mother, with two little boys, all three in poor but so
obviously festive clothes, all three lit up by the setting sun. Why
do I like it so much? I, the most unsentimental and indifferent
man, I want to cry. Why do I know with such certitude that I am
in contact with the "ultimate," that which gives total joy and faith,
the rock against which all (my little) problems crash?[5]

One longs for such "unsentimental" gifts amidst our own church's
squabbles.

4. Barth, *Dogmatics in Outline*, 123.
5. Schmemann, *The Journals*, 193.

October 27, 2004

I have been teaching a Sunday School class recently on "Sabbath as a Way of Knowing God". In preparing for that course, I ran across these words from Karl Barth, which I would share with you:

> As we all know the minister's Sunday involves both a program and work, yet does this mean that he has to bemoan it? Is not the minister the ideal case of the man who works joyfully on the holy day and in this very way keeps it holy? If it were toilsome and dull for ministers to do their Sunday work, how could they expect the congregation and the world to find it refreshing? More generally, we may ask whether even during the week theology is a *labor operosus*, a burden and anxiety, something which has to be done for professional reasons but which we should be happy to lay aside with a clear conscience. If theology as such is not a joy to the theologian, if in his [or her!] theological work, he [or she] is not genuinely free from care, what is it? Can he [or she] then abandon it on Sunday and devote himself [or herself] to all sorts of tomfoolery? Why should he [or she] not be free for theology? Fundamentally, cannot the heaviest theological working day be for him [or her] the best day of rest?[6]

Which is why one's time at seminary ought to be, despite the immense amount of travel, work, and weariness involved, the most joyful time of all.

November 2, 2005

This morning at staff meeting, I read this quote from Simone Weil which I would like to share with you. She writes:

> Will power, the kind that, if need be, makes us set our teeth and endure suffering, is the principal weapon of the apprentice engaged in manual work. But, contrary to the usual belief, it has practically no place in study. The intelligence can only be led by desire. For there to be desire, there must be pleasure and joy in the work. The intelligence only grows and bears fruit in joy. The joy of learning is as indispensable in study as breathing is in running. Where it is lacking, there are no real students, but only poor caricatures of apprentices who, at the end of their apprenticeship will not even have a trade. It is the part played by joy in

6. Barth, *Church Dogmatics* III/4, 68.

our studies that makes of them a preparation for the spiritual life, for desire directed toward God is the only power capable of raising the soul. Or rather, it is God alone who comes down and possesses the soul, but desire alone draws God down . . . [7]

"The joy of learning is as indispensable in study as breathing is in running." So may we run (and breathe and study) with such joy.

February 8, 2006

In his introduction to Nadezhda Mandelstam's memoir, *Hope Against Hope*, Clarence Brown writes of Mandelstam's husband, Osip, that he was not only one of the greatest Russian poets of the twentieth century, but also a poet who, despite years spent in exile ending in death in one of Stalin's gulags, sought to account for the joy he espied at the heart of life. In the introduction, Brown refers to a fragment of one of Mandelstam's early essays in which he writes of this inexpungeable joy, concluding finally that Mandelstam found this joy in Christianity. "In an early essay on Pushkin and Scriabin, of which only fragments remain, Mandelstam was evidently trying to find the source of this joy within the terms of Christianity. Christian art, is joyous because it is free, and its art is free because of the fact of Christ's having died to redeem the world. One need not die in art nor save the world in it, those matters having been, so to speak, attended to. What is left? The blissful responsibility to enjoy the world . . . ."[8]

I am not sure that a Reformed theologian could have said it better. This last week in theology class we read about what it means that "Jesus takes away our sins." The loss we often bewail of being exposed as a sinner who seeks in fact to be God is actually a great liberation, says Karl Barth. It is a nuisance, and at bottom an "intolerable nuisance" always to be pretending to be divine. And it is very hard work. To discover that this matter has been taken out of our hands, that we are not in fact judges of ourselves or others, is liberation. "A great anxiety is lifted, the greatest of all. I can turn to other more important and more happy and more fruitful activities. I have a space and freedom for them in view of what has happened in Jesus Christ."[9]

7. Weil, *Waiting for God*, 61.

8. Brown, *Introduction to Hope Against Hope*, xxii.

9. Barth, *Church Dogmatics* IV/1, 234.

Space and freedom to "enjoy the world." Maybe the poet Mandelstam's joy derived from the freedom he discovered in not having to undertake the hard work of saving himself.

June 21, 2006

In one of his essays, W. H. Auden comments on the difference between classical comedy (as found, say, in the plays of Plautus and Terence) and comedy in a culture that has been influenced by the Christian faith (e.g., Shakespeare). In classical comedy, the comic figures are all lower class fools, slaves, and rascals. (If you have seen, *A Funny Thing Happened on the Way to the Forum,* you will know exactly what Auden has in mind.) The comedy comes from watching these knaves connive and fool the noble classes, deceiving them with underhanded tricks. But in the end, these rascals are found out and shown to get what they deserve. Christian comedy, on the other hand, exposes all classes and conditions of folk, especially the heroic and virtuous, to the unsettling gift of grace. And at the end of the play, no one gets what he or she deserves, though all are revealed to be recipients of grace. At the end of a classical comedy, Auden notes, the audience is laughing while those on stage are weeping. In Christian comedy, he adds, both the audience and the actors are laughing together.[10]

That is how forgiveness works its healing way, and gives in the end, not what we deserve but the deep, deep joy of something better, the gift of God's grace.

October 18, 2006

More on Schmemann and joy:

> To love—one's self and others—with God's love: How needful this is in our time when love is almost completely misunderstood. How profitable it would be to think more carefully and more deeply about the radical peculiarity of God's love. It seems to me sometimes that the first peculiarity is cruelty. It means— *mutatis mutandis*—the absence of the sentimentality with which the world and Christianity have usually identified that love. In God's love, there is no promise of earthly happiness, no concern

10. Cf. Auden, *The Dyer's Hand,* 177.

about it. Rather, that love is totally submitted to the promise and the concern about the Kingdom of God, that is, the absolute happiness for which God has created man, to which He is calling man. Thus the first essential conflict between God's love and the fallen human love. 'Cut off your hand,' 'pluck out your eye,' 'leave your wife and children,' 'follow the narrow way,'—all of it so obviously irreconcilable with happiness in life . . .

What has Christianity lost so that the world, nurtured by Christianity, has recoiled from it and started to pass judgment over the Christian faith? Christianity has lost joy—not natural joy, not joy-optimism, not joy from earthly happiness, but Divine joy about which Christ told us that 'no one will take your joy from you' (John 16:22). Only this joy knows that God's love to man and to the world is not cruel; knows it because that love is part of the absolute happiness for which we are all created . . . [11]

November 1, 2006

Today is All Saints Day. The Old Testament lesson to be read today is Isaiah 25:6–9, a portion of which reads: "Then the Lord God will wipe away the tears from all faces . . . " (vs.8), an image picked up again in the Revelation of St. John the Divine, "he will wipe away every tear from their eyes." (Rev 21:4) A strange text to be read on All Saints Day, except that this eschatological vision hints that insofar as saints are those who follow Jesus Christ, their way, while not tearless, will end with One who wipes tears away. Think about what this image is portraying. At the end of all things, we are met not by the "Almighty" or "Sovereign Lord of History," but the loving parent who stoops to wipe away tears from a child who has hurt herself. What a vision of the end! What a vision of the saints who are gathered around the saint, Jesus Christ, and in whose presence have their tears and sorrows dried and healed.

A great Scottish pastor and hymn writer, George Matheson, wrote the hymn, "O Love That Wilt Not Let Me Go," whose words may seem to some old-fashioned and full of nineteenth century piety. Still, the theology of that hymn rings deeply true. In its third verse, it knows that as much as the joy of the gospel is inseparable from the pain we often suffer, the promise of God is not vain, "that morn shall tearless be." Tearless. Just as there is no crying in baseball, so there will be no crying in heaven.

11. Schmemann, *The Journals*, 291.

The saints are not sad and long-faced but joyful. May it be so on earth as it is in heaven.

January 20, 2010

Yesterday I got to meet my granddaughter, Corinne, for the first time. She was born the day before. She's beautiful. She's dainty and sweet but I suspect after a few rounds with her older brothers, she will be able to more than hold her own. I won't go on to list all her virtues here, but I do want to relate something that I was thinking about driving back home from this visit.

In Luke 15 there are three (or 3.5) parables: "The Lost Sheep," "The Lost Coin," and the somewhat inaccurately named "Prodigal Son" (which includes what Robert Capon has called the "Lament of the Responsible Child."), all of which end with an invitation to rejoice. The phrase that is used is, "Rejoice with me!" That is what the good shepherd says to his neighbors and what the woman who has found the lost coin tells "her friends and neighbors." And of course, it is basically what the father says to his elder son, whose particular hell is that he cannot rejoice.

In one sense there is nothing that extraordinary about the birth of a child. It happens every day. On the other hand, when you see such a little one begin her first day on earth, breathing with her own lungs, sleeping on her mother's breast, her fingers and toes just perfect, well you look at all of that in awestruck wonder and then say something like those folks in the parable: "Hey, look at this! Come and rejoice with me!"

I know that parallels are not perfect: my granddaughter was not lost, her parents did not have to go looking for her, etc. But the joy such a gift brings compels the telling of it to others. "Come, rejoice with me!"

There are plenty of reasons to be discouraged in this world and indeed, not all days and not all lives and not all places are so full of joy. Children who are born in Haiti, for example, are born into a very different world than my granddaughter. Still, I would venture to guess that even in that island that has known such misery, the birth of a child brings great joy.

What motivates us to care about the child in Haiti or support those who are seeking to relieve their pain is not unrelated to the joy we receive in the gifts God has placed in our hands, most especially the gift of another baby, whose life connects us to the little girl born here and the little girl born there. The only sin, I believe, is to refuse to rejoice, to choose to stay away from the party, to ignore the gifts in our midst. Joy is not the whole answer and cannot be used to do things that only medicine and money and labor can do, but it is what makes medicine and money and labor gifts that fill this world with hope.

A little baby teaches such things even to grandparents. Maybe that is why we babble on in such astonishment. "Come, rejoice with me!"

August 11, 2011

One of my favorite people is Sydney Smith (1771–1845), an Anglican divine, not much read today or even remarked upon, but who was and is as refreshing and delightful a companion as one could ever desire. As a young man, he wanted to be a lawyer, but his father prevailed upon him to become ordained. He submitted reluctantly, embarking on a career of parish ministry, political engagement, and intellectual endeavor remarkable by any standards. He was known in his day for being dangerously witty, often sending up the powerful or pompous and just as often defending the excluded or downtrodden. He is best-known today, I suspect, for being one of the founders of the *Edinburgh Review*, the first or one of the first literary and critical periodicals. But what interests me most was his allergic reaction to any form of self-pity, his *theological* refusal to play the victim, his joy in embracing the ordinary gifts of life.

He was not a Mr. Rogersish character. He did not believe in "the power of positive thinking." He would have been appalled at anyone proclaiming the gospel of "your best self now." He rarely served in a parish considered fashionable or prestigious, never made bishop, never rose to high office, either in his church or in the government. (His brother rose to a very high position in the British East India Company. Sydney, who had offended some higher-ups in the Anglican communion, once said of his brother, that "he had risen as a result of his gravity, while I have fallen due to my levity.") His only son, Douglas, an intellectually gifted young man, died in 1829, a loss that devastated his father. Sydney Smith had reason to be something less than cheerful.

But he was not. A leader in the anti-slavery movement, a proponent of Catholic emancipation and female suffrage, Sydney Smith was ahead of his time in many ways, but he never took on the mantle of an embittered prophet preaching to the incorrigible, or a self-righteous parson ashamed to be lumbered with the dullards of his own congregation.

One of my favorite quotes from Smith is contained in a letter he wrote following a visit to some puritanical sect. He wrote: "I endeavored in vain to give them more cheerful ideas of religion, to teach them that God is not a jealous, childish, merciless tyrant; that he is best served by a regular tenor of good actions—not by bad singing, ill-composed prayers and eternal apprehensions. But the luxury of false religion is to be unhappy."[12] *The luxury of false religion is to be unhappy.* This luxury is possible, I believe, only as a form of hopelessness. It is so easy to lose hope, not just about the world or our own failings, but about the church and the weakness of its message, the brokenness of its witness, the anger that seems to rage just below the surface of our attempts to live the Christian life.

So, it is good to be reminded that such luxury is not something the gospel ever affords. It is much poorer. Its people must exist on manna, on bread and wine, on words of grace. Yet, such poverty is always a happier thing. Not in the sense of being unremittingly upbeat, but happy in the simple confidence that knows the deep goodness of God, that knows something important, that knows that Jesus has won and the battle is no longer in doubt. To be unhappy in the face of that decisively good gift is to sin, to reject the manna that God daily provides.

Read Sydney Smith. He knows something about the deep joy that is at the heart of the gospel.

November 9, 2011

In a course I have been teaching this fall, we have been reading Will Willimon's book, *Pastor, The Theology and Practice of Ordained Ministry* (Abingdon, 2002). In this book Willimon has a chapter entitled, "Why Some Pastors Call It Quits." The title is not meant to be facetious. Willimon knows how hard ministry can be, how exhausting are its demands, how seemingly small are our resources, how indifferent if not hostile the culture appears to be, how frustrating the church and its governing bodies and congregations often prove to be, and how weary any pastor can become. This book is not a recruiting tool for seminaries.

But neither is it a cry of despair or a rant at the impossible nature of the job. Curiously the book inspires. So many of the reasons that are

12. Pearson, *The Smith of Smiths*, 230.

given for calling it quits are exactly what reveal this impossible work to be a gift. It is when ministry turns into a project that we are tempted to "call it quits." It is when ministry becomes a career that we burn out. It is when the impossible nature of ministry is forgotten or reduced to something that can be managed that it ceases to be a joy.

I know that ministry is hard. But it is not heavy. It becomes heavy only when we make it so, only when it becomes about our strategies for success, or more likely, our explanations for failures. No, this yoke is light. Hard but light. We are playing with house money. That is what ministry really is.

In trying to frame a response to Willimon's book, I kept thinking of Luther's hymn, "A Mighty Fortress Is Our God." We think of that hymn, rightly, as a great Reformation text and we sing it lustily at the end of October, celebrating its triumphal notes. Its lyrics constitute one of the best and most succinct statements of the *Christus Victor* theory of the Atonement. But the lyrics also have a great deal to say to those who are foolish enough or daring enough to take up the work of ministry. "Did we in our own strength confide, Our striving would be losing." What makes ministry possible, not to put too fine a point on it, is the fact that "the right man is on our side, the man of God's own choosing." Luther knows that the most implacable foes of ministry are not the relentless demands of the work or the paucity of resources but the "principalities and powers" that are capable of making us despair of God's work in the world, giving into the temptation to believe our self-doubts and manifold failures to be more powerful than God's grace. Behind such despair, of course, is an even larger pride, and behind that, an even more massive amount of self-absorption from which only God can deliver us.

"Dost ask who that [Deliverer] may be? Christ Jesus, it is he; Lord Sabaoth his name, From age to age the same." And, oh yes, lest we forget, "He must win the battle." This "little word" is stronger than all the things that "threaten to undo us."

So, knowing all of the reasons not to enter into this work becomes an occasion for laughter. Who did we think we were kidding? Did we think it was our virtues, our charming personalities, our expertise that was at stake here? Did we think this "career" would allow us to finish on top? Like who? The disciples? The prophets? Jesus? No, the only reason to go into this work is for the joy of it all, the dumb, stupid joy of it all, the joy that knows that in proclaiming the word, entering into the hearts of fellow pilgrims, pulling out of the treasure of the gospel what is new and old, we have been given a surpassingly marvelous gift, and are engaging mysteries beyond our capacity to state or comprehend.

Yes, the work is hard, very hard. But it is not heavy.

Chapter 5: Reading for Ministry

October 15, 2002

In his book, *Pastor: The Theology and Practice of Ordained Ministry*, Will Willimon reflects at length on one of the great readers of the faith, Augustine.

> One reason Augustine makes for such good reading in this century is that he had a life-long fear that we might be alone in the world. Our age is widely noted as a time of widespread alienation and loneliness. Fear of isolation, of loneliness, permeates much of Augustine's account of his life. Are we here by ourselves? Is there anyone else out there or in here, or are we left to our own devices? "Was I anywhere? Was I anybody?" he asks. Without the means to make connection with others, we are others even to ourselves. C.S. Lewis says, We read to know that we are not alone."[1]

Words are the means toward community, communion.

> *The Confessions* begins with "I, I," and ends with "You, You." All of our little words gesture toward the Word . . . . [Augustine's] life in Christ really begins by being confronted by the Word, "Take up and read, (*tolle, lege*) . . . . His is a journey through words to the Word . . . . His life culminates in, of all endeavors, biblical exegesis. The goal of life is the interpretation and performance of Scripture. All of our words are meant to find rest in the Word . . . . Augustine's testimony is an invitation to risk vocation, to go on the journey he has made, to venture forth with the expectation of discovering (or being discovered by) a new world, of learning to read as a primary way to God.[2]

1. Willimon, *Pastor,* 187–188.
2. *Ibid.,* 188, 191.

Willimon thinks that it was Ambrose who taught Augustine how to read scripture "and thus, how to read the world." I don't know if that is right or not, but I do know that learning how to read scripture teaches us how to re-describe our world, that is, to describe it not just as the scene of getting and spending or self-realization, but as the scene of God's life-giving and person-making forgiveness and grace.

The word that is spoken to us invites us not only to hear but to read.

February 23, 2005

In the most recent edition of *The Christian Century*, the editors have asked various luminaries to reflect upon the teachers they had in seminary who changed their lives. I was particularly struck by Will Willimon's memory of being at Yale in the late 1960's, and his remembering of Paul Holmer, a Lutheran theologian. Those days were turbulent times. One night the students gathered to hear Holmer and

> our great hero, William Sloane Coffin [a Presbyterian minister, and at the time, Chaplain to the University, whose most recent book, *Credo*, is currently a bestseller.] debate the role of the pastor. I don't know why someone invited Holmer to such a debate; like Soren Kierkegaard [whose work constituted part of Holmer's own field of interest], he was generally contemptuous of clergy. Coffin opened with an exciting exposition of the pastor as agent of social change. 'Because you visit and work with people in a variety of settings, you can organize them to work for justice. You will have important people in your churches—bankers, lawyers. You can do much good getting folk motivated to get together and work great change in your community.' When it came time for him to respond, Holmer said, 'I disagree with about everything that Bill has said. Your job can't be to organize people, to bring them together. People hide in groups. It's one of their best defenses against God. Your job as pastor is to break up the groups, strip them naked, render them exposed and vulnerable. That way God can get to them. Besides, Jesus despised bankers and lawyers.'

Willimon concludes: "Though that was opposed to just about everything that we believed at that time about ministry, and though I was mostly ignorant about what it took to be a pastor, I knew Holmer had it right."[3]

3. Willimon, *The Christian Century*, vol.122, No.4.

Well, I am not sure he had it exactly right. People can hide in more places than groups, and in America, one of the best places to hide out is in our own "individuality." Moreover, I don't think God is depending on me to render sinners accessible to his grace. Still, I do think Holmer was right that by preaching the gospel we bear a far more radical witness than by becoming a "change agent." We worship One whose love for us is not an agenda but a life, whose Word heals precisely as it wounds, lifts up as it casts down, inviting us to do something far more daring than "organizing" others. This God invites us all to follow Jesus Christ and in following him, to discover what it means to be taken from one place to another. That happens not as we become agents of change but as we become disciples. Holmer may have been a bit hard on bankers and lawyers, but he was right that the Kingdom does not come through better organizational skills. Rather there is something far more mysterious and miraculous in the gospel's working, a grace that can transform bankers, lawyers, and even clergy into instruments of peace.

September 21, 2005

Stephen Webb has written an important book on preaching, entitled, *The Divine Voice* (Wipf and Stock, 2012). He argues that we show that we have understood the gospel's message to the extent that we proclaim it. That is to say, the gospel is not just to be studied or thought about but finally intends its own proclamation. To miss that is to miss the gospel itself.

Like many of us, Webb thinks that he does not know what he knows until he says it. Our words do not just contain what we know, he thinks, they more often constitute what we know. In this respect, he thinks we are like God, whose triune life is constituted by the conversation made articulate in the Father's uttering the Word with the breath of the Spirit. Jesus is the way God speaks, Webb writes. And grace is God's way of uniting us to Christ so that we are included in this conversation. Baptism, the Lord's Supper, worship itself are the means of grace by which God helps us hear and teaches us how to speak, i.e., teaches us the language of praise and witness.

If what Webb is arguing is true, then his claim must represent the most difficult challenge facing a seminary. It suggests that the learning we do here is not simply digesting vast quantities of information or even acquiring certain pastoral or homiletical skills. Rather our aim must be to enable students to speak the grace of God idiomatically, helping them to become proficient in the language of praise and thanksgiving. Truly, that is the work of the Holy Spirit, i.e., to render us articulate and courageous witnesses to the gospel, but just so our teaching and learning need to reflect this gift even if we are embarrassed at our stammering timidity in making use of it.

After reading Webb's book, I have come to the conclusion that my hope for the students here is not that they become glib or chatty about the gospel but that they become courageous and hopeful speakers of its good news. Does that seem piously idealistic? Perhaps, but what will save us from such pious idealism is the fact that the word we seek to speak is not just a word but the Word made flesh, who knows how often we fail to speak, how often we prevaricate or stick to our own idiom, and yet who persists in putting his strange words into our mouths and hearts and lives. Because he speaks, the promise is that one day we will too, as timid and inarticulate (or as garrulous and foolish) as we might think ourselves to be. Because he lives, the promise is also for us that we too live . . . . and speak.

October 5, 2005

May I recommend a book for you? It is entitled, *A More Profound Alleluia* (Eerdmans, 2004) edited by Leanne Van Dyk. The book's subtitle reveals its substance: "Theology and Worship in Harmony." This book is a collection of essays that seek to relate each section of the liturgy (e.g., "Opening of Worship," "Confession and Assurance," "Proclamation," "Creeds and Prayers," "Eucharist," and "Benediction") to the theological doctrines that underpin and inform that particular part of worship. For example, the Opening of Worship is rooted in the doctrine of the Trinity; Confession and Assurance in the doctrines of sin and grace; Proclamation in Christology; the Creeds and Prayers in ecclesiology; Eucharist in eschatology; and Benediction in ethics. Accompanying each chapter are some suggested hymns.

Van Dyk's book is a marvelous way to study theology as well as to learn about worship. I commend it to you.

May 3, 2006

Recently several of us have been reading the *Study Catechism* of the Presbyterian Church (USA). Seven students and two professors gather each week to eat a meal together, to pray, and then to study. Sheldon Sorge, of our denomination's national office, helped us get started. Part of our covenant agreement with each other is to read scripture together, to follow the lectionary in the *Book of Common Worship Daily Prayer* edition, and then focus on these catechetical questions and answers. Today we read the following: "Q.71 What is baptism? A. Baptism is the sign and seal through which we are joined to Christ. Q.72 What does it mean to be baptized. A. My baptism means that I am joined to Jesus Christ forever. I am baptized into his death and resurrection, along with all who have received him by faith. As I am baptized with water, he baptizes me with his Spirit, washing away all my sins and freeing me from their control. My baptism is a sign that one day I will rise with him in glory, and may walk with him even now in newness of life."[4]

I have found it helpful work to read the catechism each day. It is not popular, I know, to teach in this way, but there is something to be said for the simple, straightforward "answer" that unapologetically points to the mysteriously large claims of the faith. I was struck today by the fact that baptism means, among other things, "that one day I will rise with him in glory," an affirmation about human destiny that is profoundly hopeful and which contrasts vividly with the hopelessness so often voiced in our own culture. The "answer" is hopeful not because it announces my "survival" or "self-preservation" but because it insists that the purposes of God, also for my life, will not be thwarted. Without such hope, we slowly begin to die, and therefore baptism is a powerful sign of God's faithfulness and therefore also our confidence and good cheer.

One could do worse than be instructed by this catechism.

February 12, 2008

One of the striking things about Father Alexander Schmemann's journal entries was the way he wrote about the day—its weather, the season, its sights, its longings, its turmoil, its simple gifts. He does this not by waxing eloquent over a beautiful sunset but by seeing a sunset or the bare empty

4. *Study Catechism,* 27.

trees of winter or snow falling on trees or rain puddling near a sidewalk—by seeing all of these as indications of life's goodness that come from God's own hand. The weather, nature, created beauty, these things are not background noise to faith's otherwise spiritual affirmations but rather are gifts which we are to receive and celebrate. Here is one entry from his journal:

> The same frosty sunshine. Yesterday I walked to church in the sunset. Brightly lit walls of houses, tops of trees. And a fleeting feeling, extremely strong, that right next to me, along with our life, exists another life, whose essence is entirely in its connection with the 'other', in its witness and expectancy. I had the same feeling in Boston where thick snow was falling, like a tale that nobody listens to. Amazing—in nature, in the world, everything moves. But in this movement (falling snow, branches lit by the sun, fields), each moment reveals a divine immobility, a fullness, in an icon of eternity as life.[5]

On some Saturdays, I see some of you eating lunch outside, enjoying the sunshine. A brief moment of quiet and sunshine in your face. On a gray day like today, I enjoy getting out for a moment after lunch, just to get out and receive a portion of the day as a gift. Some part of that in both you and me is a recognition of what Father Schmemann is talking about, an awareness "that here, right next to me, along with our life, exists another life," indeed a life in which "we live and move and have our being." That life, we believe, is definitively revealed in Jesus Christ, but as another poet has noted, "Christ plays in ten thousand places,"[6] and some of those are in the classroom, but others can be seen along the sidewalk, underneath a tree, or just walking down the street. The sense that there is "another life" nearby, perhaps right next to us, a presence that welcomes us with each new day, that is itself a gift that sometimes takes a moment to notice and acknowledge with gratitude.

September 17, 2008

I have been reading some of the novels of Peter DeVries recently, in preparation for a discussion here at the seminary with a group of pastors. DeVries is dead now but in the 50's and 60's, he was a novelist of

---

5. Schmemann, *The Journals*, 250.

6. Hopkins, *Gerard Manley Hopkins: The Major Works*, 129.

some fame and distinction. His stories consisted of a series of haphazard scenes strung together by a malaprop or ironic observation that made one laugh out loud. A protégé of James Thurber, DeVries often wrote about unglamorous people seeking to escape their humdrum existence for an ever-elusive Babylon of delights.

Ralph Wood, who has written very perceptively about DeVries, cites several instances of DeVriesian humor: A character in one of his novels desires above all to win his neighborhood's "Yard of the Month" award. He leaves a party in his neighborhood early because, he says, "I have premises to keep and miles to mow before I sleep." The mere thought of cremation makes one of his characters turn "ashen." "Like the cleaning lady, he says, we all come to dust." And on and on. In one of his novels a small town pastor debates the local atheist in a public forum, in which each of the debaters convinces the other of the truth of his position. My favorite line involves a wife who sues her husband's mistress for alienation of affection, and asks for $65.00 in damages.[7]

A recurring theme in DeVries' novels is the perduring mystery and gift of marriage. To quote Wood, "Living it up in Vanity Fair proves to be a terrible strain. DeVries' worldlings learn that there is nothing quite so time-consuming as seizing the day. To devote oneself to endless playfulness turns out to be very hard work."[8] Wood cites an aphorism of Ben Hecht's that strikes me as having direct relevance to parish ministry: "Convention has always more heroes than revolt."[9] Sometimes it takes more courage to do the next thing than to hit the road searching for greener pastures or greater adventures elsewhere.

In talking of his own marriage, one of DeVries' characters concludes (after singing, "Nobody knows the truffles I've seen"): "The conformity we often glibly equate with mediocrity isn't something free spirits 'transcend' as much as something they're not quite up to . . . . Convention calls for broad shoulders—and for all I know, more imagination than revolt."[10] At the end of this novel, the husband who has returned to his wife and rebuilt their marriage, runs across an old flame in a New York bar one night, and when invited to do something 'daring', replies: "'Thanks just

7. Wood, *The Comedy of Redemption*, 249.

8. *Ibid.*, 247.

9. *Ibid.*, 247.

10. *Ibid.*, 250.

the same,' I told her, 'but I don't want any pleasures interfering with my happiness.'"[11]

If you have read this far, you might be asking yourself what the heck does this have to do with anything. Well, it seems to me that studying to become a minister of word and sacrament is not really a very romantic undertaking. There is a difference, C.S. Lewis once said, between falling in love with the characters of *The Iliad* and *The Odyssey*, and then sitting down to learn Greek so that you can understand those characters in their native idiom. And there is a temptation to think that our real selves must be free spirits that transcend the mundane work of conjugating verbs or mastering the nuances of a doctrinal position. Imagination we associate with free spirits but in fact, I suspect that real imagination in ministry has more to do with the mundane work of listening again and again to a particular word and digging more deeply into a text we might otherwise consider familiar. Thus do we acquire the broad shoulders to do what really matters: preaching the lively word each Sunday, planning worship that is rooted in the mysterious faithfulness of God, pastoring those whose illness shows no sign of improvement, whose anger or depression cannot be immediately "fixed," and bearing witness to the Kingdom in the midst of our quite earthly communities again, and again, and again.

Eugene Peterson compares the work of ministry to mucking out a stall, a task that has to be done each day, and one that is not nearly so glamorous as riding a black stallion at the head of a parade. "What are we coming to?" a woman in one of DeVries' novels asks her husband as they are driving back from New York. "Connecticut," he answers.[12]

Well, what we are coming to is the third week of the fall term. It is not the eschaton, not the barricades, not perhaps our final or most glorious moment, but it is a moment that requires of us the most imaginative, thoughtful, creative and best service we can give. The Episcopalians have in their *Book of Common Prayer*, a prayer written by Thomas Cranmer that ends with the words, " . . . .whose service is perfect freedom."[13] We are heirs of a tradition that believes those words to be true, even though our culture might define freedom a bit differently. What the *Book of Common Prayer* and the characters in many of Peter DeVries' novels both know is that a freedom rooted elsewhere is indistinguishable from a prison,

11. *Ibid.*, 250.

12. *Ibid.*, 259.

13. *Book of Common Prayer, Collect for Peace, Morning Prayer.*

however comfortable. In any case, I hope that as this term moves forward you will not let any pleasures interfere with your happiness.

March 18, 2009

For a number of years Clara Claiborne Park taught English at a community college for working students seeking to acquire a basic degree. In 1991, she published a book of essays, entitled, *Rejoining the Common Reader,* all of which dealt in one way or another with her work with those students, who often asked her why anyone should read.

One of her essays has to do with Jane Austen. Park recalls a poem by Rudyard Kipling who imagines a returning soldier from the Great War telling his lodge brothers what it was like in the trenches. In order to sustain themselves against fear of being blown to bits, his unit decided to label themselves, "Janeites," and encourage each other by references to characters in her novels. "You take it from me," the returning soldier advises his friends, "There's no one to touch Jane when you're in a tight place."[14]

Park knows that Kipling is engaging to some extent in sentimental nonsense. Nothing could comprehend or prepare one for the miseries of that war. But in a way, Park argues, that is exactly why one reads Jane Austen. "We are reading . . . to discover how much a brilliant and not wholly fortunate woman can teach us about how to live within bounds, how to recognize them, even display them as bounds, and still not find them a prison, and still do one's serious, amused, responsible best to live well inside them and stretch them a little for those who come after . . . . Limits straiten us all. And there's no one to touch Jane when you are in a tight place."[15]

Well, you may not fancy Jane Austen, but the same kind of question might be asked of us, that is, why do we spend so much time reading texts here. The temptation, especially in American culture, is to view limits as, well, limiting, and in any case, a kind of negative thing. We read, we think, to escape limits, to transcend them. I remember a commercial for AT&T from a few years back, which invited us to "Imagine a world without limits." Such a world would be hell. A world without limits destroys marriages, families, neighborhoods, and churches. A world without

14. Park, *Rejoining the Common Reader,* 137.
15. *Ibid.,* 144–145.

limits is what brought down Enron, and what accounts for many of our troubles today.

So much of going to seminary involves getting intimately acquainted with limits: studying the original languages, burrowing into long theological readings, learning the theory and practice of teaching and pastoral care and preaching. And of course, there is never enough time, never enough energy, never enough quiet to do it all. Our days must be budgeted, or to use an older and better word, stewarded. Yet precisely in such stewardship we find the limits themselves become occasions for grace. More than one person has found that a tithe gives order to one's finances. Sabbath observance, Karl Barth has written, is the basis for human freedom.[16] Simone Weil, in one of her essays, describes how a wall in prison which separates one cell from another becomes the conducting medium by which one prisoner can communicate with another.[17] Limits can become bridges.

I suspect that most exegesis papers, sermons, and theology essays gain their value not as isolated pieces of brilliance but as carvings out of the limits that shape our days. And when you are in a tight, Jane Austen may well help. The faith that sustained her (and some of her characters, like Fanny Price in *Mansfield Park*) was one that was defined and limited by the cross. There is where our limits and our life meet.

July 8, 2009

July 10, 2009 will mark the 500th anniversary of John Calvin's birth. I suspect he might look down his long nose at all the celebrations planned for this year but perhaps he would be mollified if some of those occasions resulted in the praise and service of God and the flourishing of human life.

In preparation for a course in Ethics this fall, I have been prompted by Gilbert Meilaender to read Felix Salten's "children's book," *Bambi*.[18] I don't know if children or their parents read *Bambi* today, but it is, in its own way, a real eye-opener. The point of so many of the episodes in the book is that relationships are dangerous, and wisdom comes by remaining alone, cultivating a stoic invulnerability to pain and joy alike. Bambi takes a walk with his mother and sees a ferret kill a mouse. "Why?" he

16. Barth, *Church Dogmatics*, III/4, 71.
17. Cf. Weil, *Gravity and Grace*, 132.
18. Cf. Meilaender, *Faith and Faithfulness*, 155–156.

asks, and his mother refuses to answer. Soon his mother leaves him alone, more and more, and in the forest by himself Bambi begins to weep. The old stag hears him and asks him, "What are you crying about? Can't you stay by yourself?" To grow up is to live alone. Of all the old stag's teachings, Salten writes, "this had been the most important; you must live alone, if you wanted to preserve yourself . . . ."[19]

One day Bambi thinks he hears Faline calling him and he happily runs toward what he thinks is her voice. But the old stag blocks the way and tells a disbelieving Bambi that it is not Faline. He then leads Bambi by another way, and from the safety of cover, shows Bambi the hunter who is imitating Faline's call. The lesson is painfully evident: Bambi is most vulnerable when he gives his heart as a hostage to another.[20]

Meilaender argues that Bambi is one of the most lucid expressions of Stoicism ever written, and it is hard to disagree. So it is interesting to read what Calvin says about the Stoic effort to insulate one's heart from others. Calvin is often portrayed as a Stoic of sorts, a hard man, who emphasized the virtues of self-renunciation. And in truth, Calvin has a great deal to say about self-denial. Yet he argues that the Stoic position is selfishly ungrateful and more concerned with its "self-preservation" than in receiving the gifts God gives us daily even in the midst of pain and loss.

What drives Calvin to this position is not any inherent jolliness in his personality or some hitherto undiscovered sunniness of disposition. What drives him to this position is the way the gospel narrative portrays Jesus Christ. "For he groaned and wept both over his own and others' misfortunes. And he taught his disciples in the same way . . . . 'Blessed are those who mourn.' . . . For if all weeping is condemned, what shall we judge concerning the Lord himself, . . . who confesses his soul 'sorrowful even to death.'"[21]

Human beings are not created to be posts or pieces of iron but for that deepest relationship of all, the relationship with God. That is the vulnerability that constitutes faith and from which we are tempted daily to flee, but which reminds us also daily that there is One who will not let us go. From the cross, his cry of dereliction pierces the most well-constructed forms of isolation.

19. Meilaender, *Faith and Faithfulness,* 155.
20. *Ibid.,* 155.
21. Calvin, *The Institutes,* III,8,8.

One might think that in our "confessional age" we could use a bit more Stoicism. We are more familiar with Disney's *Bambi* than Salten's, more familiar with Dr. Phil than with "the old stag." Our eagerness to unburden ourselves is one of the best ways we have contrived to keep from hearing that piercing cry from the cross that continues to claim us. But here, Calvin is a better teacher than Felix Salten or Dr. Phil, and for that reason alone, it is more than appropriate to wish him a happy 500th birthday.

September 30, 2009

Fleming Rutledge, an Episcopalian priest who lives in New York, will be with us in October. The author of several books, many dealing with preaching, she has also written on J.R.R. Tolkien (*The Battle for Middle Earth*, Eerdmans, 2004). Here is a quote from a sermon on Psalm 16 delivered at a memorial service during Eastertide a few years ago:

> The more we know of life, the more we experience its disappointments and sorrows, the more we learn that things don't work out the way we wanted, the more the Bible has to offer us. The people of the Bible are not stained glass figures; they are like us. They are flesh and blood. They turn away from God, make deals with crooks, stab people in the back. They complain, argue, cheat, commit adultery, tell lies. They suffer . . . . Their children die, their homes are destroyed, plagues of locusts eat their crops. But here is the central fact. All of this happens in the sight of God and in the context of his faithfulness. That is why we often find two seemingly contradictory things in the same psalm, for instance in Psalm 40: "Though I am poor and afflicted, the Lord will have regard for me." Or Psalm 38: "My loins are filled with searing pain, there is no health in my body; I am utterly numb and crushed . . . . [but] in you, Lord, have I fixed my hope; you will answer me, O Lord my God."
>
> How can the Psalms be so filled with despair and hope at the same time? Is this what is frequently called "the triumph of the human spirit"? No, it isn't. One of the central truths of Biblical faith is that the human spirit left to itself is doomed to self-destruct. The Biblical man or woman does not say, 'I am the master of my soul, I am the captain of my fate.' We do not say, 'I did it my way.' [Instead, we say] 'Thou dost show me the path of

life; in thy presence there is fullness of joy, in thy right hand are pleasures evermore." (Ps 16:11)

This is a way of saying what is unsayable. God has promised to us the abundance of his own inexhaustible riches, not because we deserved them—Scripture teaches us we most decidedly did not deserve them—but because it was his purpose to give them to us out of his unbounded, indeed immeasurable love . . . . What a strange story it is that the church tells! . . . . The promise of abundant life, the hope of glory, the guarantees of the fullness of joy lie in our recollection of the mighty act of God who raised Jesus from the dead and has promised that we will be raised with him. We trust him for the future because in our own day we have heard afresh the ancient Easter message. 'The Lord is risen! The Lord is risen indeed!'[22]

Fleming Rutledge is worth reading and listening to, something we will have the opportunity to do next month.

October 6, 2010

In 1989 I had just moved from one small Texas town to another slightly larger one, from a redeveloped congregation to a much more established one. I had been a pastor for 13 years and had experienced some ups and downs in the ministry but I thought I knew what ministry was about, mostly. However, I was having a hard time relating to my new congregation and found myself struggling with a kind of vocational depression. I couldn't understand why folks didn't think my sermons just marvelous, why the town didn't flock to First Presbyterian Church each Sunday to hear the pure gospel unfolded, why ministry itself seemed such a struggle for me.

I don't remember who put the book into my hands but one day, I found myself reading Eugene Peterson's *Working the Angles* (Eerdmans 1989). That book came to me like water in the desert, manna in the wilderness. It was one of the very few books I wished that I had read while in seminary. And it wasn't because Peterson explained it all for me or gave me some surefire sermon tips or managerial strategies for garnering market share. None of that. Indeed, I found myself in the company of someone who found ministry mysterious and hard, beautiful and

22. Rutledge, *The Undoing of Death*, 331–332.

demanding, a form of discipleship that was serenely uninterested in what my colleagues, and in truth, what I myself fretted about: numbers, success, therapeutic solutions, etc. Here was someone who insisted on calling the place where he worked his "study," who kept appointments to read novelists and poets who spoke about the mystery of being human and the deeper mystery of God's grace. Here was a pastor who thought his parishioners were not numbers but storied people, carrying burdens and facing challenges of which one could scarcely guess, and who were in need, as I was, of some water in the desert, manna in the wilderness. Here was a preacher drenched in scripture's story, who studied it not to become an expert, but as if it were a great treasure that delighted one's heart. Here was a man who praised Sabbath, and saw in Sabbath rest true liberation, a minister who was suspicious of modernity's 24/7 efficiencies. Here was a minister of the Word who, because of that, loved words, loved how they could be well-crafted to serve the Word.

I remember trying to gather other area ministers to "come and rejoice with me" in what I had found in Peterson. I thought we might read some of his books together and so find a joy in ministry that could be shared. They, however, were not interested.

Years later, when I came to Charlotte to undertake this work, I decided that one of the first books I wanted students to read was Peterson's book on Jonah and the task of ministry: *Under the Unpredictable Plant: An Exploration of Vocational Holiness* (Eerdmans 1994). Could one really speak of "holiness" or the "holy life" or "holy vocation" without the quotation marks? Could the pious ooze and the pretentious righteousness be drained from the word to reveal its terrifying glory? Peterson does that in this book, and does so in a way that makes the call to ministry appear as dangerous and as difficult as it really is.

Peterson will be with us this coming weekend. I hope you will be able to engage him in conversation. He will be, I think you will find, a good conversation partner.

May 11, 2011

When I was about about 45 years old, I started reading Jane Austen. One might think that was pretty late in the game to become interested in one of the world's great novelists, but I have always been a slow learner, and in my immaturity, I am not sure I could have appreciated her before then.

She was and is a great artist but she also knows a thing or two about ethics and I would argue, even theology.

Alasdair McIntyre, whose book, *After Virtue*, first drew my attention to Jane Austen's "profoundly Christian moral vision," calls her, "the last great effective imaginative voice of the tradition of thought about, and practice of, the [classical] virtues . . . ."[23]

The chief virtue of Jane Austen's heroines and heroes is "constancy." Constancy is that virtue, which as the presupposition of all others, enables a person to live in accordance with the end for which he or she is made. It is a kind of faithfulness to a particular vision of human life, a vision of the human being as a creature of God, whose integrity is not to be violated or manipulated for lesser ends than the service of God and the enjoyment of our own and others' humanity. None of this, or very little of this, is made explicit, but all of this forms the plot and character of her great novels and informs the Christian self-understanding of her heroines. Hers is a "Christian rather than a Socratic self-knowledge which can only be achieved through a kind of repentance."[24] "Till this moment I never knew myself," says Elizabeth Bennet. "How to understand the deceptions she had been practicing on herself, and living under," thinks Emma. As McIntyre notes, "Self-knowledge is for Jane Austen both an intellectual and moral virtue . . . ."[25]

So how does one come by such self-knowledge? It is difficult. Many people who should be guides to us are not (e.g., Mr. and Mrs. Bennet, Mr. and Mrs. Bertram, Mrs. Norris), and are, in fact, potentially dangerous. We ourselves do not possess this knowledge innately, and we acquire it only through time and often through failure and suffering.

And yet there is something or better, Someone, whose life comprehends the purposes of our own, and whose grace enables us to see what we otherwise would miss. Moreover, this grace, which resists the reduction of human life to socially constructed ends, enables a constancy that is rooted in God's own faithfulness to his sinful and broken creatures. In Jane Austen's novels there is both a searing critique of a commercial and class-dominated culture as well as a depiction of the deep mercy and even contented happiness of those such a culture overlooks or dismisses.

23. McIntyre, *After Virtue*, 279.

24. *Ibid.*, 241.

25. *Ibid.*, 241.

Fanny Price is one of those easily overlooked creatures, whom the wealthy and clever and self-absorbed inhabitants of *Mansfield Park* regularly dismiss, often in patronizing tones of pity and contempt. Yet Fanny, a poor relative of the Bertram family, learns and exhibits constancy. In ways that are not always clear even to herself, she seems to have an inner gyroscope that prevents her from being reduced to something less than a child of God. This is not easy, and for Fanny, this comes at great cost, especially when she is offered everything that the society of her day and her own guardian regard as "salvation." Something in her thinks that there are more important things than being "saved" (or to put it in the terms of the novel, accepting, in her poverty, the proposal of marriage from a wealthy but deceitful suitor). What could enable a person to reject such a "salvation," especially when it contains everything we are told we should want? At this point, Jane Austen's vision strikes me as uncomfortably contemporary and almost Reformed.

We live in a culture that purveys salvation as the highest good. Politically, religiously, economically, socially, medically, denominationally,—we will justify anything in order to be saved. Narratives that question such an idolatry of salvation run deeply counter to our culture, which is another reason Jane Austen's novels are worth reading. Another way of making this point is to insist that knowledge of self derives from that one who, when offered salvation (" . . . save yourself, and come down from the cross!" Mark 15:30), refused it, enacting a constancy entirely cruciform in shape.

So read Jane Austen. Her novels are delightful, witty, and if you are not careful, theologically encouraging.

September 28, 2011

In the past three years I have required my students in Ethics to read an article by Kathleen Norris on the sin of "Acedia," a form of slothful despair about oneself and the world. In that article she tells the story of being a bratty teenager, who, when her mother asked her to make up her bed, replied, "Why bother? I'll just have to unmake it again at night." She continues: "To me, the act was stupid repetition; to my mother, it was a meaningful expression of hospitality to oneself and a humble acknowledgement of our creaturely need to make and remake our daily environments. 'You will feel better,' [my mother] said, 'if you come home to an orderly room.' She was far wiser than I, but I didn't comprehend that for many years . . . ."[26]

So much of learning and of pastoring is repetition. Memorizing texts and hymns has gone out of fashion these days, which, in my judgment, is more the pity. When I would lead worship in a nursing home in my days as a pastor, I would always be struck with how the lyrics from an old hymn, or the voicing of a familiar Bible verse, or even the response of a catechetical answer would light up a face or broaden a wrinkled smile. As threadbare as many of those words were, they were sources of strength to the residents of those "homes." They knew the words, as we say, "by heart." Yes, by heart.

More than sentiment is involved here. Repetition can help shape the path of discipleship.

This summer I was given the opportunity to live for a week near the Abbey of St. John's in Collegeville, Minnesota, where Benedictine monks gather to worship 4 times a day (7 a.m., 12 noon, 5 p.m., and 9 p.m.), reading the lectionary texts and psalms for the day. Same texts, same feasts, same movement from Advent to Epiphany to Lent to Easter to Pentecost to Ordinary Time to All Saints Day, Christ the King and back to Advent. These repetitions are strangely not boring. Instead their rhythms draw one more deeply into the mystery of God's daily, unspectacular, life-giving grace. One soon grows accustomed to these rhythms and even is carried along by them.

Eugene Peterson has compared ministry to farming. So many of the chores have to be repeated each day. So many are not dramatic but quite ordinarily mundane. Often they are messy. I think that people who study here learn very quickly the truth to which Peterson and Norris are pointing. The sense of call to ministry in one's own life may or may not be dramatic but in any case, represents a passionate claim that deserves immediate attention. We want to do something right now! But then we are told to study for 5 or 6 years in seminary, memorizing Greek verbs or identifying the Satisfaction theory of the Atonement or learning from Hildegard of Bingen. Why so long? Why so much repetition, when after all, God has called me to be about God's work right now?

As you no doubt have discovered, I am not a Biblical scholar, but I have always been intrigued with the account Paul gives (not through Luke but in his own account in Galatians) of his seminary experience.

26. Norris, *"Wasted Days"* in *The Christian Century,* Sept. 23, 2008, 30.

Few have received a more dramatic call than Paul. He refers to that in Galatians 1:13, noting his persecution of the church, his zeal for "the traditions of my ancestors," and God's sudden revelation of Jesus Christ to him. Paul makes it clear that he did not immediately preach, did not suddenly proclaim his conversion experience in Jerusalem. Rather, "I went away at once into Arabia, and afterwards, I returned to Damascus. Then after three years, I did go up to Jerusalem . . . " (Gal 1:17)

After three years. Of what? Study with others, prayer, re-reading of scripture, silence, sorting things out, learning some things by heart? We don't know. But in any case his journey of learning and doing and re-doing step by step was a journey of learning how to follow. Kathleen Norris tells of her desire at one point in her youth, "to do everything once and for all and be done with it," a kind of deep impatience that is a close relative to the *acedia,* whose despair can breed such impatience.

So how are we delivered from such slothful self-absorption? By the Holy Spirit, no doubt, but the Holy Spirit who teaches us to love the ordinary, to bless the daily gift of life, to be content with the "long obedience in the same direction" and resist the temptation for quick fixes. Only such a miracle can help us. Only such a miracle can introduce us to the repetitious gifts Jesus insists on giving his disciples. He has a way of taking us to "Arabia," of slowing us down, of giving us direction amidst the mess of life. He does not hold that mess in contempt but precisely there, in the daily repetition of worship and study and life together is where the Incarnate takes shape in our lives. There is where the beauty of what is small, ordinary, daily, and unremitting begins to shape us into disciples fit for Jesus' ministry.

January 18, 2012

I have been reading a book by Julie Canlis recently, entitled, *Calvin's Ladder* (Eerdmans, 2010), which interprets Calvin's theology not just in terms of its systematic or historical significance but also in terms of its spiritual and "lived out" commitments. Canlis stresses the importance for Calvin of the liturgical phrase, "Lift up your hearts." This phrase is important because Calvin sees our union with Christ as an upward movement, the rising of the believer who has been lifted up through union with Christ into the presence of God. The "ladder" is not metaphysical or mystical or philosophical. The "ladder" is deeply Christological, with Christ lifting us up from the grave of our own self-centeredness to the light and self-forgetting joy of life before God.

This is an interesting book that warrants further attention.

January 23, 2013

In preparation for a class I will be teaching with John Rogers, I have been re-reading Richard Lischer's book, *Open Secrets*. It is such a great book, a classic really, that describes Lischer's first pastorate in a small, rural, Lutheran congregation in southern Illinois. Lischer had come to this church directly from finishing his PhD in London.

Sometimes we talk about the importance of "exegeting the congregation" as well as the text, and I think it fair to say that Lischer had a lot of exegeting to do. He was a city boy, trained in the best schools that his tradition had to offer, a highly educated, not to say, learned reader of texts. The church he was called to serve was populated largely by farming families, most of whom had not attended college and many of whom had not graduated from high school.

One of his chapters begins by reflecting on his effort to preach to these folks. It is entitled, appropriately, "Help me, Jesus" and deals with a sermon he preached during Epiphany. He writes:

> Like most preachers, I grossly overestimated the importance of my part of the sermon. When I thought of preaching, I did not consider it to be the congregation's reception of the word of God, but a speaker's command of the Bible's hidden meanings and applications, which were served up in a way to showcase the authority and skill of the preacher. In those days, the gospel lived or died by my personal performance. My preaching was a small cloud of glory that followed me around and hung like a canopy over the pulpit whenever I occupied it. How ludicrous I must have appeared to my congregation .... In my first sermon I explained the meaning of *an* epiphany, not *the* Epiphany of God in the person of Jesus—no, that would have been too obvious— but the category of epiphanies in general .... Before I could talk about Jesus, I apparently found it necessary to give my farmers a crash course in the angst-ridden plight of modern man .... It didn't occur to me that the problem of meaninglessness had not occurred to my audience or that Marx's critique of religion rarely came up at the post office .... Aside from the formulaic complaints about Communists, perverts, and radicals, they did

not engage the modern world . . . . But then I did not bother to
engage their world either . . . . Why couldn't I see the revelation of God in our little church? In our community everyone
pitched in and learned how to 'pattern' a little girl with cerebral
palsy. We helped one another put up hay before the rains came.
We grieved when a neighbor lost his farm, and refused to buy
his tools at the auction. As a people, we walked into the fields
every April and blessed the seeds before planting them. Weren't
these all signs of 'church' that were worthy of mentioning in the
[Epiphany] Sunday homily? Whatever lay closest to the soul
of the congregation I unfailingly omitted from my sermons. I
didn't despise these practices. I simply didn't see them.[27]

A long quote, I know, but Lischer's words remind me that one of the
congenital failings that Jesus regularly addresses in the gospel is blind-
ness. He helps people see. He helps us see. What is hardest for us to see
is the beauty of the church itself. We labor so hard to make it something
good or important or strategically useful. We miss its particular glory. It
takes an epiphany for us to see the glory of God in our midst, the Epiphany of Jesus Christ to open our blind eyes to the glory of the ordinary
all around us.

You might want to read Lischer's book. His recounting of his first
three years of ministry describes a blind man who is slowly given his
sight and enabled to see the rare beauty of the congregation he had been
called to serve. It took awhile. It often does. But God is patient and God
still opens the eyes of the blind.

27. Lischer, *Open Secrets*, 73.

Chapter 6: Theology and Poetry

September, 2002

Do you know George Herbert? He was, like most of you, a second-career student, who, after a career in Parliament and the academy, became a priest in 1629. He served the parish church of Bemerton, England, near Salisbury. He died in 1633.

Perhaps you know one of his hymns, "Let All the World in Every Corner Sing". In any case, he wrote several poems about the church, its worship, its architecture, its ministers, its mission, all collected in a book of poems entitled, *The Temple*.[1] Herbert is not just a remarkable poet. He knows something about the faith and how the grace of God sustains those who follow Jesus Christ, especially those who enter the ministry. I have returned to him again and again in my own ministry, not to pretty up my sermons but to understand better what I have been called to do.

Herbert was an Augustinian in his theology. We have been reading Augustine's *Confessions* in class, so I thought I could do worse today than to end this brief note by printing out for you one of Herbert's poems that illustrates his understanding of our "restless hearts."

The Pulley

When God at first made man,
Having a glass of blessings standing by,
Let us (said he) pour on him all we can:
Let the world's riches, which dispersed lie,
Contract into a span.

So strength first made a way;
Then beauty flow'd, then wisdom, honor, pleasure:

1. Cf. *The Complete Poems of George Herbert*, 3–178.

When almost all was out, God made a stay,
Perceiving that alone of all his treasure
Rest in the bottom lay.

For if I should (said he)
Bestow this jewel also on my creature,
He would adore my gifts instead of me,
And rest in nature, not the God of nature:
So both should losers be.

Yet let him keep the rest,
But keep them with repining restlessness:
Let him be rich and weary that at least,
If goodness lead him not, yet weariness
May toss him to my breast.[2]

February 26, 2003

Next week many churches in our area will be observing Ash Wednesday. One of George Herbert's poems, *The Agonie*, helps us think faithfully about this coming season in which we reflect on Jesus' long walk toward Jerusalem and his embrace of the events that took place there. I will close this brief note to you by sharing with you Herbert's poem.

The Agonie

Philosophers have measured mountains,
Fathomed the depths of seas, of states, and kings,
Walked with a staff to heaven, and traced fountains:
But there are two vast, spacious things,
The which to measure it doth more behove:
Yet few there are that sound them, Sin and Love.

Who would know Sin, let him repair
Unto Mount Olivet: there shall he see
A man so wrung with pains, that all his hair,
His skin, his garments bloody be.
Sin is that press and vice, which forceth pain
To hunt for his cruel food through every vein.

2. *Ibid.*, 150.

Who knows Love, let him assay
And taste that juice, which on the cross a pike
Did set again abroach; then let him say if ever he did taste the like.
Love is that liquor sweet and most divine,
Which my God feels as blood; but I as wine.[3]

June 30, 2005

My father might be best described as a Liberal Protestant Evangelical, a combination one does not see much of today. He loves the Presbyterian Church, thinks we ought to be starting new churches, and he loves this country. He is a Calvinist whose deep faith has never seen a conflict with the broadest learning. He has always feared any kind of faith that would seek to dictate what could be learned in the world, just as he has been suspicious of any kind of learning that thought itself exempt from the workings of God's providence. In a book that he wrote some time back, he quoted a piece of doggerel that summed up his own views and represented what he thought best of the Reformed tradition. I leave it with you.

A Calvinist, he thought, never

Dreads the skeptic's puny hands
While near the school the church spire stands;
Nor fears the blinded bigot's rule
While near her church spire stands a school.[4]

September 14, 2005

This morning at staff meeting the devotional dealt with one of God's attributes: mercy. There is a debate of sorts going on among some academics today as to whether Shakespeare was a crypto-Catholic or a moderate Protestant. I don't know enough to enter that debate, but based on Portia's speech in *The Merchant of Venice*, I would affirm that Shakespeare knew something about the doctrine of grace and how justice, pursued without mercy, soon becomes lethally unjust. As a piece of theology, Portia's speech on mercy is worth remembering, not least in our day when

---

3. *Ibid.*, 33.

4. Currie, Thomas W. Jr., *The History of Austin Presbyterian Theological Seminary*, 25.

"justice" has become such a self-evident good. Let's hear the speech from
Portia again, if only to reflect on the gift of mercy.

> The quality of mercy is not strained,
> It droppeth as the gentle rain from heaven
> Upon the place beneath:
> It is twice blessed;
> It blesseth him that gives and him that takes;
> 'Tis mightiest in the mightiest; it becomes
> The throned monarch better than his crown;
> His scepter shows the force of temporal power,
> The attribute to awe and majesty,
> Wherein doth sit the dread and fear of kings,
> But mercy is above the sceptered sway,
> It is enthroned in the hearts of kings,
> It is an attribute to God himself,
> And earthly power doth then show likest God's
> When mercy seasons justice. Therefore, Jew,
> Though justice be thy plea, consider this,
> That in the course of justice, none of us
> Should see salvation: we do pray for mercy,
> And that same prayer doth teach us all to render
> The deeds of mercy.[5]

Not bad theology, whether Roman Catholic or Protestant. And good
to remember, when we plea so ardently for justice, "that in the course of
justice, none of us should see salvation."

October 13, 2005

I have always loved Psalm 127. It begins: "Unless the Lord builds the
house, those who build it labor in vain." But it is the second verse that
is my favorite part of the psalm. It reads: "It is in vain that you rise up
early and go late to rest, eating the bread of anxious toil; for he gives to
his beloved sleep."

For he gives to his beloved sleep. As I grow older, that gift seems
more and more precious.

Charles Peguy, a French Catholic writer and poet, died in the early
days of World War I. He wrote a remarkable poem entitled, "Sleep," a
portion of which I would like to share with you, in part because I find

---

5. Shakespeare, *The Merchant of Venice,* Act IV, Scene 1.

myself so deeply implicated in this poem's lyrics and wonder if you might find its words equally troubling.[6]

Sleep

I don't like the man who doesn't sleep, says God.
Sleep is the friend of man. Sleep is the friend of God.
Sleep is perhaps the most beautiful thing I have created, and
I myself rested on the seventh day.
He whose heart is pure, sleeps, and he who sleeps has
    a pure heart.
That is the great secret of being as indefatigable as a child,
Of having the strength in the legs that a child has.
Those new legs, those new souls,
And to begin afresh every morning, ever new,
Like young hope, new hope.

But they tell me that there are men
Who work well and sleep badly.
Who don't sleep.
What a lack of confidence in me. I pity them.
I have it against them. A little, they don't trust me.
Like the child who innocently lies in his mother' arms,
    thus they do not lie
Innocently in the arm of my Providence.
They have the courage to work.
They haven't enough virtue to be idle.
To stretch out. To rest. To sleep.
Poor people, they don't know what is good.
They look after their business very well during the day.
But they haven't enough confidence in me to let me look after it
    during the night.
As if I wasn't capable of looking after it during one night.
He who doesn't sleep is unfaithful to hope.
And it is the greatest infidelity.

June 4, 2006

This afternoon, Susan Hickok and I had lunch with a fellow who is going to give the seminary some money to help with our scholarship program.

---

6. Cf. Peguy, *Basic Verities,* 209–215.

He is a very successful businessman and a member of one of the churches in Charlotte. During the course of the conversation, he said that every morning when he wakes up, he says . . . . And I waited for him to say something like, "I am going to make a million dollars today," or perhaps, "I am going to do something strikingly generous and philanthropic today." But what he said was: "Every morning, when I wake up, I say, 'Thank you.'"

This "you" he thanks, he went on to say, is the One who gives us our days and our daily bread. He went on to observe, "Life is a blessing."

Which reminded me of some words in Auden's poem, "Precious Five" in praise of the five senses. There he invites the reader to "bless what there is for being."[7]

Why are you going to seminary? To know stuff? To acquire certain skills? Perhaps all of that and more, but we will have failed if in doing all of that you are unable at the end of your time here, to "bless what there is for being," to be able to say at the beginning and end of each day, "Thank you."

January 10, 2007

In one of Auden's poems ("As I walked Out One Evening"[8]), he writes:

> In headaches and in worry
> Vaguely life leaks away,
> And Time will have his fancy
> Tomorrow or today.

This poem ruefully acknowledges the fragility of our sunny optimism, the brevity of all our promises of love, the inadequacies of our most sincere affirmations. Time has a way of having his fancy despite all our protestations. But the poem does not end in a sigh of wise despair. Rather, it celebrates that in the midst of the dailiness of ordinary life, amidst the routines of study, work, and obligations owed to others, there is a blessing to be found, and even in our weakness and sinfulness, we are summoned to bless, and in all our frailty, to love one another. Listen:

> O look in the mirror,
> O look in your distress;

---

7. Auden, *Collected Poems*, 591.
8. Auden, *Collected Poems*, 133.

Life remains a blessing
Although you cannot bless.

O stand, stand at the window
As tears scald and start;
You shall love your crooked neighbor
With your crooked heart.

Loving crooked neighbors with our own crooked hearts describes, in fact, the work of ministry, the impossible work which we undertake only through the power of the Holy Spirit. Only a miracle enables us to bless the mess we find ourselves in, especially when we cannot see it as a blessing. Only a miracle can enable us to love our crooked neighbors with hearts as crooked as our own.

So, as you are studying your Greek this term or buried under assignments in Contemporary Theology, and are, perhaps, having trouble blessing this mess, know that it remains a blessing, even a gift that will bless you, and enable your crooked little heart to love others whose hearts are crooked as well.

June 10, 2009

When I was a child, my mother would come into my room at night to tuck me in and say prayers with me. My childhood prayers, like the ones I pray now, were often scattered, unformed, and often unfocused. But my Mom prayed with me each night.

Recently I have come across a poem by W. H. Auden, entitled, "Lullaby,"[9] which he wrote shortly before he died. The title might indicate that it is a song to be sung to an infant, but in fact this is a song of an old man sung to himself before he falls to sleep, or perhaps before he falls into that final sleep. There is one line in this poem that has stuck with me all week and has found its way into my morning and evening prayers. The line goes: "Let your last thinks all be thanks . . . ."

Let your last thinks all be thanks. Some days are not so good; some are very busy; some just mercifully come to an end. But insofar as a day is a life, young in the morning, at full strength at noon, slowly yielding to dusk and then darkness, then at the end of the day, Auden's words strike just the right note. "Let your last thinks all be thanks." The work of ministry is full of all sorts of days, just as the work of preparation for

9. Auden, *Collected Poems*, 875–876.

ministry is. I hope that at the end of them all, you will be able to let your last thinks, all be thanks.

May 19, 2010

As I grow older, I have realized how much I have come to love poetry. When I was in school, I rather dreaded the section of my "Literature" course that dealt with poetry, fearful that it would be boring or unintelligible or worse, sweet. I did not want to have to write a paper on something I couldn't understand or didn't care about.

When I was in seminary, my homiletics professor warned us against using poetry in our sermons. He thought the use of poetry would inevitable sentimentalize and smooth over the gospel's rough edges. I now think he was wrong. There is something piercingly beautiful about words that do not say too much but in saying what they say, help us see more than we can articulate. Poetry is mysteriously powerful that way. It can also be obscure, heavy, and stupefyingly tedious, but when it works, it brings delight and insight as nothing else.

Which is why the church has never been able to worship God with only prose. God is not prosaic. There are things that God unveils of God's love, indeed, of God's very being, that can only be described poetically. That is why the book of Psalms was so crucial to Israel's worship.

Recently I was listening to a sermon at presbytery (a more prosaic setting cannot be imagined) on the text of Psalm 133, a psalm that celebrates the unity of God's people. "How good and pleasant it is when kindred live together in unity!" How good that is in truth! But the way this song of ascents describes that goodness is not simply in terms of earnest exhortations or more detailed abstractions, but in the unlikely form of oil that runs "down the beard, on the beard of Aaron, running down over the collar of his robes. It is like the dew of Hermon, which falls on the mountains of Zion. For there the Lord ordained his blessing, life forevermore." (vs.3)

This is a vision of abundance, of almost uncontrolled plenty, of blessing unmerited and overwhelming, blessing that comes upon us without our even asking it, a gift that falls on us. This is not a unity that we contrive or make but that we discover. There might have been lots of ways to say this, but these images are so rich that we are left breathless.

At this same meeting of presbytery a young woman and a young African American man preached and were examined. After they were examined and approved, an older man, who was a retired pastor, was received as transferring from another presbytery. He had been ordained in this presbytery in 1954, a year which many might consider a high water mark for our denomination: post-war families joining the church in droves, expanding congregations, building programs, and new churches. Everywhere there was abundance, especially in comparison to today. But the old retired minister did not point to 1954 as a time of abundance. Instead, he reminded us that in 1954, this presbytery would not have been able to hear either of the sermons that were preached that day. "Do you see what we would have missed?" he asked us. He pointed to some oil that was flowing down our robes at the moment, oil supplied by this young woman and this African American man, oil that signaled abundant blessing.

The old pastor was not a poet, but somehow the psalmist's words seem to capture the abundance of the moment in a single image. It was a poetic word in a prosaic setting that stirred the heart and made me glad for that unity that is ours in Christ.

October 10, 2010

William Cowper (1731–1800) was, unfortunately, a manic-depressive, who, on at least one occasion, attempted to take his own life. Still, like many who, for one reason or another, refuse to accept what is called "reality," Cowper saw things that the rest of us regularly miss. Recovering from one of his depressions, Cowper (pronounced Cooper) was invited by John Newton of slave-trading fame, to join him in his Olney parish to write some hymns, many of which we still sing.

Newton's most famous hymn is "Amazing Grace, How Sweet the Sound." Cowper wrote a couple that are still familiar to many of us: "God Moves in a Mysterious Way" and "O For a Closer Walk with God," and some we (Presbyterians anyway) don't sing so much anymore: "There is a Fountain Filled with Blood," "The Spirit Breathes Upon the Word" (a great piece of Reformed theology), and "Sometimes a Light Surprises" (a hymn whose lyrics speak powerfully to those who have first-hand acquaintance with depression).

Cowper's hymn, "God Moves in a Mysterious Way" is often trivialized today as a way of talking casually about the strange workings of God's providence. In fact, however, the hymn makes the consistent point that what we fear most, what we flee from, what we dismiss is often the very point of entry that God uses to bless this world and grant us unexpected gifts. Of course, this is thoroughly scriptural. Where is the Prince of Peace born? In a palace, in a place where we would all like to be? No. He is born in a manger because "there was no place for him in the inn." (Luke 2:7)

It is the contradictory nature of God's grace which Cowper praises. There are two lines in the hymn that have always struck me. The first one is:

> Ye fearful saints fresh courage take;
> The clouds ye so much dread,
> Are big with mercy, and shall break,
> In blessings on your head.

Big with mercy.

The other line in Cowper's hymn that is so profoundly Reformed that I am tempted to label Cowper a Barthian, goes like this:

> Blind unbelief is sure to err,
> And scan his work in vain;
> God is His own Interpreter,
> And He shall make it plain."

God is his own interpreter. God is the subject of being God, the "indissolubly Subject" of all theological predicates. God defines what grace is, what love is, what mercy is. To paraphrase Eugene Peterson, the God of Jesus Christ is the dictionary in which we are to look up the meaning of the words of our lives.

Which is liberating news because, as Cowper knew very well, not all who suffer from "blind unbelief" are atheists or agnostics. A good many of them are Christians whose fears cause them to want to define God for themselves, perhaps to get a god that meets "my needs". We are always tempted to be the subject ourselves, determining what God can and cannot do. The clouds we so much dread are full of "blind unbelief," and keep us from seeing and enjoying God's self-interpretation and the blessings that flow from that Word.

November 10, 2010

Psalm 118 vs. 24 reads, "This is the day that the Lord has made; let us rejoice and be glad in it." When things get busy around here or I lose something important or my frustrations get the best of me and I utter some expletive that would have been better deleted, a colleague here, Susan Griner by name, quotes this verse to me and smiles. This has happened so often that even I now know this verse by heart and can even sing a song with its lyrics.

One of my mother's favorite writers was Phyllis McGinley, who is not read much today but who in her time (the 1950's and 60's) was a Pulitzer Prize-winning poet. I have come to enjoy her as well. A Roman Catholic, she often put her faith into song. Here is a portion of one of her poems, entitled, *Sunday Psalm*[10], for your reading pleasure.

> This is the day the Lord hath made,
> Shining like Eden absolved of sin,
> Three parts glitter to one part shade:
> Let us be glad and rejoice therein.
>
> Tonight—tomorrow—the leaf will fade,
> The waters tarnish, the dark begin.
> But this is the day which the Lord has made:
> *Let us be glad and rejoice therein.*

April 18, 2012

During this Easter season I ran across a poem by John Updike, a portion of which I would like to share with you. In addition to being an extraordinarily gifted writer, Updike was also a student of theology. This poem, reflecting on Easter and the appropriate response to this good news, was written when Updike was an undergraduate at Harvard.

Seven Stanzas at Easter[11]

> Make no mistake: if He rose at all
> it was as His body;

10. McGinley, *Times Three*, 82.
11. Updike, *Collected Poems*, 20–21.

if the cells' dissolution did not reverse, the molecules
reknit, the amino acids rekindle,
the church will fall.

The same hinged thumbs and toes,
the same valved heart
that-pierced-died, withered, paused, and then
regathered out of enduring Might
new strength to enclose.

Let us not mock God with metaphor,
analogy, sidestepping, transcendence;
making of the event a parable, a sign painted in the
faded credulity of earlier ages:
let us walk through the door.

Let us not see to make it less monstrous,
for our own convenience, our own sense of beauty,
lest, awakened in one unthinkable hour, we are
embarrassed by the miracle,
and crushed by remonstrance.

In some ways Updike's poem reminds me of the famous encounter that Flannery O'Connor had with Mary McCarthy at a cocktail party in New York. The conversation concerned the Eucharist and McCarthy, an indifferent Catholic, opined that it was okay to think about it as long as one thought of it as a symbol, to which O'Connor replied, "If it is only a symbol, then to hell with it." Updike would have understood.

May 9, 2012

Sometime in the 19th century, and probably before, a growing number of people lost their faith in God. The big name for this is "secularization," whose roots go back to at least the 17th century. The "melancholy, long, withdrawing roar" of faith's retreat manifested itself not in the pugnacious atheism of today but in a recurring sadness, and sense that something important was fading away. People like Nietzsche, Dostoyevsky, Matthew Arnold, Herman Melville, and others heard that roar and commented upon it, sometimes, like Nietzsche, celebrating the end of a weak and hypocritical Christianity, but more often like Dostoyevsky, fearing that without God, our worst demons would be unleashed. One person who

heard that roar and felt very keenly the absence of God was Emily Dickinson, whose poem #1551 bears eloquent testimony both to her sense of
loss and to her prescient description of what life without faith might look
like. The poem goes like this:

> Those—dying then,
> Knew where they went—
> They went to God's right hand —
> That hand is amputated now
> And God cannot be found —
>
> The abdication of Belief
> Makes the behavior small —
> Better an *ignis fatuus*
> Than no illume at all —

Roger Lundin has written that the middle two lines of the poem
"may be the most succinct description we have of the consequences of
modern unbelief."[12] So much of modernity (even more post-modernity)
seems made up of small behavior, small convictions, small deaths, small
betrayals, small hopes. Faith carries too much baggage for so many. We
want "simply Jesus," that is, a Jesus without the church. And if we have to
have a church, we want a church without the embarrassments of creeds,
confessions, and doctrines, a Jesus without the Christ, and without com-
plicating things like long term commitments issuing in budgets, buildings,
and committees. We do not seem to be able even to summon the strength
to light an *ignis fatuus* (a trivial fire or light); it all seems too much.

I believe that to the extent that theological seminaries represent an
enormous investment in the deepest convictions of the church, requiring
costly commitment to study and preparation and growth, to that extent
what we do here may look increasingly odd to a culture that has grown
comfortable with "small behavior" and expects nothing more.

What we do here may be modest but the work is not small. And
what we are called to live out as pastors and teachers is not small either,
but rather life-encompassing, bearing witness to the Lord Jesus Christ
who rose from the dead, who is alive, and who calls disciples to live lives
of daring faithfulness and costly joy. Theological education, like faith itself, does not narrow life but enlarges it, casting it against the brilliance of
the Light of the World. His is not an *ignis fatuus*.

---

12. Lundin, *Emily Dickinson and the Art of Belief,* 151.

What people like Emily Dickinson felt is real and true, as many of the psalmists and the prophets and Jesus himself bear witness. There are times when God seems distant indeed, times when God seems unforgivably absent. Yet even the sense of longing, the sense of absence, even the sense of God-forsakenness makes for a larger and more compelling life than the 'modesty' of hopelessness, with which our own day is so well-acquainted.

I sometimes think that the troubles our church is facing today have little to do with debates about sexuality or politics or any of the things we fight about and split over. Rather, I think we have lost sight of the largeness of faith's convictions and have accustomed ourselves to a smaller faith, one that will not trouble or surprise us, one that will not tempt us either to hope or to joy. "The abdication of belief makes the behavior small." If our church is acting small today, maybe it is because we have learned to live with less embarrassing claims.

Chapter 7: Theology and Theological Education

September 16, 2009

How does one become encouraged? The other day I saw an advertisement for a "Motivation Workshop" here in Charlotte which, for a fee, one could attend. I have never understood such things. Apart from the fact that I cannot see the point in paying someone else to get me motivated—the very idea leaves me depressed—I suspect that such attempted manipulation is a sin against the Holy Spirit.

But encouragement comes in some strange ways. Good preaching, I would argue, never has motivation as its primary goal. The Gospel, when it is proclaimed and heard, however, always encourages the heart and enlivens the imagination.

I think we become encouraged when we hear the truth articulated. In one of his essays, Alexander Solzhenitsyn tells about his decision to join with others to try to live truthfully in the midst of a culture of constant and pervasive lies. The group drew strength from each other, determining to live counter to the culture of lies surrounding it.

We live in a culture that bombards us with much more pleasant lies but lethal ones nonetheless. And it is easy to despair, especially when we are told how to "motivate" ourselves into one or another state of salvation. All of which helps explain why I was so encouraged by yesterday's meeting of Charlotte Presbytery. I must confess, sinner that I am, that presbytery meetings do not always have a positive effect on me. But this one did.

A student, who did not graduate from this seminary, but who took some classes here, was being examined on the floor of presbytery. In her introductory remarks, she reported that her faith story was not really about her seeking God. She had sought God all of her life, but in the course of her pilgrimage had discovered that God "was long beforehand" with her soul, and had moved her heart to seek the One who had already found her. The verse she quoted was from 1 John 4:19: "We love God because God first loved us."

The examiner asked her to "explain" the Reformed doctrine of election, and she quoted a well-known Swiss theologian to the effect that the doctrine of election was the sum of the gospel, because in this teaching all of God's ways and works are revealed, namely, that in Jesus Christ God loves us and claims us for God's own before we can ever stir or summon a response.

She was asked why Presbyterians baptize infants, and she referred back to the doctrine of election, and though she did not quote the French Reformed baptismal formula, I could hear it in her words ("Little child, for you Jesus Christ came came into the world, for you he did battle in the world, for you he suffered and died . . . . And you, little child, do not yet know anything about this. But thus is the statement of the apostle confirmed, "We love God because He first loved us."[1])

And then she preached. And she never tried to motivate me or whip me into some moral or political shape; she just proclaimed the gospel of the God whose love will not let this world go.

And I came away greatly encouraged about things. I came away hope-filled, grateful, eager to be about the work of ministry. Good theology will do that for you. It directs us away from ourselves, pointing us toward Jesus Christ, and when that happens, we do indeed hear the gospel gladly.

March 3, 2010

It will come as no surprise to you that since my seminary days, I have been enthralled with the way Karl Barth undertakes the theological task. One of the most remarkable aspects of his work is his deep conviction that the whole theological task is undertaken for the sake of the church's proclamation. That, he thinks, is the only reason we do theology: to help the church with its task of preaching the good news. We do not do theology as the academic study of religion, or as a form of our deepest religious feelings, or to give an account of our own spiritual journeys. Theology is

1. Cf. Robert McAfee Brown, *The Spirit of Protestantism*, 149.

done to help the church provide nourishing food for the souls the gospel gathers to eat.

However, I have noticed that the church is not always interested in this food or in this task. I have reached this conclusion reluctantly and only after considerable reflection, because I always took it for granted that a nourishing meal was what sustained the church's life. But I have noticed the church often seeks to be fed in other ways and to undertake what it considers to be more urgent and compelling tasks. Some of the congregations that nurtured me in my youth and indeed, in my ministry, no longer find the task of preaching, much less theology, to be at the heart of the church's mission. In fact, they seem embarrassed by all of that and view such as an outworn burden that can only impede their work. Many of these same congregations, I have noticed, were and are segregated by race. They are affluent, most of them, and full of well-educated types who are busy doing good things. But the role of theology in the church is viewed with some skepticism, and preaching seems to be something, perhaps a performance to be endured.

Living in Charlotte has introduced me to a number of strong, vital, and remarkably joyful African American congregations. Interestingly, in those congregations preaching is central to their life and worship, so central, in fact, that its task is embraced by both congregation and preacher with great joy and expectation.

Our denomination (PCUSA) worries a good deal about its declining numbers and lack of attractiveness in the marketplace of religion. Many pastors work hard to remake their congregations into something emergently hip. Yet, when I worship in an African American Presbyterian Church, I find none of these worries. Which is not to say they have none. Many of them face big concerns over budgets, missional efforts in near and distant place, staffing, etc. But their worship is confident and joyful. And their preaching is powerful. I suspect that we have much to learn from the African American church as to why preaching is so vital. Which might lead us also to a new and deeper appreciation of theology's role in helping us preach.

March 14, 2012

One of my heroes is Dr. Samuel Johnson, who seemed to spout quotable aphorisms as easily as breathing. One of his that I often repeat to myself goes like this: "Depend upon it sir, when a man knows he is to be hanged in a fortnight, it concentrates the mind wonderfully."[2]

Every sophomore cramming for a final exam knows the truth of Dr. Johnson's words. And indeed, I must confess, getting ready for an accreditation visit from a joint team of SACS (Southern Association of Colleges and Schools) and ATS (Association of Theological Schools), has something of the same effect on me. I have been studying our proposal for "Quality Enhancement," re-reading the focused report we have already sent in, and trying to think how best to respond when asked about this or that aspect of our program. I don't know if my answers will satisfy but I think I am getting pretty good at self-justification.

Which is kind of scary when you think about it, and has made me reflect yet again on the relationship between Gospel and Law. Our Reformed faith takes the law seriously, in part because we have a healthy respect for the fallen condition of humankind. The gospel bears witness to Jesus Christ's victory over sin and death, making clear once and for all that as powerful as these demonic powers are, they are not more powerful than God and cannot and will not thwart God's redemptive will. Yet though they are defeated, sin and death are not rendered powerless, and we struggle, sometimes not very convincingly, to bear witness to Christ's victory in our own lives. The cross has redeemed us but it has not made us angels. We still have some ways to go. As Martin Luther once said of that sin that clings to us even after baptism, "the Devil is a very good swimmer."

But since we are not angels, the law has a sanctifying role in helping us become what God intends us to be. Justification, says Barth, is summed up in the words, "I will be your God," while our sanctification is captured by the words, "and you shall be my people."[3] The law helps us become God's people, sometimes goading us to do better, other times holding us accountable to each other, always directing us toward more faithful discipleship with Christ.

What the law does not do is justify us. That matter has been taken care of. And yet, since we live in a culture of credentialing, and since we value, rightly, the virtue of accountability, we are tempted sometimes to think that justifying ourselves before the law, i.e., proving ourselves before others, is the way we are to live out our vocational lives. The danger is not really that we will violate some notion of grace, but rather that

---

2. Boswell, *Life of Johnson*, 748.
3. Barth, *Church Dogmatics* IV/2, 499.

we will get good at our self-justifications, that we will become captive to them and the various "proofs" that we contrive rather than enjoying the liberation with which Christ has set us free.

That would be a great sadness. But what Jesus Christ does in liberating us from the captivity of self-justification is to give us the law—the important work of credentialing, accreditation, etc.,—*as a gift*—not the main thing, but a way of living together that reflects the main thing. The 10 Commandments do not save us. Jesus Christ does. But the 10 Commandments are a gift, a way of drawing us more deeply and faithfully into Christ's own life.

The Christian life is not a slovenly thing. Nor is it easy. Grace is never cheap. Living faithfully has nothing to do with pretending that we are either above or beneath criticism. The law, in this sense, though it does not justify us, does help us to press forward and to try to do better than we might otherwise do if left to ourselves.

So, come Monday, when the questions from the visitors come thick and fast, we need not fear getting "hanged" even if our minds have, at that prospect, become a bit clearer. We need only (!) bear witness to that One whose gift makes us more, not less, accountable.

May 30, 2012

I am always surprised that there are people in the world who are not as interested in theology as I am. Perhaps you think I live a sheltered life and need to get out more, and perhaps you are right. But what makes theology so interesting is what I hear in that unsheltered part of my life when I encounter various folk expressing a desire for a church "liberated" from all the theological baggage with which it is lumbered, or desiring a faith that is "personal" and non-creedal, one that promotes an ethic that is, above all, compassionate.

What's wrong with me, I ask, that I should oppose such things or find such earnest and heartfelt sentiments to be so dangerously inadequate, even ridiculous? Who could be against "compassion"? Who after all, thinks creedal statements will be our salvation? Who has ever participated in a theological debate of real intensity and not come away feeling slightly dirty, as if the matter of God could ever be reduced to argument or a winning (or losing) proposition?

The gospel, whatever else it is, is not theology, and we are not called to preach theology. Rather, we are called to preach the gospel. Yet the gospel of Jesus Christ cannot be preached without theology, that is, without our words being held accountable to and reflective of the One to whom our sermons would point. Absent that, and what we are preaching, as my son, Chris, has reminded me recently, is one version or another of a "prosperity gospel." Perhaps such a "gospel" will not be as blatant as equating the Kingdom of God with our material success, though that version is popular enough, but my self-realization or success or "authenticity" or "happiness" will serve just as well.

If theology has anything to teach us, it can teach us grammar, and perhaps it is best to think of it that way. We don't speak "grammar." We speak English or French or Swahili. But in order to be understood, we must speak grammatically, that is, in accordance with what our sentences intend to say. Theology is the way our words about God attempt to keep faith with the way God has spoken to us. Speaking faithfully alway entails then, speaking theologically. If we think that does not matter, or if we think God has not really spoken to us, then theology can be whatever we want it to be, and given our proclivities, the result will be that theology will, in the end, be about "me."

Well, what is so wrong with that? After all, don't each of us have our different ways of approaching the truth, and who is to say the church's grammatical rules (or creedal statements) are more authoritative than my feelings or sentiments? Even Calvin warned against "implicit faith," arguing that every believer ought to affirm the faith sincerely for him or herself, and not rely simply on the adequacy of the church's confession of the faith.

But what theology asks us to do, and what we find so difficult, is to acknowledge the Subject of our sentences as the Subject. Karl Barth once wrote an important essay in the middle of the German Church Struggle, entitled, "The First Commandment as a Theological Axiom." "Thou shalt have no other gods before me," is also true for theology. God is the Subject of this good news. God is the Subject of our theological sentences as well. (A good test when listening to a sermon or reading one of your own is to see how many sentences have God as their subject.) What God has done in Jesus Christ is *not* primarily about me or my faith. By God's grace what God has done in Jesus Christ includes me, and by God's grace, I have an important role to play in this story, but I am not the subject of the gospel's sentences. I want to be. And jettisoning the bothersome creeds of the faith is one of the ways I try to be. But in truth, such is fruitless and finally tedious work.

One of the reasons people find theology difficult to appreciate today is that it has a nasty habit of asking our "selves" some inconvenient questions. Like, "Who is Lord over the story I am telling?" A good question and sometimes a painful one.

When Karl Barth died in 1968, his memorial service was held in the Basel Cathedral. One of the speakers at that service was his assistant in the last years, Eberhard Busch. Busch took as his text, Psalm 103:1: "Bless the Lord, O my soul, and all that is within me, bless God's holy name." Busch began his reflection on this text by noting that all theology is rooted in this text's first verse. This is where theology begins, in doxology for what God has done: "Bless the Lord . . . ." We do not begin by blessing "all that is within me." "All that is within me" is not the source of our faith or our theology. We are summoned first to attend to what is first: "Bless the Lord . . . ."[4] The Lord, who has blessed us beyond measure, the Lord who has spoken and speaks to us, the Lord who delivered Israel, the Lord who raised Jesus from the dead, the Lord is the One who has made a beginning with us. "All that is within me" is not unimportant or ignored but it is not where we begin. When we "bless the Lord," then "all that is within me," finds its rightful and important place in the praise and service of God.

Theology matters not because theology matters but because God does, and God will not let us trivialize our witness or our words with the "whatevers" we might contrive or be tempted to say. Theology is not easy, but it is harder and much more tedious to attempt to live un-theologically or to seek or even want an un-theological church. One might wish it all were easier, that we could travel with less baggage and fewer questions. Scripture is full of such "murmurings" in this very vein. But God's love for us is not indifferent or cheap. Left to "me," theology would become a trivial matter and offer at best a trivial witness. But as long as God is the Subject of this story, theology's task will be to remind "me" that the gospel has no intention of letting this story be about "me."

4. Busch, *"Lobe den Herrn" in Karl Barth Gedenkfeier,* 13. My translation.

October 10, 2012

Recently, my Ethics class has been watching the German movie, *The Lives of Others*. This movie is set in East Germany a few years before the fall of the Berlin Wall. It concerns a zealous East German police interrogator, who is given the task of spying on a gifted, young playwright, who has fallen under suspicion because one of the higher-ups in the State Security system (the STASI) wants to capture the affections of the playwright's girlfriend, and therefore needs him removed. Simply to rehearse the plot in this sketchy way hardly does justice to the depth of the movie's narrative, which mainly concerns itself with the slow transformation that takes place within the heart and mind of the zealous and true-believing police interrogator. From being a convinced soldier in the state's "sword and shield" secret police, the interrogator gradually changes, discovering that the subject of his investigation is not a subversive artist at all but a genuinely good man. Along the way, the interrogator begins to lose faith in the system he has been charged with serving, finding a goodness far deeper and more mysterious than a person's usefulness to the state.

The movie excels in showing how this discovery takes place. I ask my students to identify the moment when the police interrogator begins to change. At what point does he leave his old self behind and venture into a strange new world of humanity. If you have seen the movie, you know there are several places which one might single out: when the interrogator's immediate superior betrays his own lack of faith in the values of the Marxist state; when a little boy asks the interrogator if he works for the Stasi, the "bad guys;" when the interrogator learns that the point of his investigation has nothing to do with state security but everything to do with the furtherance of unwanted advances on the part of a higher-up. All of these moments help map the change.

There is one point in the movie, however, which struck me as pivotal. The playwright's best friend and mentor was a director who had been blacklisted by the East German state for committing some form of political incorrectness. Before committing suicide, the director sends a piece of music to his playwright friend, a composition entitled, "A Sonata for a Good Man." The playwright ignores this gift until he learns that his mentor has taken his own life. That evening he takes the composition down and begins to play it on the piano. Since his apartment is bugged, the interrogator listens as the music is played. The music is deeply moving and very beautiful, and the interrogator is transported, even moved to tears. Something has touched his humanity and rendered him quite unfit to be the interrogator and spy he is charged with being.

I won't tell you the rest of the movie—I have told you quite a lot already—but I want to pause for a moment over that music.

We don't always think of theology, preaching, worship, as beautiful. We tend to talk about these important things in terms of their truth or goodness, and we often fight about them on those terms. But I wonder. Maybe you and I are doing what we are doing because at one time or another we heard the music of the gospel; we discovered, perhaps inadvertently, the beauty of life in Christ, or of Christ himself, and against our better judgment, risked following. Which is to say, we were not in possession of all the truth or even a big chunk of it, and may well have found our notions of goodness completely undermined. But there was a beauty there we could not ignore. Do you think that is possible?

Yesterday, I received a call from a journalist asking me to comment on the fact that Protestants are no longer in the majority in this country, and the fastest growing group are, supposedly, the "nones," that is, people not affiliated with any denomination or church. I don't know that I had much wisdom to share. Such questions alway seem somehow pointless to me, smelling as they do of some invitation to self-justification. But I suspect we would do well to worry less about how to defend our market-share and instead, simply play our music, our beautiful music, as best we can. You can never tell who is listening, and even in our awkward and unpracticed hands, the music is quite capable of transporting the lives of others and ourselves to places we never thought we would be.

That is the gift of music, and that is the beauty, the true beauty of theology.

January 9, 2013

When Karl Barth was a youngster, his pastor was a man named Abel Burckardt. Burckardt was not a great theologian, according to Barth, but he was a theologian to whom Barth felt greatly indebted. The Rev. Burckardt composed and edited a collection of songs for children, which served as Barth's first textbook for theological instruction. Barth writes: "And what made an indelible impression on me was the homely naturalness with which these very modest compositions spoke of the events of

Christmas, Palm Sunday, Good Friday, Easter, the Ascension, and Pentecost as things which might take place any day in Basel or its environs like any other important happenings. For these songs were sung in the everyday language we were then beginning to hear and speak, and as we joined in singing, we took our mother's hand, as it were, and went to the stall at Bethlehem, and to the streets of Jerusalem, where, greeted by children of similar age, the Savior made his entry, and to the dark hill of Golgotha, and as the sun rose to the garden of Joseph . . . . All very naive, and not worth mentioning at all in academic circles? Yes, it was naive, but perhaps in the very naivete there lay the deepest wisdom and greatest power, so that once grasped it was calculated to carry one relatively unscathed—although not, of course, untempted or unassailed—through all the serried ranks of historicism and anti-historicism, mysticism and rationalism, orthodoxy, liberalism, and existentialism, and to bring one back some day to the matter itself."[5]

The matter itself. To believe that these things took place and are taking place in our midst; to believe that Jesus is walking the streets of Charlotte or Greensboro or Spartanburg or Anderson or Columbia or High Point or Asheville or wherever, and is calling us to take each other by the hand and enter into his story, even to follow him, that is "the matter itself." Naive? Perhaps.

This afternoon I was interviewed about what I thought of a local TV evangelist who is preaching a "prosperity gospel," inviting listeners to send him dollars so that they will receive a blessing, usually a car or house or some other desired commodity. Not everything is simple in the gospel but some things are simple. People who prey upon the poor in the name of Jesus Christ have long since ceased to believe in "the matter itself." They are false prophets. For them, Jesus is merely an object to be used in achieving their own selfish goals. Such prophets will one day reap their reward, as one day we will all see more clearly.

But what concerns me more even than the sins of the false prophets is the ease with which we ourselves so easily dismiss "the matter itself" or seek to turn it to our own advantage. It matters so much what you believe Jesus' story is about. If you don't believe scripture is about Jesus Christ, the crucified and risen Lord, a friend of sinners, whose humility exposes our pride, then scripture can be about anything we like, even prosperity, and we have no reason to object.

5. Barth, *Church Dogmatics* IV/2, 112, 113.

Sometimes naivete in regard to the faith is the best part of faith. It is what gives us the strength to say, "No!" when that is *the theological word* that needs to be said. Pastors like Abel Burckhardt and the songs he composed are critically important gifts that help us see what the gospel story is about. They also help us see what the gospel is not about and why those who prey upon the poor in the name of Jesus Christ or discover some more respectable way of avoiding "the matter itself" are purveyors of bad theology, weakening the church's witness and endangering their own souls (and those of others) with their fatal lack of naivete.

Which is why you are in seminary, because among other places, as we seek to learn more about the matter itself, Jesus is walking these halls and setting tasks for us to do in his company.

January 16, 2013

We are nearing our nation's annual celebration of Dr. Martin Luther King Jr., concerning which some thoughts.

Having grown up among privileged white people in a segregated South, I have always been reluctant to write about Dr. King, feeling that I had no right to express an opinion about one who suffered all manner of evils from people like me. Though we are often importuned to have a "conversation about race," in truth, I have found that difficult to do, perhaps because I have never suffered any real kind of discrimination. But there are other reasons as well.

When I was serving in my first parish, there was a farmer in the church whose deceased father had been both the sheriff of the county and the leader of the local Klan. In addition, he was head of the county Democratic Party. The son, my parishioner, was, when he grew to maturity, also active in politics, and the first year I was pastor was actively soliciting support for President Carter. Later when the Republicans took over the county, the son, who was by no means a liberal, fought a valiant rearguard effort to preserve things like food stamps and Head Start funding from being cut.

As a pastor I had a hard time processing all of this. How could the son of a Klansman who had no love for the federal government and in many respects was more conservative than I, work so hard for the least of these in our community. A mystery. Later, I know he was active in helping "illegal aliens" find work in our community, protecting them from deportation.

In Taylor Branch's book, *Parting the Waters* (Simon and Schuster, 1989), he writes about King's predecessor at Dexter Ave. Baptist Church in Montgomery, Alabama, a man named Vernon Johns. Johns was originally from Prince Edward County, Virginia, the county where our seminary was founded in 1812. Johns was a true non-conformist, as hard on his own African American congregation as he was on the white racists who were oppressing them. (If you have not read Branch's book, you need to do so. He spoke on our Richmond campus a couple of years ago.) In any case, the saints at Dexter Ave. Baptist Church finally had enough of Johns and his antics (e.g., He pressed them to work harder, become more entrepreneurial, earn and save and give more, and he did so in some prophetic and outlandish ways. He was truly fearless.) and eventually forced him out in 1952. They wanted someone a bit more refined, polished, less eager to take on the various demons of the day.

What they got was a newly-minted PhD from Boston University, the son of a prominent pastor in Atlanta, who seemed to be just the person who would suit. Be careful what you pray for.

So, in thinking of Dr. King today, I like to think of him not just as a great Civil Rights leader, which he was, or a great orator and public speaker, which he also was, but as a young pastor going down to Montgomery, Alabama, in a deeply racist and segregated world, to preach the gospel. There is a mystery here too.

When he died, or rather, when he was killed, much of the commentary understandably focused on his political and social and even economic achievements. Sometimes forgotten, however, was the fact that he was a preacher of the gospel, a pastor of a church who was trying to help his people hear the gospel and participate in what God was doing in the world. I wonder if we might best honor Dr. King this year with joint or community worship services in which we remember his work as a minister of the gospel of Jesus Christ, the One who so mysteriously and disturbingly makes it really difficult to keep our political, social, and racial categories straight.

As a character in one of Flannery O'Connor's stories observes about Jesus: "He thown everything out of balance."[6] Indeed, he did and does, thank God.

January 8, 2014

Recently I have been reading a book, edited by Dean Stroud (full disclosure: he was a seminary classmate), entitled, *Preaching in Hitler's Shadow* (Eerdmans, 2013). The book is a collection of sermons preached in Germany during the 1930's. Some of the preachers are well-known (e.g., Karl Barth, Dietrich Bonhoeffer, Martin Niemoller), while others much less so, at least to me (e.g., Paul Schneider, Julius von Jan, Clemens August von Galen). In some cases the preachers of these sermons paid for their words with their lives (Schneider, Bonhoeffer), while others paid in terms of exile, imprisonment, torture, forced labor, loss of job, etc. None of the sermons preached in this volume were cheaply given. To read such costly witness is humbling and frankly troubling amidst the comforts and unthreatening trivialities of our day.

When Mary Mikhael was here this past fall, she showed pictures of Christian churches in Syria that had been bombed or otherwise destroyed by the terror and strife consuming that country at the moment. As she spoke to us, I wondered what it must be like to pastor in such a context.

When I think about our own ecclesiastical troubles and differences, I feel ashamed when reading these sermons. We seem like poseurs of the faith rather than witnesses. But the point of these sermons, as the point of Mary Mikhael's pictures, is not to make us wallow in our guilt. That is a luxury that tempts us in our comfort but does little good either for us or for those in great need. No what is called for is not guilt but remembrance of what is truly important, what is central to the faith, who is truly the Lord. These witnesses offer that to us as a gift. And that is no small gift. We need reminding of that to do the little or the much that we will be called upon to do.

If I had been living in Germany during the 1930's, I don't know what I would have done. I'd rather not think about that because I fear my voice would have been inaudible, if not more deeply compromised. But what is the appropriate response to these witnesses today? What might

6. O'Connor, *"A Good Man Is Hard To Find"* in *Flannery O'Connor, The Complete Stories*, 131.

we faithfully offer in our own witness? Let me suggest, and only suggest, three avenues that might be open to us.

1. These sermons ought to help us *remember* what is at stake when we preach and hear the gospel. There should be no cheap words in our sermons, which is to say, every word we preach is a witness to Christ crucified and his lordship over this world.

2. These sermons ought to help us *remember* that those who preached were themselves ordinary, flawed, compromised, sinners who dared to offer their witness to Jesus Christ. They were not moral paragons. They were not superheroes. They were scared. And they had no more strategies for dealing with what appeared to be the triumph of evil than we would have. So, all they did was preach. That is enough. The Nazis, like other oppressive regimes (e.g., Herod) paid the faith a great compliment in acknowledging how dangerous the gospel was to their purposes. If the gospel no longer seems dangerous to us, I wonder who will do us the favor of seeing what we no longer see. I suspect that if we dare to offer our ordinary, compromised, flawed witness, even that will be enough to find the trouble that will clarify the gospel for us.

3. These sermons ought to help us *rejoice and be glad* that God does not allow his words to return to him empty. In truth, to read these sermons is to become inspired—not just ashamed or fearful—but inspired to risk offering ourselves in our own calling and contexts.

Remembering like this, even rejoicing like this can be hard, even painful. But remembering and rejoicing is the way all true ministry begins. That is one of the reasons we begin here with courses in Church History and The Christian Life. If we cannot or will not remember, we cut ourselves off from the very sources that sustain and nourish the witness we are called upon to make in our own day.

The "German Christians," that is, those who embraced the Nazi takeover of the church, despised theology and church history, regarding such subjects as impediments to constructing a new and more up-to-date church. The church needed to be made relevant to the new order of things. In one of their very few attempts to articulate their confessional position, they drew up in 1933, the "Rengsdorfer Theses" in which they argued that the Reformation was significant because it made the gospel accessible to the German national character. Unless the gospel can speak to the German national character, they went on to confess, it will lose its relevance and usefulness to the people. "History," they claimed, "confirms that this proclamation of the gospel of the Germanic race is appropriate."[7]

At one point Karl Barth penned a counter-thesis. It read: "The Reformation as renewal of the church based on God's word is 'made accessible' for Germans, not in accordance with their character but rather in accordance with the wisdom and will of divine providence. It was and is appropriate and inappropriate for the Germanic race as for any other race. Whoever treats the Reformation as a specifically German affair today interprets it as propaganda and places himself outside the Evangelical Church."[8]

Perhaps all of this seems at the moment to be so much rhetoric from long ago, but as we move forward this spring term, I invite you to "remember" and to "rejoice:" to remember the witnesses with whom you are walking along this path; to remember the privilege of sharing in the story that cost them and other saints their lives; and to rejoice that this story is also yours and mine and will hold on to us long after we are able to hold on to it.

Welcome to the bracing task of ministry!

7. Stroud, *Preaching in Hitler's Shadow*, 24.

8. *Ibid.*, 24.

Chapter 8: Preparation and Prayer

March 26, 2003

If you are like me, your prayer life may be somewhat confused and erratic. I find it relatively easy to pray for peace but in truth, such prayers are easy because they do not cost me much. And given the horrific things happening in Iraq, for example, both to the Iraqis and to American soldiers, prayer seems like a weak effort to undertake.

Moreover, I must confess to a deep admiration for the way our military prepares for battle. Though one may reject the use of force to settle conflicts, the soldiers know that you don't face an enemy without preparation, without planning and practice, and without the awareness that there will be a cost. Maybe our prayers for peace and our study together should reflect something of that awareness, and be undertaken with the same degree of preparation and energy.

A student I interviewed for admission here once told me that the reason he refused to seek ordination in a church that did not require the M.Div. degree was because he had been a soldier and he knew that one should not enter a battle unprepared. "I want to come to seminary to get prepared," he told me.

So, I invite you, as part of that preparation, to pray regularly, perhaps at a set time and place of your choosing, and to pray for peace in a world that is at war, and to study that peace and seek to embody it in your own life.

Secondly, I would invite you to offer a prayer of thanksgiving for the beauty of this spring in Charlotte. The Bradford pears and weeping cherries, the redbuds and daffodils may not be the answer to the world's evils, but they have a way of keeping us from despairing over such evils, and are, in any case, some of God's most wonderful gifts.

I wish I had more specific advice to offer you. The Benedictines know more about this than I do. Their motto is: *Ora et Labora*. Work and Prayer. Work that is performed as prayer and prayer that is a daily, regular work. I commend this to you and to myself.

May 27, 2004

Recently I have been reading Diarmaid MacCulloch's biography of Thomas Cranmer (Yale University Press, 1998), an English Reformer who is credited with creating the Anglican Book of Common Prayer, and who, with two others, was burned at the stake in Oxford under the reign of Mary Tudor. In reading about Cranmer, I was drawn to what is known today as the "prayer of humble access," which also is in the Presbyterian *Book of Common Worship*, though in the part called, "Preparation for Worship" and not in the Communion Service itself.

The "prayer of humble access" was originally prayed by the whole congregation immediately prior to taking communion. The words, I believe, are not just "beautiful" or "pretty" or even "pious." Rather, they are profoundly true and express as few other words have ever done, the nature of the gift that awaits us at the table and the grace that enables us to approach and eat and drink.

In Cranmer's 16th century words, the prayer reads

> We do not presume to come to this thy Table, O merciful Lord, trusting in our own righteousness, but in thy manifold and great mercies. We are not worthy so much as to gather up the crumbs under thy Table. But thou art the same Lord, whose property it is always to have mercy: Grant us, therefore, gracious Lord, so to eat the flesh of thy dear Son Jesus Christ, and to drink his blood, that our sinful bodies may be made clean by his body, and our souls washed through his most precious blood, and that we may evermore dwell in him and he in us. Amen."[1]

But thou art the same Lord, whose property it is always to have mercy . . . Amen.

January 22, 2005

The mother of my assistant, Terry Johns, died last night in Front Royal, Virginia. We need to keep Terry and her family in our prayers.

---

1. *Book of Common Worship*, 20.

Terry's faith tradition is Episcopalian and she often cites the *Book of Common Prayer* to me for my instruction and benefit. There is a prayer in that book, a version of which appears in our own *Book of Common Worship*, a prayer I frequently prayed at the graveside, when I was a pastor. It reads: "Into thy hands, O merciful Savior, we commend thy servant (name). Acknowledge, we humbly beseech thee, a sheep of thine own fold, a lamb of thine own flock, a sinner of thine own redeeming. Receive her into the arms of thy mercy, into the blessed rest of everlasting peace, and into the glorious company of the saints in light. Amen."[2]

Sometimes the old words express better what our words cannot. The rhythm and cadence of the words and the theological acuity of the petition itself—"a sheep of thine own fold, a lamb of thine own flock, a sinner of thine own redeeming"—render this prayer achingly beautiful and pastorally helpful.

July 14, 2005

As this summer term winds its way toward the end, I would like to leave you with this prayer taken from Stanley Hauerwas' book, *Prayers Plainly Spoken*. It reads:

> Lord of all Time and Space, we come to the end of this course grateful for the time and space you gave us together. For you all endings are but beginnings. We ask you therefore to make more of this time than we can imagine. You make our past more than we knew and our future full of surprises—and then our present is wonderful joy. May that joy stand as an alternative to the world's despair, so that the world might know that your truth is deeper than our violence. Amen.[3]

September 7, 2005

The fall term is about to commence. Welcome. I would like to welcome you with a prayer taken from the *Book of Common Worship*. It is a prayer that has often been prayed here at the seminary on various occasions, in part because it describes so well our hopes as a new venture in theological

2. *Book of Common Worship*, 1028.

3. Hauerwas, *Prayers Plainly Spoken*, 131.

education for the church. I have come to think of this prayer as "our" prayer, and so I offer it to you as we begin a new term together. It reads:

> Eternal God, you call us to ventures of which we cannot see the ending, by paths as yet untrodden, through perils unknown. Give us faith to go out with courage, not knowing where we go, but only that your hand is leading us and your love supporting us; through Jesus Christ our Lord.[4]

The good news, the prayer implies, is not that we know where we are going or even that our paths will always be straight, but that there is a hand that is leading us and a supporting love that will never let us go, and One who will in the end draw us unfailingly to Jesus Christ, in whom there is only joy, and in whose presence we find our true home.

October 19, 2005

I am aware that we are a seminary and not a church. Our business here is teaching and learning, not baptizing or preaching. Still, we are commissioned by the church to help train pastors for service in the church. Most of that training takes place either in the classroom or in a congregational setting. However, some of it happens as we live together, share meals with one another, and pray with and for each other and the world.

Not everyone enters the same disciplines for undertaking this part of the training, but I do think that seminary can encourage students to take up certain practices that will help sustain them in their ministry. Two of those practices that the church has exercised for the last 2,000 years, are the practice of daily Bible reading and prayer.

There are a number of ways these disciplines can be undertaken. For example, I use the Moravian Daily Texts, which are sent (free!) to my email address each morning. You can access this service at www.moravian.org/daily_texts/. When I come to work in the morning and turn on my computer, there is a set of readings waiting for me, which will eventually lead me through the whole of scripture and which will serve to direct my prayers for that day.

Another site that many have found useful is the PCUSA website, which lists the lectionary's Daily Readings as a link.

If you prefer books, I recommend the *Book of Common Worship*, which comes also in a handy *Daily Prayer* edition. I would recommend

---

4. *Book of Common Worship*, 501.

that you purchase this book in any case, because as a pastor you will find it an invaluable resource. It has lectionary readings spread over a two-year cycle, and is full of helpful ways to begin praying.

There is much more to the Christian life than prayer, and prayer is certainly not a substitute for faithful action. Still, as a little known Swiss theologian of the last century has said, "To fold one's hands in prayer is the beginning of an uprising against the disorder of the world."[5] I encourage you to participate in this "uprising" by engaging in the discipline of prayer.

May 24, 2006

In the hope of inoculating you against earnest exhortations you may hear this commencement season encouraging you to do something important as a change agent for the future, I would like to draw your attention to volume III/4 of Karl Barth's *Church Dogmatics*, where he is concerned with the matter of confessing the faith. There he writes: "A confessor is one who is not ashamed to do something quite useless in a world of serious purposes."[6] Just so does worship call into question the "serious" business of the world (and most surely also, our own pious "seriousness") revealing the idolatries we so carefully construct, which with all their "seriousness" seek to obscure from us the joy of the gospel.

May 9, 2007

Recently I have been reading Robert Jenson's two-volume *Systematic Theology*. Jenson is a Lutheran, who is now retired but who has been called by some the leading theologian in America today. I don't know how such titles are determined or in the case of a Christian theologian, whether that would be a title one would want, much less seek. Still reading Jenson is an instructive experience, whether one agrees with him or not. One of the things I admire about him is that he actually produces a "systematic theology" and does not spend a whole career rehearsing issues of method or critique.

In a section of the second volume, he deals with the doctrine of creation, particularly the creation of humanity, and he asks what is it that

5. Cf. Migliore, *The Lord's Prayer*, 18–19.

6. Barth, *Church Dogmatics*, III/4, 78.

is distinctive about human beings. Throughout this section he is exegeting Genesis 1–3. At one point Jenson concludes that what differentiates
human beings from other animals is that "we are the ones addressed by
God's moral word and so enabled to respond—that we are called to pray.
If we will, the odd creature of the sixth day (created humanity) can after
all be classified: we are the praying animals."[7]

Jenson is not a pietist and is not here expressing a merely religious
sentiment. Instead, he actually thinks that our humanity is characterized,
fulfilled, defined as human in that we pray to God. Not *homo sapiens* or
homo faber but *homo orator*.

We are the creature that asks. I mention this because I suspect
that most of us find asking difficult if not embarrassing. It is easy to be
ashamed of one's own prayers as paltry, weak, formulaic things. At the
beginning of a chapter in *The Brothers K*, David James Duncan offers this
epigram: "If I were God, I wouldn't answer my prayers either."[8] Prayer
can be humiliating work. But our humanity, Jenson argues, is discovered
at that point where we ask: for bread, for life, for love, for purpose, for joy.

Modernity, in many ways, exists to keep us from being in the embarrassing position of ever having to ask. That is one of the reasons that
people shaped by modernity (and even more by post-modernity) find
it so hard to pray, and also why they find scripture to be so baffling. Yet
Jesus not only was unafraid to ask (asking for his Father's blessing on
bread and wine, for strength in the face of betrayal and loss, even for
his disciples to wait and watch with him for a while) but he also never
seemed to be ashamed of others who were asking so many things of him.

Asking is the way we make progress in the Christian life. It is a terrible self-sufficiency, according to Jenson, to be unable to ask. Indeed, that
must be what hell is like. No one asks there. To turn to God in petition is
to claim our humanity, and it is what connects us with human beings in
a fellow-humanity of asking, companions who are merely desperate, that
is, who are hungry, homeless, in prison, and in despair, all of whom are
unashamed to ask God for help. With them we learn to ask together, even
to pray, "*Our* Father . . . ."

"Ask," Jesus says to us. "Knock." "Seek." These are not words inviting
us to explore ourselves in some endless round of self-absorption, but to

---

7. Jenson, *Systematic Theology,* Vol. II, 59.

8. Duncan, *The Brothers K,* 150.

learn the humbling yet finally joyous work of looking to God for our life, that is, of becoming the human beings we were created to be.

June 13, 2007

This summer a group of us have been studying prayer. I have been struck how in two of the novels we have read, *The End of the Affair* by Graham Greene and *The Brothers K* by David James Duncan, there is a great deal of praying going on. In Greene's novel, published in 1951, a man comes to engage with God not out of piety or sudden conversion but out of hatred. Bendrix sees God as the One who has stolen the love of the woman with whom Bendrix is having an affair. She has prayed to God in the hope that God would spare Bendrix's life after a terrible bombing in London. And in the event, Bendrix is spared, a gift which his lover regards as an answer to her prayer. In response, she begins to turn toward God and away from the affair. When he discovers what has happened, Bendrix, though he has no faith, begins to accuse God of taking from him the one person whom he loves, thus ruining the one chance he had for happiness. "Oh no," he prays, "it wasn't You that took, for that would have been magic and I believe in magic even less than I believe in you: magic is your cross, your resurrection of the body, your holy Catholic church, your communion of the saints . . . . You can't mark a two-year-old child for life with a bit of water and a prayer. If I began to believe that, I could believe in the body and the blood. You didn't own her all those years: I owned her. You won in the end. You don't need to remind me of that . . . ."[9]

Strangely, ironically, Bendrix's anger at God has led him into a rather serious conversation with God, and in the novel, this conversation eventually leads him to even stranger places of grace. "You" is a dangerous conversation partner.

In David James Duncan's novel, *The Brothers K*, "You" reappears, this time in a prayer that a young man offers who is serving time in prison for avoiding the draft. A determined agnostic, a scorner of his parents' faith, this young man writes a letter to his girlfriend from his prison cell that something inside of him "keeps wanting to thank God." His father is dying of cancer, one of his brothers has been placed in a VA mental ward, and his girlfriend has moved several states away and he is not even sure if she will read his letters. Nevertheless, he writes to her these words:

9. Greene, *The End of the Affair*, 164–165.

Why does my whole heart, every beat, round the clock answer my mind's constant groaning with: 'but wait, but wait, but wait'? Of course, I want to shout, 'Because of you, Tasha [his girl-friend] . . . . Yet knowing me, my weakness, my tedious anger, this tedious darkness, I know I could lose my hold on you . . . . Not you, Tasha. I mean this other you. I refuse to resort to Uppercase here. But you hear me. And I feel you. I mean you, the who or whatever you are, being or non-being, that somehow comes to us and somehow consoles us. I don't know your name. I don't understand you. I don't know how to address you . . . . But you alone, I begin to feel, who sends me this woman's love . . . .and this new hope and stupid gratitude . . . . So, O thing that consoles, how clumsily I thank you . . . .[10]

The great temptation that faces those who study theology, Bonhoeffer says, is to speak of God as if God were not in the room. Or, to put it another way, to speak of God as if God were not a "You," a "Thou." You. That is why theology has finally to become doxology, why the point of all our studies here is praise, thanking this You who speaks to us, who has become a You for us in Jesus Christ.

It is scary to be loved like that, but only such love consoles.

10. Duncan, *The Brothers K,* 613.

Chapter 9: Worship

The answer to the question of "How?" in the Christian life (and in theology) is always the same: "the Holy Spirit." How does one move forward in the faith, how is one sustained in the face of great adversity, how does one grow in grace, how does one engage others in the name of Jesus Christ, how does one try to hold it all together when it appears everything is falling apart? The Holy Spirit. Don't get me wrong: saying all of that is a miracle of the Holy Spirit is not to say that any of that is easy or simple or quick.

Not all miracles happen fast, and many of the best ones take a very long time. Some take a lifetime. Baptism tells us that getting through life, growing up and finally growing old takes a miracle. We get through life in the company of One whose Spirit empowers us to do things we could not otherwise do, things we are not good at and might not even choose to do. Baptism tells us that we do not walk this way alone, and are not burdened with the heavy responsibility of making something of ourselves. Baptism is the sign that we are not and never will be self-made people. We belong to Another, who is at work within us. There is nothing, absolutely nothing that we have, that we have not received from him. And finally, it is baptism that sticks us with others whom we have not chosen but who are gifts to us along this walk.

That is how we move forward, by the power of the Holy Spirit, who "makes me wholeheartedly willing and able from now on to live for him." (Heidelberg Catechism, Q.1)

July 22, 2009

This summer I have been reading a couple of books on John Nevin, a 19th century American theologian, who is not as well known as he should be. He and his Swiss-born colleague, Philip Schaff, formed what came to be known as the "Mercersburg School of Theology," centered around the seminary of the German Reformed Church located in Mercersburg, Pennsylvania. Later, Schaff went to teach at Andover Seminary, and then on to a very distinguished career as professor of church history at Union Theological Seminary in New York. Nevin remained in Pennsylvania, eventually merging the Mercersburg seminary with what later became Franklin and Marshall College, of which he served several years as President.

What set Mercersburg apart was, among other things, Nevin's conviction that Reformed theology, at its best and in its classic expressions, held to a very high doctrine of the Eucharist, believing the risen Christ to be truly present in the celebration of the sacrament. Nevin was opposed by the leading American theologian of the day, Charles Hodge, who saw the sacraments more in Zwinglian terms, that is, not so much as the gift of Christ offering himself to us in the bread and wine, but more in terms of our remembering and recalling Christ's sacrifice for us.

Who cares about all of this today and why might it be important? I guess it comes down to what we think worship is about. Is worship, God's making space and time for us to participate in the life of Jesus Christ, finding in him the shape of our own discipleship? Or is worship an expression of our own religious sensibilities, a form of self-expression, grounded in our own context and offered out of our experience?

No doubt, worship always has elements of both these definitions, and will in any case, always involve our self-expression and cultural understandings. We cannot jump out of our own skins. And indeed, we shouldn't. But worship is not about us. And celebrating the sacrament is not about our memories and devotion.

This Saturday, we will mark the end of a long summer term, full of the study of Hebrew, Children's Literature, Understanding Congregations, Presbyterian Polity, and the Reformed confessions. A long term. But in worship on Saturday, we will not be celebrating our labors here but rather the gift of God's sustaining presence in Jesus Christ, the living Lord, who feeds us the bread and wine that is his own life, inviting us to share in this meal together with him.

April 30, 2012

Last Sunday I had the privilege of worshipping at Sugaw Creek Presbyterian Church, where a group of West African immigrants gather in the afternoon for a service led by one of our students here at the seminary, Thomas Agbemenou.

Thomas is from Togo, a country in West Africa that recently celebrated the 50th anniversary of its independence from France. Thomas designed the worship service, in part to thank God for the end to colonialism but also to caution his West African friends against other forms of bondage that freedom and independence can sometime bring in their wake.

It was a happy day. The preaching was excellent. Thomas preached in French, and in a native tongue I did not recognize, and occasionally in English. His text was Isaiah 61:1-2, and he spoke on what it means "to proclaim liberty to the captives."

The congregation was filled with young people. The music was impressive—various drums, piano, and much, much singing. One of the most joyous displays of gratitude to God was the dancing of 8 children, aged (it seemed to me) 5 to 13. They wore their native dress, with some kind of decorative tracing on their shoulders and necks, and they sang and danced with great exuberance. They sang the music to which they danced. So lovely. And all of their songs were in praise to God for God's deliverance of them.

You can't imagine a more white, Western, proper Presbyterian than I, but I was sitting there in a church organized in the 18th century by tough Scots-Irish immigrants, and finding myself deeply moved by the singing and swaying and dancing of these West Africans, all in the praise of God. Amazing!

One thing I noticed is the extent to which these folks worship God with their bodies. They clap, they dance, they move, they lift up their arms. I got tired doing all of that. Worship here made me tired, not bored, not despairing, but bodily tired—a strange gift that does not usually happen to me in church. It was a good tired, as if worship were a kind of workout. In any case, if the chief end of human life is to glorify God and enjoy God forever, as those Scots-Irish settlers knew so long ago, then maybe these recent immigrants have more in common with us and we with them than might be apparent at first glance.

Where is the church? We did not celebrate the sacraments but we did hear the gospel proclaimed, albeit in a different tongue and with different music. Where will the church be in the future? I don't know. And I am not real sure that other people know. But I wonder if the church is not going to look more and more like what I saw on Sunday.

In the congregation not everyone was from Togo. There were also some Vietnamese women worshipping there. They might have seemed incongruous as I myself, except they could follow what Thomas was saying because they understood French. God is sneaky. Our church tries so hard to be multicultural, and here is the confluence of many cultures right in our midst, coming to us as a gift.

A final note: Jesus is very important to these new immigrants. They talk about him a lot and they insist that he is King of kings and Lord of lords and that he is very powerful. Some of us might recoil at such triumphalistic language, but the words are utterly scriptural. When you are poor, homesick, and struggling to make it in a strange land, affirmations like these lose their smugness and become daring affirmations of the truth. I don't know that I saw the future of the church but on Sunday during worship, I believe I was given a vision of the Kingdom.

July 11, 2012

Last week I read a review of R. Jay Magill's book, *Sincerity*,[1] in which he argues that at least since the time of Rousseau, and perhaps going back to the Puritans themselves, we have put far too much stock in this alleged virtue. If one reads sermons or responses to sermons by Jonathan Edwards and other American Protestants, one is often struck by the individual's quest for a sincere repentance or evidence of true redemption. Rousseau thought that sincerity of heart was the key to living the "authentic" life, which would be manifested most compellingly in self-expression. He did not write the lyric, "I've got to be me," but he could have.

Magill is rightly suspicious of all this talk of sincerity, whether it comes in the form of religion or politics or art. As the cynic might say, "Once you have learned to fake sincerity, the rest is easy."

Last Sunday, my wife and I were in Scotland, where we worshipped at a church in St Andrews. It was a summer Sunday so the choir was on vacation and the parish minister also. In his place the Kirk session had

1. Akst, *The Wall Street Journal*, July 8, 2012.

invited an American missionary, who preached on Acts 10, the story of Peter and Cornelius. The point of the sermon was that until we are truly sincere in seeking our salvation, we will fail to reach that goal. Cornelius, the American preacher maintained, truly sought to be born again, and because he was sincere in his faith, he was able to receive the gospel and be saved.

The question the American preacher posed to each of us was whether we were equally sincere, whether we really wanted to be saved.

Well. At first I was discouraged that there were not more people in worship on this glorious summer Sunday, but after the sermon I was grateful that the crowd was so sparse. Somewhere Nietzsche says something to the effect that one begins to understand what sincerity really means when one recognizes how good we are at lying to ourselves. Few people were more sincere than Hitler or Torquemada or Pol Pot.

The theological issue here is the same one that Augustine dealt with in his struggle against the Donatists. Is it the sincerity, i.e., the purity of the priest that makes the sacraments effective? The Donatists thought so, but Augustine said, "No." We are not saved by our sincerity but by God's grace to undeserving sinners.

Our quest for authenticity is just another way of keeping ourselves at the center of the story, another way of seeking to avoid the piercing light of God's grace. The truth is, we are never entirely sincere. This side of the Kingdom, our motives will always be mixed. And in any case, God does not wait until we achieve an acceptable level of sincerity before granting us grace. Thank God.

I don't mean to be too hard on that American preacher. He was a good man, no doubt, but he seemed offended by the radical nature of God's forgiveness. The Luke who tells the story of Peter and Cornelius also tells us that the scribes and Pharisees murmured against Jesus, grumbling that "this fellow welcomes sinners and eats with them." (Luke 15:2) Yes. That is true. Here, as in other places, the scribes and Pharisees unwittingly proclaim the gospel. Jesus welcomes sinners and eats with them. Thank God.

The gospel is so much better, so much more joyful, so much more beautiful than our tiresome efforts to be worthy of it. That was what I was hoping to hear in the story of Peter and Cornelius, whom the Holy Spirit—not their sincerity—had brought into proximity to each other and into the realm of the Kingdom.

Chapter 10: Stories that Sustain the Faith

October 1, 2003

I have been reading Ralph Wood's book, *The Gospel According to Tolkien*. Wood will be lecturing here in February. In the book, he quotes Sam, Frodo's friend and companion, on the nature of stories. Sam's words reminded me of what you might be feeling as a new seminarian embarked on a long course of study (viz., "What have I got myself into?").

Sam tells Frodo:

> We shouldn't be here at all, if we'd known more about it before we started. But I suppose it's often that way. The brave things in the old tales and songs, Mr. Frodo: adventures, as I used to call them. I used to think that they were things the wonderful folk of the stories went out and looked for, because they wanted them, because they were exciting and life was a bit dull, a kind of sport, as you might say. But that's not the way of it with tales that really mattered, or the ones that stay in the mind. Folk seem to have been just landed in them, usually—their paths were laid that way, as you put it. But I expect they had lots of chances, like us, of turning back, only they didn't. And if they had, we shouldn't know, because they'd been forgotten. We hear about those as just went on—and not all to a good end, mind you; at least not to what folk inside a story and not outside it call a good end. You know, coming home, and finding things all right, though not quite the same—like old Mr. Bilbo. But those aren't always the best tales to hear, though they may be the best tales to get landed in! I wonder what sort of tale we've fallen into?[1]

Do you wonder that as well? Well, whatever it is, it is a tale that will demand more courage than we have and will take us to places we never dreamed of going. And the home we find may not be at all "back there"

---

1. Wood, *The Gospel According to Tolkien*, 146.

but still up ahead. Still, I am glad to be "landed" in the story with you and to have such good traveling companions along the way.

January 21, 2004

In the novel, *The Brothers Karamazov*, Dostoyevsky creates a remarkable character, Father Zossima, an Elder among a group of Orthodox monks living in Russia. At one point, Father Zossima preaches a sermon to his fellow monks, in which he says the following:

> My friends, pray to God for gladness. Be glad as children, as the birds of heaven. And let not the sin of men confound you in your doings. Fear not that it will wear away your work and hinder its being accomplished. Do not say, 'Sin is mighty, wickedness is mighty, evil environment is mighty, and we are lonely and helpless. Evil environment is wearing us away and hindering our good work being done.' Fly from that dejection! There is only one means of salvation. Make yourself responsible for all men's sins. As soon as you sincerely make yourself responsible for everything and for all men, you will see at once that you have found salvation. On the other hand, throwing your indolence and impotence on others, you will end by sharing the pride of Satan and murmuring against God.[2]

What does Father Zossima mean when he says, "make yourself responsible for all men's sins"? Does he mean that we are to cultivate a stronger sense of guilt? I do not think he means that, though I suspect he believes that guilt does have its redemptive purposes. I think, rather, he means that because Jesus Christ is risen and is Lord, human sinfulness ought not to frighten us as much as it wants to, that we should not grant to sin that much power, such that it paralyzes us and renders us unable to embrace the sinner.

Earlier in the novel, Father Zossima says that hell is the suffering of being unable to love. That would indeed be hell. And that would keep us, as hell is designed to do, in splendid isolation, surrounded only by our worries. So, it is liberating to hear words like these: "Do not worry about your life, what you will eat or what you will drink, or about your body, what you will wear. Is not life more than food and the body more than clothing?" (Matt 6:25)

2. Dostoyevsky, *The Brothers Karamazov*, 340.

Perhaps it seems the height of pomposity for me to tell you, as busy as you are, "not to worry about your life," but I risk such foolishness because we are all so busy that we might be tempted to think that our life is about being busy, about checking things off a list, about being the main character in our particular stories, and so come to forget that our life and even our life together here is a gift. Such a gift is the only thing that enables us to hear that worry is not to be the center of our lives. There is Another who occupies that space and has lifted that burden from us. So, do not worry.

Hard to do? To be sure. It is not easy to become a lily of the field or a bird of the air. All it takes is a miracle. Which is why it is a good thing to listen to Father Zossima and "pray to God for gladness."

April 29, 2004

This spring I have been re-reading Mark Twain's *Huckleberry Finn*. An interesting resource to read alongside it is William Phipps' book, *Mark Twain's Religion* (Mercer University Press, 2003). Phipps makes much of the fact that Twain grew up in the Presbyterian Church and was familiar with the Westminster Shorter Catechism. In that catechism, the purpose of human life is described not in terms of salvation of self but in terms of glorifying God and enjoying God forever. In *Huckleberry Finn*, there is a recurring critique of religious and other kinds of efforts to save oneself, and also, a laying bare of a kind of faithfulness that is characterized by the willingness to lose oneself for another. That kind of faithfulness is not depicted as adherence to a given principle so much as it is shown to be the faithful love for another person. The novel turns on Huck's decision to be faithful to Jim even if it means going to hell. In this, Huck exemplifies the Reformed insistence that a believer should not make an idol of his or her own salvation, and should even be willing to be damned for the sake of Jesus Christ. Which is to affirm that one does not follow Jesus Christ for the sake of one's own selfish gain but to witness to him and his Kingdom. This, of course, is just another way of affirming that the gospel is not about "me" but about God's redemptive purpose in the world.

To be sure, Twain is writing a novel, not a Sunday School lesson. Indeed, in the preface to the novel he warns that people attempting to find a moral in this story will be "banished." But his warning is aimed at those who would reduce the narrative to a moral principle and thereby miss the story being told, a story that, in fact, has to do with the quite moral issue of slavery and freedom, and even more with the mysterious gift of our own humanity.

Twain has no problem revealing 19th (and 21st?) century America's lust for salvation, and he amply offers illustrations of the ways in which that lust disorders and violates human fellowship. But Twain also knows of a different kind of "Providence," one that is "not ashamed" of God's creatures, however humble. Early in the novel, after being chewed out by Miss Watson for not accepting her god of conditional and contractual "love," Huck concludes: "I judged that there were two Providences, and a poor chap would stand considerable show with the widow's Providence, but if Miss Watson's got him, there warn't no help for him anymore. I thought it all out, and reckoned I would belong to the widow's if he wanted me, though I couldn't make out how he was going to be any better off then than what he was before, seeing I was so ignorant and so kind of low-down and ornery."[3]

Such is the real mystery of God's grace, that God would love us even in the midst of our "low-down orneriness," or to use Paul's language: " . . . perhaps for a good person someone might actually dare to die. But God proves his love for us in that while we were still sinners Christ died for us." (Rom 5:8) In Jesus Christ, God is faithful to us and even puts that faithfulness above his own life, time and again refusing a separate peace, a private salvation, or any that does not include "low-down and ornery" sinners.

So, maybe Twain knew more Reformed theology than he is given credit for. In any case, many theologians, Reformed and otherwise, could learn a thing or two from the story Mark Twain tells.

December 1, 2004

Reading Simone Weil is not always easy but in engaging with her thought there is, I believe, great reward. At one point she writes the following:

> There are people who try to raise their souls like a man continually taking standing jumps in the hopes that, if he jumps higher every day, a time may come when he will no longer fall back but will go right up to the sky. Thus occupied he cannot look at the sky. We cannot take a single step toward heaven. It is not in our power to travel in a vertical direction. If, however, we look

3. Twain, *Huckleberry Finn*, 11.

heavenward for a long time, God comes and takes us up. He
raises us easily. As Aeschylus says: 'There is no effort in what
is divine.' There is easiness in salvation which is more difficult
to us than all our efforts . . . . In one of Grimm's stories there
is a competition between a giant and a little tailor to see which
is the stronger. The giant throws a stone so high that it takes a
very long time before it comes down again. The little tailor lets
a bird fly (from his cupped hands) and it does not come down
at all. Anything without wings always comes down in the end
. . . . In the parables of the gospel, it is God who seeks man . . . .
Nowhere in the gospel is there question of a search undertaken
by man. Man does not take a step unless he receives some pressure or is definitely called . . . . Waiting for goodness and truth
is, however, something more intense than any searching . . . .[4]

"Waiting," in Simone Weil's terms, is what we are doing here in
seminary. It is intense and in any case, more intense than any searching.

January 25, 2006

I have been reading Alan Jacobs' book, *A Theology of Reading* (Westview
Press, 2001), which in turn spurred me on to read Charles Dickens' novel
Hard Times. Jacobs spends the last chapter of his book examining Dickens' novel and suggesting that at its heart it has something to say to us
about God and the nature of God's love for sinners.

Hard Times opens with a description of the school run by Mr.
Thomas Gradgrind (whose name tells you all you need to know about
his educational practices) who wants his own children and the other students in his school located in "Coketown" (the miserable town created
in the wake of the industrial revolution) to know what he calls "facts."
Knowledge of facts and nothing but "facts" will lead, Mr. Gradgrind is
sure, to the greatest happiness for the greatest number.

But starved of imagination, not to mention images of love, his students, and especially his own children fail miserably as models of the new
way, and his son is eventually revealed to be a thief who avoids arrest and
jail only through the merciful intervention of a man Mr. Gradgrind has
criticized and dismissed. The arresting officer is one of Mr. Gradgrind's
students, and in pleading for mercy for his son, Gradgrind asks the police-
men, "Don't you have a heart?" only to be told in reply that the policeman

4. Weil, *Waiting for God*, 127.

does, and that a heart is a muscle within the body whose purpose is the distribution and circulation of blood.[5] He has learned his lesson all too well from his teacher. There will be no mercy.

Near the town there is a traveling circus that visits on occasion. It is operated by a Mr. Sleary, who has a severe speech impediment (a lisp) and whom Mr. Gradgrind has always viewed as a nuisance and something of a fool. Toward the end of the novel, it is Sleary who helps Mr. Gradgrind's son escape to freedom, and it is to Sleary, that Mr. Gradgrind turns for consolation. Mr. Sleary talks to Mr. Gradgrind about love, in this case, the love of a dog for his master. He contrasts that with Mr. Gradgrind's conviction that only self-interested happiness is sufficient to motivate a person. In describing the beauty of love to one who believes only in "facts," Mr. Sleary says (I paraphrase.): "There is a love in the world that is not entirely self-interested, but is something different, a love that has a way of mysteriously calculating what is valuable, almost like a dog loves."[6]

A dog's love, Mr. Sleary implies, is marvelously instructive, suggesting that there is a mystery at the heart of life that cannot be reduced to facts, anymore than a person can be reduced to a number. What sustains such love, what reveals such a mystery? Though Sleary does not say it, as the head of a "traveling circus," he knows a great deal about the comedy of redemption, about the grace that can only appear disturbingly comedic in a world dedicated to its own "facts." Fools and sinners have always understood each other, just as they have always known how to celebrate their mutual forgiveness by a grace whose calculus is difficult to figure. The "traveling circus" will always constitute a dangerous presence in "Coketown" because it brings joy to a world preoccupied with the serious business of its own "happiness." In that respect, the circus resembles the gospel itself, and does not have to do much more than sing its song to surprise the inhabitants of "Coketown," drawing them away from the misery of their own distractions.

I mention all of this to you to remind us that going back to work after such a wonderful break, should not return us "to the grind" but rather to the learning of the ways of that "traveling circus" which is the life of the church. There we will find that "practicing the scales of rejoicing"[7]

5. Dickens, *Hard Times*, 275.

6. 99 *Ibid.*, 280.

7. Cf. Auden, 'For the Time Being," in *Collected Poems*, 400.

brings its own joy and introduces us to music that regularly interrupts our work, rendering it both happy and fruitful.

A final note: the subtitle of Jacobs' book is "the hermeneutics of love," which has application, I would think, for the way we read scripture.

February 1, 2006

When I was in college, I was invited to read *The Diary of Anne Frank*. Somewhere, toward the end of that deeply moving witness, Anne writes: "I still believe that people are really good at heart."[8]

At the time that I first read those words, I thought them painfully sad and ironic. "Well," I thought, "she knows better now. She has learned what human beings can do to each other. To believe that they are "really good at heart" seems almost criminally naive. Anne can be forgiven because she was still a young girl and still unaware of the darkness of evil that awaited her and so many others. But we, we know better now." Or so I told myself.

This past week I have been reading *Hope Against Hope* by Nadezhda Mandelstam, the wife of Osip Mandelstam, one of Russia's great 20th century poets, who was executed by the Communists in a Soviet Gulag in 1938 for writing a poem critical of Stalin. Nadezhda Mandelstam's memoir of her husband came out in 1970. In the book, she writes that after her husband was arrested and sent to Siberia, many friends came to their aid, even at a great threat to their own well-being. She writes: "In periods of violence and terror people retreat into themselves and hide their feelings, but their feelings are ineradicable and cannot be destroyed by any amount of indoctrination. Even if they are wiped out in one generation, as happened here to a considerable extent, they will burst forth again in the next one. We have seen this several times. The idea of good seems really to be inborn . . . ."[9]

As a Calvinist, I might want to question all of this but what do you make of this insistence by two very different women who were facing frightening evils, that there is a goodness that is "ineradicable," a goodness that is even capable of regenerating itself despite all that might threaten to exterminate it. I am not so sure, as I once was, that Anne Frank was sinfully "naive." Maybe she possessed the wisdom of serpents

8. Frank, Anne Frank *The Diary of a Young Girl*, 263.
9. Mandelstam, *Hope Against Hope*, 39.

and innocence of doves. Maybe Nadezhda Mandelstam knows things about goodness than I, who have enjoyed a much more comfortable life, could never know.

The Apostle Paul knew a thing or two about "our righteousness," which he thinks is "hidden with Christ in God." (Col 3:3) That suggests to me that the goodness that is "ineradicable" exists there, centered not in us or the "human spirit" but in Christ, who by his resurrection is able to regenerate it in the face of death again and again. This does not make goodness any less mysterious, nor does it confine its regenerative powers only to Christians. In fact, as the poet reminds us, "Christ plays in ten thousand places," showing up where we think he has no business being.

Maybe the way to think about all of this is to take the mystery of goodness and its presence in the world more seriously than we do the presence of evil, not forgetting the latter or papering over it, but trusting that if people are "good at heart," that can only be the residual witness to the One who really is good at heart, and who is able to make the rest of us dare to live more faithfully out of his goodness. The evil that human beings do is not the light. It is the darkness that can only be seen when the light shines to reveal it. And the darkness cannot, and will not ever, master this light.

March 17, 2010

Today a group of alums and pastors met here at the seminary to discuss a book of sermons by Karl Barth. I must confess that this morning was one of the best mornings I have experienced here. Some of our recent graduates, who are now pastoring congregations, gave excellent presentations and led us more deeply into fruitful discussion. A feast.

Which made me think of Jan Parler. Last week, her husband, Rick, came by and dropped off a book of her collected sermons, entitled, *For the Beauty of the Earth.* As you may remember, Jan very much wanted to be ordained, a gift that was denied her by reason of illness and death. But while she was in seminary and especially after she graduated, she preached on several occasions and in a variety of settings. Her family collected those sermons and had them bound in this lovely volume.

I read one this morning as part of my devotionals. Its title is "Standing on the Rock." In this sermon, Jan tells of her remarkable experiences as a novice chaplain at Presbyterian Hospital. On the third day of her time there, she was sitting in the chaplain's office waiting for instructions, when a call came that a patient had just died and the family was requesting a chaplain. The secretary turned to Jan and asked if she would take this one. Jan replied, "Don't you think they need a real chaplain?" The secretary looked at her and said, "Today, you are a real chaplain."

Jan gulped and took the elevator up to the floor and walked into the room where a 92 year-old African American woman had just died, surrounded by her daughters, granddaughters, and great-granddaughters. They invited Jan into the room and graciously made space for her to sit down. Jan listened. They began to share stories of the deceased woman, and through laughter and tears, they recounted something of her life. Jan asked if they would like her to pray, and they said they would, very much. In fact, some of the family members began praying before Jan could get a word out. In the midst of this ministry, Jan discovered that what she was doing was a shared work, into which she had entered, and that she was receiving as much, if not more, than she was giving.

After the prayers were prayed, one of the daughters commented on how much her mother loved to sing. Jan asked what her mother's favorite hymn was. All the women in the room smiled; they all knew the answer to that question. "On Christ the Solid Rock I Stand," they said, almost in unison. Jan's final comment: "This woman had lived her whole life grounded in that understanding. I left the room that day, suddenly recognizing I was already empowered for the journey ahead."[10]

To which I do not have much to add, except that Jan's sermon reminds me that good ministry depends on hearing such stories, which help us find our footing on that Rock, and teach us how to sing.

November 3, 2010

In Dostoyevsky's novel, *Crime and Punishment*, the main character is a self-centered sometime university student, who thinks his "smarts" are sufficient to justify himself, even to the point of murdering someone he considers unworthy of life so that he can spend her money on "good deeds." The story is about how he is relieved of his self-sufficiency, that is, how he is redeemed. His particular redemption is one that mercifully impoverishes what he had thought was his wealth, even as it grants him the unexpected grace of needing and receiving another's love. Raskolnikov

10. Parler, *For the Beauty of the Earth*, 9.

is the young man and the unexpected grace that comes to him is being loved by Sonya, a prostitute. The climactic scene in the novel takes place in Sonya's room, where Raskolnikov asks her to read to him the story in John's Gospel about the raising of Lazarus. She is surprised because he has given no previous indication of being interested either in scripture or its message, but she reads. Her reading of the passage occasions the conversation that enables him to confess to her his crime, the point being that what he needs is not just punishment or even reform, but to be raised from the death of his own self-centered despair.

Raskolnikov is dying of hopelessness. And he has been trying to live in a world in which there is no such thing as hope: only power, only smarts, only the success of the self-justifying I. In that world, he has become lethal to others and himself. He needs to be raised from the dead.

In the Ethics course this fall, we have been reading another novel, Graham Greene's, *The End of the Affair*. In this novel too, the main character, Bendrix, is not very nice. He is rich in intellect, in novelistic skill, in cleverness, all of which he has enjoyed quite without worrying about God or other people. In this novel, he too is ravaged, robbed of the one person he loves, a theft that, quite against his own will, draws him closer to God.

Bendrix is also living in a world without hope but unlike Raskolnikov, he is comfortable in that world, assiduous in his manipulation of it. The theft of his lover is what upsets things and results in his calling the "end of the affair" not so much a love story as a hate story. He hates God, the great thief, who has stolen his lover from him. God, as far as Bendrix is concerned, is a far more accomplished manipulator than he is a source of benevolence. Yet, just so, is Bendrix forced to consider God and to wrestle with God's grace. Gradually, and with very little fanfare or pious celebration, Bendrix begins to show kindness to another human being and be introduced, however reluctantly, to hope. His is not a pretty story nor does this novel have a completely happy ending but its very messiness is the way discipleship often looks in a "hopeless" world. It is how modern day Lazaruses are gradually unwrapped from their grave clothes and called into resurrection life.

What has prompted these reflections is my own perception that the threat we face today, both as students and faculty, is really not lack of money or enough time or smarts or all the other things we think prevent us from preparing adequately for this work. Rather, the threat we face is a kind of hopelessness. We know its world and we know how to operate in its environs. And like Bendrix, we can even resent Lazarus' bothersome presence, a hope that is almost embarrassing in its lack of strategy, technique, or wealth. How does one "practice resurrection" in the face of all of that?

Not by ignoring the facts, that is for sure. The gift is, as the line from Wendell Berry's poem reminds us, to *"Be joyful though you have considered all the facts."*[11] The fact is that Lazarus died. The fact is that Raskolnikov murdered his landlady and deserves punishment. The fact is that Bendrix is a selfish purveyor of his own desires, whose loss of the one person he loves and who loves him would hardly seem regrettable, and might even appear a fitting end for one so self-centered. These are the facts.

But there is another fact that these facts do not know. And that fact is what enables us to believe in something more than our own smarts or wealth or savvy or success. This fact contradicts all our facts and is, in truth, difficult to explain. This fact is what enables people like Raskolnikov and Bendrix to begin to hope. This fact is what enables us, *having considered all the facts,* to be joyful.

Although the church, Calvin claims,

> is at the present hardly to be distinguished from a dead or at best a sick man, there is no reason for despair, for the Lord raises up his own suddenly, as he waked the dead from the grave. This we must clearly remember, lest when the church fails to shine forth, we conclude too quickly that her light has died utterly away. But the church in the world is so preserved that *she* rises *suddenly* from the dead. Her very preservation through the days is due to a succession of such miracles. Let us cling to the remembrance that she is not without her resurrection, or rather, not without her many resurrections.[12]

So, let us be of good cheer, despite all the facts we have to consider. There is another fact that takes us more seriously than all the other facts put together. "And he must win the battle . . . ."

---

11. Berry, *"Manifesto: The Mad Farmer Liberation Front"* in *The Selected Poems of Wendell Berry,* 88.

12. Cited in Barth, *The Word of God and the Word of Man,* 135.

Chapter 11: Language Study

May 7, 2003

I know that many of you are taking Greek this summer. For the students who have already had Hebrew, the anxiety that arises from trying to learn another language is, perhaps, not so severe. But for those who are coming to Greek for the first time, trying to learn another language well enough to read it, can be a stressful thing. Concerning which, I want to say two things.

The first is this: Fear not. That simple message is one that recurs throughout scripture. It is in the 23rd Psalm. It is what the angels tell the shepherds, what Gabriel tells Mary, what the angels tell the women at the tomb: "Fear not." We dismiss such words too quickly sometimes, thinking the angel's grasp on reality is not that firm, but when we do that, we are the ones who lose our grip. "Fear not," does not mean that things will be easy or that there will be no struggle or that you will make an "A" in Greek. "Fear not," means, rather, that none of the things you fear will be able to overcome you. None of them will defeat you or your calling to be a pastor. None of them will unclasp the hand of the most real person in the world who has a hold of your hand even now and will never let it go. So, fear not. Greek will not get the best of you. Do not take counsel with your fears.

The second point is this: this seminary lives from that "Fear not." We have a lot invested in you and your future ministry and we are going to do everything we can to help you master this challenging course of study. We believe that by doing so, we will be helping you to hear "Fear not" even better and more faithfully. So, the only way you will not succeed in this course will be if you give up on yourself and give into your fears. We are not going to give up on you or your gifts.

So keep studying, keep learning that vocabulary, mastering those verb tenses, and do not give up on yourself.

"Do not fear, for I have redeemed you; I have called you by name, you are mine. When you pass through the waters, I will be with you; and through the rivers, they shall not overwhelm you . . . . Do not fear, for I am with you." (Isa 43:2,5)

Isaiah's word is a good one to keep beside you as you study.

January 11, 2006

Many of you are carrying a heavy load this term, with Greek and Theology I or Greek and courses in teaching or preaching. Words of comfort and encouragement can be cheap things, especially when delivered by those who are not facing what you are facing. This morning, I was reading a selection from Dietrich Bonhoeffer's *Letters and Papers from Prison*, in which he was trying to encourage his friend, Eberhard Bethge. Bethge was getting ready to return to the Eastern Front, and to what he suspected would be his death. Bonhoeffer was writing to him from a Gestapo prison, suspecting that death might be awaiting him as well.

In the letter, Bonhoeffer urged Bethge not to despair, but to hold on tightly to his earthly affections. These affections, Bonhoeffer claimed, do not distract us from God but rather bear witness to God, much in the same way that the harmony of a song bears witness to its melody, without replacing it. What is vital is to hear the *cantus firmus*, the melody, so that we can catch the tune and find the courage to risk our little harmonies.

In a similar vein, Frederick Buechner writes: "'He who loves fifty has fifty woes . . . . Who loves none has no woe,' said the Buddha, and it is true . . . . [But] side by side with the Buddha's truth is the Gospel truth that 'he who does not love remains in death.'" (1 John 3:14)[1] The point? The point is that in all the pressure to learn, to study, to master Greek or read theology, there is a great temptation just "to get it done," i.e., to take the course, even excel in it, but then be done with it. What Bonhoeffer and Buechner remind us of is that there is no point in learning anything about Christian discipleship, if it does not issue in love: love of this world, love of this world's people, love of Christ's church, love of God.

In scripture, knowing and loving are deeply related things. Only in our modern world have the two fallen apart. Only fairly recently has it been possible to study theology lovelessly, as if it were some kind of neutral information to be categorized and stored in the academy.

1. Buechner, *Now and Then*, 54–55.

So, as busy as you are, I hope that your studies here lead you to become more faithful lovers of Jesus Christ and his gospel. Sometimes that will actually cause you to fall in love with Greek and theology, and one day, with the people of God whose lives will depend on your interpretation of the story that sustains you both.

February 15, 2006

Last week I was asked by a student here why the seminary requires the study of Greek and Hebrew. I was just finishing lunch and on my way to another appointment, and so I ventured a quick but hardly satisfactory response. The question has gnawed at me since then, and deserves a better answer than I gave then.

So, here's what I think:

1) Perhaps it should be noted at the outset that knowledge of Greek and Hebrew does not deliver the Gospel into one's hands or even make one, automatically, a good interpreter of the Bible's story. It takes a miracle for any of us to hear the gospel, which is why we pray for the Holy Spirit before we dare to read the scripture in worship and preach each Sunday. You will find also, if you have not already, that a member of your congregation or Sunday School class will know the gospel better than you and may well be a better interpreter of its story than you. Kierkegaard, a layman, offers several helpful reminders in this regard, when he insists that knowledge of Jesus Christ is equally offensive to all, and most especially offensive to those who attempt to "explain" it to others. In any case, people do not come to worship to hear you display the extent of your knowledge of Greek or Hebrew. Much less have they come to hear your "explain" the gospel to the "dullards" in the congregation who have not taken the original languages.

2) However, the study of Greek and Hebrew can be and one hopes actually is a way of becoming a more faithful student of the gospel's story, and to that extent, a more faithful disciple of the Word made flesh. John Calvin thought that knowledge of the liberal arts was a good preparation for ministry. The reason he thought that was that ministers of the Word are called to be lovers of words. That is to say, they are not called to be garrulous, wordy, or pedantic but to become students who are at least as interested in the way the Word enfleshes itself in language as they are in preaching and using words themselves. Why should we apologize for

being in love with words? The Word we struggle to hear and to proclaim speaks itself into the flesh of a particular language, with its own idioms and metaphors, some quite earthy and specific. To attend to this Word, indeed, to become a "Minister of Word and Sacrament" is to know the language well. People who hear you preach do not have a right to expect that you are an expert retailing your expertise, but they do have a right to expect that you know the story well enough not to hold it captive to our own idioms and metaphors. They have a right to hear something of the strangeness of this word. Knowledge of the original languages works to liberate us from the temptation to reduce the gospel to the sameness of our words, our culture, whatever direction we find the prevailing wind to be blowing at the time.

3) Requiring knowledge of the original languages assumes that God loves us in a strange way. We spend a great deal of time complaining at the inefficiencies or even weirdness of this love, and often would prefer that God be more direct, transparent, even obvious and quick. But instead the gospel, which in some places seems nothing more than a love letter, comes to us in Greek and Hebrew. We can't read it without help, just as we can't become Christian without the help of others. The languages drive us toward the community of faith, the community that is extended in time and has struggled with these words for centuries, and the community extended in space that seeks to understand this word for today. Not learning the languages is one way we can pretend that we are exempt from bonds of faith and can deal more directly with God ourselves.

There are some in our culture who think that our way of training pastors and teachers does not take scripture seriously. And it is true that we are not always able to memorize verses or quote texts as well as others. But how does one measure seriousness here? If we are serious lovers of this word, why should we not want to hear it in its own idiom and grammar and language? Do we know the culture of these words so well that we can dismiss its language? I am weary with the accusation that we do not take the Word seriously here. Fully 25% of our required courses focus on the languages, the language that shaped Israel and the early Church. We have many faults as a seminary and as a tradition, many faults, but spending time listening to these words is not one of them.

Love seeks to learn the language of the One who loves us in this way.

4) Finally, the study of the original languages works to slow the preaching task down. That may seem an odd virtue to you, but consider: even if you graduate from this institution and enter ministry and do not

use the Greek or Hebrew each week, or its use falls away after awhile into neglect, you know that writing a sermon is not just putting down big ideas or what you thought about that week. You know that listening is hard and takes time and requires a lot of digging. Calvin called prayer a kind of digging, a digging out of the gospel's treasures. Such a humble analogy, such humble work. Preaching is like that. It is very humble work. It is like digging a trench or mucking out a stall. It requires some advanced preparation, at least enough to slow us down long enough to attend to this story. To be sure the Holy Spirit will have to work the usual miracle of giving us something to say, but the Holy Spirit does not work those miracles only in the moment, but more often in and through the work of study and listening and thinking and writing.

I know this is hard. Mastering Greek and Hebrew is not easy. It is also, however, a gift. There are no Cliff Notes for preaching a good sermon anymore than there is for becoming a faithful pastor. This story seeks those who will listen to it afresh and proclaim it, in all its offensiveness and comfort, gladly.

May 16, 2007

Cornelius Plantinga has written an essay on "glory," the substance of which I would like to share with you. His essay concerns more particularly a German Jew named Viktor Klemperer, whose ambition it was to write the definitive account of 18th century French literature. "If he succeeded," Plantinga writes, "he would be eminent throughout academe and thus could hold his head up in the faculty lounge."[2] He could go to conferences of the learned and be acknowledged as one of the masters in the field.

But, unfortunately for Viktor Klemperer's ambitions, the Nazis came to power and bit by bit he was frustrated and reduced, unable to achieve his goal. The Nazis took away his office, telephone, typewriter, literary privileges, and canceled his courses. They even took away his home. In response, Klemperer began to record—very carefully and very completely—each humiliation, each detail of his oppression. He wrote: "I want to bear witness, precise witness, until the very end."[3]

2. Plantinga, "Deep Wisdom" in God the Holy Trinity, ed. Timothy George, 149.
3. Ibid., 150.

Clearly he could see where this road was headed. So he wrote in his diary every day about the small things, ordinary daily indignities and little "murders" that happened all around him. One day the Nazis came for him and put him on the train to one of the death camps, where he died.

Klemperer, Plantinga notes, did not find the glory he sought in writing about 18th century French literature. Instead, another kind of glory was thrust upon him, a glory he did not seek but for which he is remembered and celebrated today.

His diary survived his death to bear witness, precise witness not only to "man's inhumanity to man" but also to the remarkable acts of courage ordinary people sometimes were capable of, and the equally distressing acts of cowardice.

He became a martyr for the truth. Klemperer never knew that this would be his glory, and indeed, it is not one he sought. But this glory is so much brighter and more vivid than the glory of the faculty lounge might afford. Indeed, this glory is so bright (and so terrible!) that it is hard for us even to look at it.

Studying Hebrew may not strike you as particularly glorious. But this course requires close attention to detail, daily discipline, and ordinary but unrelenting sacrifice. The whole purpose of taking this course is to assist you in bearing witness, to tell the truth in your own day and time. And the work brings with it its own glory, not perhaps the glory we envision for ourselves, perhaps not even the glory that will make your face shine, but a glory nonetheless.

What kind of glory? Some years ago, my daughter, Kate, gave me a print by Van Gogh, which is hanging on a wall where I can see it each morning. It is a simple painting, depicting a pair of well-worn work boots. These boots are not pretty or particularly stylish, but rather, beat-up, almost worn out, and old. But they shine with an illumination from beyond the painting. They proclaim, in all their weary earthiness, the glory of the one who puts on those boots each day and goes to work. They tell me something of the ineradicable dignity of human beings. I love this print.

When Moses came down from Mt. Sinai, his face glowed though he did not know it, anymore than Viktor Klemperer knew of his true glory, or those old boots, with one lying on its side, knew of theirs. And perhaps you can, as they say, relate. Studying Hebrew may not strike you as glorious work. I understand that. But though you may not sense either the beauty of your labors or the beauty of this language, the glory of God is shining through your study and efforts.

"Look to him and be radiant, and your faces will never be ashamed." (Ps 34:5)

May 1, 2013

There is a lovely Simon and Garfunkel song describing the course of a brief romance: "April, come she will/ When streams are ripe and swelled with rain;/ May, she will stay, Resting in my arms again . . . ."/ After that, everything goes pretty much downhill in this relationship, and by August and September, whatever was cooking in April and May is finished and done.

I always thought of this song as a melancholy riff on love's unsmooth course, but recently someone has suggested to me that what it is really about is baseball, and how in April every team, even the Cubs, are full of hope, but by June most of them start to swoon, and by August, their hopes are dashed, and by September, it's over. Very few make it to October.

Maybe baseball is the better analogy, so I will go with that. It's May now and time to play ball.

A few years ago, George Will wrote an excellent book about baseball, entitled, *Men at Work* (Harper Perennial, 2010). Tommy Lasorda, not known for his literary criticism, took exception to the title of Will's book, reminding Will that when a game of baseball begins, the umpire does not say, "Work ball!" but rather, "Play ball!" It is, after all, a game, a game of skill and craft, to be sure, but a game.

Changing the respective terms, I would like to remind you as we begin this summer term, that we *get* to learn Hebrew. I am not being facetious. There is, after all, something of the joy of "playing ball" that is true of learning itself, the joy of preparing ourselves for the work (and the gift!) of ministry.

Going to school here is not the easiest way to attend seminary. Lots of weekends and not a few nights are taken up with classes. And all of that in addition to your earning a living and caring for a family. Yet if theological education were not a joy, I doubt any of us would undertake it. I once heard a seminary president say that learning was inherently sanctifying. I am not quite convinced of that; I have met my share of learned sinners. But I do believe that learning can be one of the ways we grow in faith and deepen our commitment to Christ and his mission in the world. It is not the only way, but whatever faith we have is faith that seeks understanding, and it seeks understanding in no small part for the joy of it all.

At the turn of the 11th and 12th centuries, there was a great theologian named Anselm, who began the theological task by praying to God to grant him the joy of knowing God. The joy.

So may we begin this May in the confident hope that our time together this summer will be a time of sanctified learning, of true joy in getting to study the Word as it is enfleshed in the words of the text and of life.

July 10, 2013

Last week, my wife had me cleaning up in our attic, getting rid of old papers and copies of old sermons. (It is a separate and not uninteresting question as to why pastors save old sermons. As a rule, a sermon has a very short shelf-life, but perhaps this discussion will have to wait for another time.) In any case, I was reading one of these sermons when I stumbled across a story involving my older daughter, a story that made me smile. One day when Kate was in the 8th grade, I had come to pick her up from school and we were driving home. As we were going along, a car slowly passed us on the right. It was a late model convertible, driven by a high school senior girl, whose blonde hair was flowing in the breeze. My daughter stared at this phenomenon for a moment and then turned to me and said, "When I go to high school, I want to be just like that; I want a car just like that."

I said nothing for a moment as I drove along, and then opined that I thought Kate's wish represented an unlikely prospect. She turned to me and asked with some asperity, "Why? Why not?" I could see that my response would require thought, and so, after some reflection, I decided to offer a bit of parental jujitsu. "Because," I said, "you are too rich." Kate looked at me, stunned, and asked, "What do you mean?" "Well," I replied, "you have two parents who love you deeply and who are determined to give you the very best we can. One of those very best gifts is a college education, which, we hope, will provide you with nourishment and strength far in excess of a temporary mode of transportation. That girl's parents may love her as deeply as we love you, but if the only evidence of their love is that new car, then she is poor indeed." My daughter stared out of the window for awhile, and then turned to me and said, "I wish we were poor."

All of which, for some reason, puts me to thinking about Hebrew. Those of you who have been on the long march through Hebrew this summer may be wondering if all of this is absolutely necessary. Well, I am here to tell you that your seminary is very rich. I am not talking about money (obviously), but I am talking about being rich in expectations and commitment to the work of ministry. We want to give our students the very best gift we can, and part of that gift is the skill and facility with the original languages, so that when they get up to serve as preachers of this word, they have something to say that is rooted in the text and not just what the culture wants to hear or is used to hearing.

Our seminary is not unique in wanting to give you this gift, but our decision to provide this gift to you in this way places us more and more in the minority among our peers. So, I can hear you saying, "I wish we were poor." That is a common response, I believe, to the gospel. Both Israel and the disciples often preferred to try to live off their own poverty rather than the abundance of God's many gifts. But God insists on making us rich, rich in the abundance of the feast God provides, rich in the life that is life in Christ.

So, enjoy your wealth in the remaining weeks of this term. You will have a lifetime of ministry to spend it all.

Chapter 12: Gratitude

November 24, 2004

In Christopher Lasch's remarkable book, *The True and Only Heaven*, he notes that for Jonathan Edwards "the essence of true virtue" is "consent and good will to Being in general." What this means for Edwards is that "gratitude has to be conceived . . . .not as an appropriate acknowledgement of the answer to our prayers, but as the acknowledgement of God's sovereign but life-giving power to order things as he pleased . . . ."[1]

What might one call Edwards' sense of gratitude? Awe before God's gracious presence? Faith? Clearly, it is not a counting of one's blessings. Rather, it seems to be a kind of deep-seated contentment that knows that Jesus Christ is Lord and all that is "hangs together in him." This does not mean that all that is is good or that this kind of contentment is smug, oblivious to the needs all around us. But it does mean that there is something at the heart of things that is deeply, deeply right; that whatever else our task is, we are not called to the impossible labor of having to re-invent ourselves; that one attempts to love one's neighbor not out of some scrupulously moral obligation but out of a deeper sense that one's neighbor is a gift from the "Lord and Giver of life."

It is this "givenness" in life that makes life bearable, I think, and keeps us from reverting to a spirit of resentment, which is the characteristic 'spirit' of our age. When life is centered on me or on my politics or my consumer choices, then justice becomes a matter of getting what is due to me, and resentment is what is inevitably produced when that does not happen.

We live, we are often told, in a divided country (red and blue states), in a divided church (liberals and conservatives), and perhaps also in divided selves, where gratitude seems an increasingly elusive gift, and where

1. Lasch, *The True and Only Heaven*, 249–250.

contentment can even seem "un-Reformed." I want to suggest to you this week that faith in God implicates us in a life of deep contentment. That is what baptism means, what the Christian life discovers and rediscovers, and that is also why the only real remedy of our culture's resentments is the joy that faith in Jesus Christ makes possible.

The third section of the Heidelberg Catechism deals with the Christian life and takes as its title, "Thankfulness." Thankfulness is what those who follow Jesus Christ discover, what they enjoy, what they profess—not because for them times are always good or because they are such virtuous and successful people, or because they have received blessing upon blessing, but because they follow One whom to serve is to be deeply contented. Do not misunderstand me. I don't mean Christians are to be content with everything or every societal structure. Contentment in Christ is not the same thing as blessing the status quo. But contentment in Christ is that liberation from the hard labor of serving as my own lord and finding, instead, the joy of following him. There is a blessed order in that, an acknowledgement of our "consent and good will" to his "life-giving power to order things" that frees us from the tangles of our self-ordered resentments and gives us a true reason to be thankful.

Happy Thanksgiving!

July 6, 2006

As I write this note to you, I am looking at a freshly grown tomato on my desk, which is staring back at me in all its red/orange glory. It is a beautiful thing. This tomato was grown in Jim Johns' garden. Jim serves as the pastor of Indian Trail Presbyterian Church and is the husband, of my assistant, Terry Johns.

Looking at this tomato, I am struck with the goodness of God. I know that the place of Natural Theology has been extremely problematic in the Reformed tradition and that Karl Barth had nothing much good to say about theologizing on the basis of our experience of the natural order. But this tomato is so firm and ripe and beautiful, and seems so full of sunshine and moisture and other good things that, though I cannot reason from it to God, I cannot help being grateful to God for creating such a beautiful thing.

Maybe in our theological tradition that is the way things like tomatoes work: they cause us to be grateful to God.

Recently, I was reading some of the letters of Sydney Smith, a 19th century Anglican priest and critic. He was beloved by some for his stories and wit and feared by others for his stories and wit. At one point he was sent to serve a parish in the depths of Yorkshire. One day a member of that parish brought to him some strawberries. Here is his thank you note to her, written with tongue only partly in cheek: "What is real piety? What is true attachment to the Church? How are these fine feelings best evinced? The answer is plain: by sending strawberries to a clergyman. Many thanks."[2]

True piety and attachment to the church, no doubt, cost more than a gift of strawberries, but a gift of strawberries, like a gift of a ripe tomato, is a good place to begin practicing true piety and real gratitude.

November 19, 2008

This coming week will mark our last classes before Thanksgiving. *Tempus*, as has been noted before, *fugit*.

Often at this time of the year we hear exhortations to be grateful or perhaps to be more grateful than we are. And it is true that gratitude is the chief virtue of the Christian life. So, why is it that when I hear "Count your blessings, name them one by one," that my neck stiffens and something smart alecky wants to come out of my mouth? To be sure, this might be yet another sign of my own sinfulness, and I am prepared to admit that. But I wonder if it's the being told to be grateful that irks.

I remember once when I was a pastor, encountering one of my congregants and her 4 year-old son in the grocery store. I had stooped down to tie his shoes. "Say thank you," the mother implored her son; "Tell the man, 'thank you.'" The little boy wasn't having any of it and refused even to look up from the ground. The Mom kept insisting and finally I said something noble about not needing any thanks and then getting the heck out of there. Gratitude had never seemed such a miserable thing.

In one of his essays, Ralph Wood calls Flannery O'Connor's understanding of morals and manners, an "obedience to the unenforceable."[3] There is no great virtue in doing what you are told to do, or else. And indeed, there is not much more virtue in doing what you are nagged to do.

---

2. Pearson, *Smith of Smiths*, 224.

3. Cf. Wood, *"Obedience to the Unenforceable"* in *Flannery O'Connor Bulletin, 1996–97*, 153–74.

"Obedience to the Unenforceable" is doing something not out of obligation or fear of the consequences, but freely, offering it as a gift. Such a gift is what creates that living space that enables people to live and work together.

There is not much nagging in scripture, I believe. Rather, words like the 10 Commandments are more of an invitation to a life before God in which enforceability (even of the guilty) is not the chief characteristic. Jesus does not nag his disciples, much less those to whom he ministers, though he is certainly not above bidding them "to go and sin no more." But in his mouth, even those words sound more like an invitation to freedom than a reminder of guilt.

The gift of Thanksgiving is not its piety or our dutiful observance of the holiday, but the joyful offering of self that in its own very small way echoes God's lavish and abundant self-giving that has created space for us. God, Karl Barth reminds us, is the One who has time for us. Accordingly, we do not *have* to say, "Thank you;" that is not what we are commanded to do. Instead, we *get* to say those words; we *may* say those words.

Given what this year has brought to many in our country and to some of our own students—economic downturn, loss of job, loss of health and even life—finding blessings to count may seem more difficult than in the past. But if what truly occasions gratitude is the grace of that One whose promise is never to be without us, that One who makes time for us, then Thanksgiving will simply be gratitude for the time and space given to us to share in this life together. That is not a small thing. It is a gift.

December 3, 2008

I have been thinking this week of a friend of mine who died earlier this fall. He was 57 years old, a small town pastor in Oklahoma. I had known him since he was a little boy. I once shot him in the buttocks with a BB gun. We played football with his brothers in their backyard. Well, he grew up, went off to college, and worked for a while at a summer camp in Colorado. About the time I entered seminary, he was finishing at the University of Texas, and soon after that, he entered seminary himself. Later, he moved to Oklahoma and went to law school there. I thought that would be the end of his ministry but he kept his ordination and after graduating from law school, accepted a call to a small Presbyterian church in Wewoka, Oklahoma. The call was to a tent-making ministry. During the week, he provided legal services to many of the Indian tribes in the area, and would preach on the weekends. He served the church and those people until he died. He never went anywhere else; never "advanced" beyond that small congregation. He suffered a stroke in October and died on the way to the hospital in Tulsa, leaving a wife and three children.

In some ways there is nothing particularly remarkable about this story or this ministry. Yet I have been thinking about my friend as this term concludes and as Christmas lurks on the horizon, only in part because I miss him and grieve for his family. Only in part . . .

The end of term is a vivid reminder that work ends. Life ends. One of the reasons we often find scripture so baffling is that scripture seems so unsentimentally well-acquainted with ends. The gospel we preach centers on a man dying on the cross. The creed insists that he died and was buried.

Simone Weil once wrote that the one absolutely indispensable prerequisite for entering eternity is death.[4] I am not sure we believe that. We like our endings happily uninterrupted. But when a child is baptized in church, is that not a recognition that this life is not about some endless pursuit of happiness, but that this life has been marked with Christ's death and has been given an end in him. Christ is our end. We are not endless creatures. We are given an end. And from that end is where we begin, being baptized into Christ's death. Only from that vantage point can we speak of resurrection or risk the venture of "practicing resurrection" by living a life not out of the myth of never-ending plenitude of self or time, but out of the daily gift of the risen Lord's own hand.

But such a life has death behind it. Such a life can risk spending its ministry in Wewoka, Oklahoma, and not think of it as a sacrifice or even noble self-expenditure, but a joy. And when the end comes, whether suddenly or in a long, lingering illness, it is not viewed as a tragedy, for all its pain, much less as a welcome oblivion, but as a gracious ending kept safe in the hands of that One in whose end we were all baptized.

So, as the end of term approaches, it too comes as neither tragedy nor oblivion but as a gracious gift, and one that can be received only with a grateful heart. Even Christmas, with all its overwhelming "muchness" finally bears us the one gift that makes all our beginnings and endings occasions for gratitude.

4. Weil, *Gravity and Grace*, 32.

November 30, 2011

Over Thanksgiving I began reading a book about G. K. Chesterton written by Ralph Wood (*Chesterton: The Nightmare Goodness of God*, Baylor University Press, 2011). I recommend it.

Chesterton was a genius at the well-turned phrase, the paradox that startles, the insight that makes the obvious suddenly appear wondrous. Since it was the Thanksgiving holiday and since we are approaching both the end of the term and Christmas, I have been paying particular attention to what Chesterton says about gratitude. Let me share with you some quotes.

Chesterton writes: "I would maintain that thanks are the highest form of thought, and that gratitude is happiness doubled by wonder"[5] He goes on to add: "The test of all happiness is gratitude.... Children are grateful when Santa Claus puts in their stockings gifts of toys or sweets. Could I not be grateful to Santa Claus when he put in my stockings the gift of two miraculous legs? Can I thank no one for the birthday present of birth?"[6] Of this excerpt, Ralph Wood comments: "Gratitude of this kind prevents the irrationalist madness that seeks ever more intense forms of subjective self-satisfaction. It plants the flag of loyal indebtedness to the world and its cornucopia of blessings, preventing the false presumption that we deserve such benefits and that we may exploit them heedlessly."[7]

Two more quotations from Chesterton himself, one having to do with love and the other, faith. "The ultimately free decision," Chesterton declares is "the liberty to bind myself." Discipline and fidelity, oaths and obligations are means, not obstacles to joy. Wood concludes: "The making and keeping of promises, especially in marriage, provide the key to happiness. 'Love is not blind,' Chesterton keenly observes. 'Love is bound; and the more it is bound the less it is blind.'"[8]

And as for faith, what is the difference between "losing one's life for the sake of the gospel," and despair, between martyrdom and suicide? "A suicide is one who has given up on life and thus desires death; a martyr is one whose strong desire to live takes the form of readiness to die ...." The soldier of the Cross "must not merely cling to life, for then he will be a coward, and will not escape. He must not merely wait for death, for then

5. As quoted in Wood, *The Nightmare Goodness of God*, 35.
6. *Ibid.*, 36.
7. *Ibid.*, 36.
8. *Ibid.*, 36.

he will be a suicide, and will not escape. He must seek his life in a furious indifference to it; he must desire life like water and yet drink death
like wine."[9]

As we approach the end of this term, I wish you a full measure of
that "furious indifference" that can embrace this last stretch of work and
enable you to drink to your fill the wine of preparing for ministry.

March 6, 2013

This morning I received word that Virginia Wehrung died. You don't
know her. There is no reason you should. Virginia was a farmer's wife,
who worked for the Washington County (Tx) welfare department and
served as clerk of the session of the first congregation I was privileged to
serve as pastor. She and her husband, George, who worked for the telephone company, originally lived in Houston, where George had grown
up. Sometime after W.W. II, George and "Ginna" decided to pool their
life savings and borrow themselves into serious debt and buy a farm
in Washington County, about 75 miles northwest of Houston, where
George could work for the telephone company to pay the bills and where
they both could try to manage the farm. There they raised their only son,
Bub, who soon grew big enough to help them with the chickens, tur-
keys, cattle, and whatever else they could find to help make the farm pay.
Eventually, Ginna got a job with the county welfare department, which,
meagre as the salary was, paid better than the farm.

The Wehrungs were Methodists and members of the German Methodist Church in Brenham, Texas. Around 1953, the two Methodist congregations in town merged to form First United Methodist Church, and
to help pay for their new building, sold the German Methodist sanctuary
to the Presbyterians, who were in need of one. George and Ginna liked
the old sanctuary so much that they stayed and became Presbyterian,
when the others moved. George served on the session for many years
and later, when women were declared eligible to serve, Ginna became an
elder and then the clerk of session.

George and Ginna were salt of the earth people. My first day on
the job as pastor began with George coming by in his pickup at 7 a.m. to
take me out to the country to meet all the members who did not live in
town. We went all over Washington County. It was a long day, but George

9. Wood, *The Nightmare Goodness of God,* 37.

wanted to make sure I knew everyone in the church and how to get to their farm. Ginna was the best. She would tell me every Sunday what a great sermon I had preached. I knew many of them stunk. Didn't matter. She loved me. She encouraged me in the work of ministry. If someone in the church needed a pastoral visit or some special attention or was ill and I did not know it, she would call and let me know. She never bugged me or prodded me, she would just encourage me.

While I was serving as pastor of this congregation, the church built a small educational building, on the first floor of which was a nursery. On the door in front of the nursery was (and perhaps still is) a large photograph of Ginna holding two of the children in that church, both of whom have now graduated from university. She is smiling. She was always smiling.

Most ministers worth their salt will tell you that they receive so much more in ministry than they ever provide. I went to Brenham with no experience as a pastor and not much of a plan beyond sensing that God was calling me to serve in that place, and I received so much more than I ever gave. I received the gifts of one of God's saints, Virginia Wehrung, who told me I was doing a good job even when I wasn't, and who loved me through many a dark night of the soul.

I know today that that congregation in Brenham will be rejoicing in all their sadness, happy that her baptism is now complete, and she has entered the rest that remains for God's people. I will always be grateful for Virginia Wehrung.

> "O blest communion, fellowship divine! We feebly struggle,
>   they in glory shine;
>
> Yet all are one in Thee, for all are thine. Alleluia! Alleluia!"

Chapter 13: Weather

February 18, 2004

This winter has been cold and hard, and the days seem so short. I hope, however, that you are enjoying the lovely sunshine today, whose beams are pouring through my office window. I am reminded of Emily Dickinson's poem that begins, "I taste a liquor never brewed," the last line of which, sings, "Till seraphs swing their snowy hats, And saints to windows run, To see the little tippler, Leaning against the sun!"[1] I feel as if I could lean against the sun today.

March 25, 2004

As Mr. Rogers might say, "It's a beautiful day in the neighborhood" today. The sun is shining, the birds are singing, and as Mr. Browning did say or at least write:

> The year's at the spring
> And day's at the morn
> Morning's at seven;
> The hillside's dew-pearled;
> The lark's on the wing;
> The snail's on the thorn;
> God's in his heaven—All's right with the world.[2]

Well, in truth, all is not right with the world, but there are some days so beautiful that one is tempted to think so. God is in his heaven, we confess, but God's glory fills the whole earth, and just as that glory is mirrored in the day's beauty, it also reveals the day's misery and heartache,—empty places that compel us to cry out to the Lord.

1. Dickinson, *The Complete Poems of Emily Dickinson*, 214.
2. Browning, *Pippa Passes and Shorter Poems*, 47.

Last Sunday, I worshipped at Matthews-Murkland Presbyterian Church, an African American congregation whose pastor is Alex Porter. He preached a great sermon. One of the gospel songs we sang, had the lyric, "a saint is a sinner who got back up." Alex's sermon took that as his theme. It was not a "how to" sermon, not even a "feel good" sermon, but a deeply encouraging word for sinners, who Alex insisted, were justified and enabled to stand up by the grace of God. His scriptural text was Luke 15, what is sometimes called "the parable of the prodigal son". I have often thought that parable might better be called "the parable of the prodigal father," who was, if anything, much more prodigal in his love for both of his sons than either turned out to be towards him.

Since we have been studying the doctrine of Justification in our theology class, I was interested in how Alex would speak about this word. At one point in the sermon, he asked everyone in the congregation to respond verbally with the words, "I am a sinner." And then he read Romans 5:8 to us. "But God proves his love for us in that while we still were sinners, Christ died for us." And again, he read Romans 8:1 to us. "There is therefore now no condemnation for those who are in Christ Jesus." None. A saint is a sinner who gets back up, who knows there is no condemnation in Christ Jesus. Sorrow, yes. Remorse, repentance, hope, yes. But no condemnation.

As I left worship on Sunday, I felt like "getting back up." Indeed, I felt like the answer to question 52 in the Heidelberg Catechism, a question that asks what comfort comes to us from knowing that Christ will come one day to judge the living and the dead. The answer reads: "That in all affliction and persecution, I may await with head held high the very Judge from heaven . . . ." With head held high—that is how we should leave worship, confident that God's love and mercy are greater than anything in our world or in ourselves that would seek to frustrate or undermine his purpose. In Jesus Christ it is true, "God's in his heaven, and all's right with the world," or as Paul might put it, "Nothing can separate us from the love of God in Christ Jesus our Lord." (Rom 8:39) Nothing.

November 10, 2004

As I write this note, the sun is shining through my window and the day is just beginning to unfold. What a lovely place the world seems to be today. I know that the world does not look this lovely everywhere. Children are starving in Dafur. War is tearing apart nations in near and more distant places. There are mean streets in our own city that offer little promise or hope for those who tread them daily. And here we are, in the midst of all of this, studying theology, translating Hebrew verbs, seeking to make sense of pastoral care verbatims or traditions of moral discourse or mapping "the Christian life." A strange way to practice loving the world, one might think.

Living in Warsaw and working with the resistance to the Nazis in W.W.II, Czeslaw Milosz witnessed some of the most brutal and horrifying scenes the 20th century had on offer. Yet in the midst of such darkness, Milosz continued to write lyric poetry. After the war, reflecting on what had happened, he wrote: "Life does not like death. The body, as long as it is able to, sets in opposition to death the heart's contractions and the warmth of circulating blood. Gentle verses written in the midst of horror declare themselves for life; they are the body's rebellion against its destruction."[3]

Or as the psalmist might say, "I will sing to the Lord as long as I live: I will sing praise to my God while I have being." (Ps 104:33) Maybe what our world needs most of all today is a voice that sings such praise, and sings it joyfully and well, that knows that this too is the day the Lord has made and that our happy task is to rejoice and be glad in it. And to do this, not as a Pollyanna or Dr. Pangloss or Mr. Rogers, but as a bird of the air or lily of the field whose life simply cannot help reflecting the glory of God, even amidst all that is not so evidently glorious.

I think we go to seminary to learn how to sing, to learn how to reflect the glory that is all around us.

January 19, 2005

"Good King Wenceslas" is a hymn written by John Mason Neale, an Anglican Divine of High Church vintage (1818–1866). Neale performed a great service for the whole church by helping to recover and translate into English many ancient hymns. "All Glory, Laud, and Honor" is one of these, as is, "Come, Ye Faithful, Raise the Strain," "Christ is Made the Sure Foundation," and "O Come, O Come, Emmanuel."

"Good King Wenceslas" Neale composed himself. As one who detests cold weather, I have always loved this carol because it describes, in

3. Milosz, *Milosz's ABC's*, 40.

some measure, the victory of Jesus Christ in terms of warmth, which to me makes beautiful sense. The deepest regions of hell, Dante thought, were frigid, not hot, just as the most imprisoning of sins are the cold ones, the ones that require calculation and finally frigid indifference to others. So, John Mason Neale's hymn that tells the story of "Good King Wenceslas" concludes with the king's page crying out that he cannot go on; the weather is just too brutally cold.

> "Sire, the night is darker now, and the wind blows stronger.
> Fails my heart, I know not how; I can go no longer."
> Mark my footsteps, my good page, tread thou in them boldly.
> You shall find the winter's rage freeze your blood less coldly.
>
> In his master's steps he trod, where the snow lay dinted:
> Heat was in the very sod which the saint had printed.
> Therefore, Christian men be sure, wealth or rank possessing,
> You who now will bless the poor shall yourselves find blessing.

Stay warm.

March 2, 2005

I don't know about you, but I am glad to see the back of February. Yesterday, as I was walking to my car and the March wind was blowing an icy blast, there was, nevertheless, a spring in my step because I somehow felt that winter, or most of it, was through. Natives of this area are quick to instruct me that snow in March is not an unknown phenomenon in Mecklenburg County, but I find such a prospect too horrible to contemplate and prefer to think of daffodils.

You will not be surprised, therefore, that in preparing for my theology class, I ran across this quote from Barth, who was commenting on the Christian life, particularly that portion of it that might be called, "bearing the cross." He cites Paul Gerhardt, the great Lutheran hymnwriter and poet of the 17th century on this theme: "Our Christian cross is brief and bounded, One day 'twill have an ending. When hushed is snowy winter's voice, Beauteous summer comes again; Thus will be with human pain. Let those who have this hope rejoice."[4]

I guess Gerhardt didn't like winter either. In any case, as he notes, "beauteous summer" is on the way, of which, March, it seems to me, is

---

4. Barth, *Church Dogmatics* IV/2, 613.

but a windy harbinger. Barth concludes: "There cannot lack a foretaste of joy even in the intermediate time of waiting, in the time of sanctification, and therefore, in the time of the cross . . . ."[5]

For example, pitchers and catchers have already reported and spring training is underway!

June 14, 2005

I love summertime. I love the hot days and the long days and especially the long, twilight of evening, when one's work is done and the day is still far from over, and there's time to enjoy a refreshing drink, good conversation, and friends.

When I was a child, we lived next door to an ancient, childless couple, who would invite my two older sisters and me to come over to their side porch to drink iced tea and play Canasta. We were young enough to think this was a big deal, and I remember my Mom rehearsing us as to our manners, and making sure that we would say, "Thank you." I need hardly mention that this was in pre-air-conditioning days and even pre-TV. Still, we enjoyed sipping iced tea and listening to the katydids chirping as the day cooled off and the darkness gradually descended. The couple would always send us home with treats, usually candy, and they would watch us as we tromped home.

I wonder if people even play Canasta anymore. Regardless, summer is one of God's best gifts.

October 5, 2005

I do not know the poet, Humbert Wolfe, but I ran across the following piece of doggerel that reminded me of how lovely these October days and evenings have been lately. He writes:

> Listen! the wind is rising, and the air is wild with leaves,
> We have had our summer evenings, now for October eves![6]

So, Mr. Wolfe.

I talked to a former parishioner of mine the other day, who had moved to Bismarck, N. Dakota. I asked her if the leaves had started to fall there, and she replied that what leaves they had were indeed falling. Moreover,

5. *Ibid.*, 613.
6. Wolfe, *"Autumn-Resignation"* in *Humoresque*, 62.

she said, the weatherman was calling for snow this weekend. Which is one of the reasons why I remain grateful that God has not yet, at least, called me to N. Dakota.

Still, these "October eves" are lovely, and I am grateful to be sharing them with you.

April 25, 2007

Last summer, I was driving by an elementary school here in Charlotte, and read on the sign in front a quotation from a poem by William Carlos Williams that goes: "In summer, the song sings itself."[7]

A lovely sentiment, I believe, and one with which I am in full accord. It is easier to believe this when you are relaxing at the beach on a long summer afternoon, or napping in a hammock under a copious shade tree. However, I doubt if studying Hebrew sings itself, or mastering Presbyterian polity, or the other course offerings listed for this summer's term. But they too are songs. They are songs that require a good deal of preparation and risk-taking and sheer hard work. But they make music, and one day in the pastors and teachers who study here such songs will make music for the church to sing.

God seems to love music. God's people have sung psalms, God's anointed ones have played the harp, God's prophets, teachers, and preachers have made music even in prison, and God's theologians exiled on distant islands have seen the heavens open and "myriads of myriads" singing to the Lamb.

Not to stretch the metaphor, this summer term will be a time for learning to sing . . . . So, it is good that we are learning to sing—even in Hebrew!—this summer, because in truth, we are made for singing, for learning to praise, for glorifying God and enjoying God forever. The song may not sing itself this summer, but it sings a lot better when we help each other catch the tune and sing together.

February 4, 2009

This morning the seminary opened late because of the snow. I know that it goes against every rule of good management, but in truth, I was glad not to have to come into work at the usual time. I enjoyed the pause. In

7. Williams, *"The Botticellian Trees"* in *Selected Poems,* 81.

my neighborhood the streets were covered with snow. Everything was so quiet. I went for a walk about 7 a.m. and listened to the quiet for a while: snow on trees and branches, snow on the banks of the nearby creek, animal footprints (Dogs? raccoons? possums? I am no outdoorsman but for a moment I felt like one.). The sun was just beginning to shine on it all so that it all glistened. I felt as if I had wandered into a Brueghel painting, and expected to see hunters returning from the hunt and peasants lugging firewood home.

Of course, since this was not a Friday or Saturday, I could take all of this in with a grateful eye and not worry about classes or deadlines. If the snow had fallen on the weekend, I assure you I would not be thinking such beautiful thoughts. But the gift came today and so I enjoyed it, especially the quiet that snow makes. Such a lovely quiet.

Another surprising gift was the way the snow rendered even more vivid the colors of the birds that were out. Cardinals look intensely red against the snow. A robin, evidently confused about the season, looked positively radiant with his orangey-brown breast protruding against the snow.

I don't know what to make of all of this, and I don't want to wax eloquent about nature or the gift of having some free time, but I do want to bear witness to the mystery of the goodness of the created order that is all around us, the astonishing beauty of the ordinary gifts of life. Perhaps that is enough, even more than enough to acknowledge here on the occasion of this "winter event" of a mild snow in Charlotte. Praise God for the beauty of snow and bird, tree and bush, quiet walks and morning sun. Praise God for this day.

November 11, 2009

The rain is falling steadily today. On days like this my father would often recite a piece of doggerel that went like this:

> The rain, it raineth all around,
> On the just and unjust fella,
> But mostly on the just,
> Because the unjust has stolen the just's umbrella.

Not much of a poem or joke but it appealed to my father's Calvinistic sensibilities.

This particular rainy day is also Armistice Day, which in its own way bears witness to a form of "total depravity." On this day in 1918, on the 11th day of the 11th month at the 11th hour, the guns mercifully ceased firing and the Germans and the Allies brought the horrors of W.W. I to a close.

This day's memories and celebrations are made even more poignant, I believe, in light of what took place this past week at Ft. Hood, Texas. There 13 soldiers were shot dead (and several others wounded) by a man who, judging by what has been reported, thought he was doing the will of God. Our president spoke very eloquently at a service yesterday, rejecting the notion that such an action could ever be construed as the will of a loving and just God. I found myself deeply moved by the scraps of the service I saw on TV and, particularly, by the images of helmets placed atop guns stuck in the ground with an empty pair of boots in front.

We Presbyterians do not like to think of ourselves as "militants" (e.g., "Onward Christian Soldiers" is no longer in our hymnbooks), and we have been rightly suspicious, at our better moments, of jingoistic calls to arms. We prefer to speak of peace and work to pursue it. And I would not want to change any of that. But in witnessing those turned down guns and empty boots, I could not help but think of the fact that those men and women gave their lives for something they believed in, and in any case, for their country.

There are so few areas of modern American life where it is even possible to sacrifice one's life for what one believes, where it is clear that engaging in a certain activity may well require of one that "last full measure of devotion." Coaches and athletes sometimes talk about "sacrifice," and they are often called upon to sacrifice their bodies, but most of the time the pay is good and the "sacrifice" is hardly ultimate.

We preachers also talk on occasion about sacrifice, though most of the time we employ the word metaphorically rather than literally. And indeed, one of the burdens of an affluent Christianity is that it makes such talk increasingly metaphorical to the point of meaninglessness.

Yet for soldiers (and public school teachers, nurses, social workers, and others) sacrifice is a daily reality. I suspect that seminarians could learn a good deal from soldiers in this regard. I do not wish to romanticize the military but I suspect that there are few experiences more formative for one's vocational identity than serving in the Marines or Army. And part of that surely has to do with the ready acceptance of sacrifice and the deep reliance upon comrade that enables a unit to remain a unit.

So, on a rainy Armistice Day, I would like to acknowledge with gratitude the sacrifice of those who have given so much to the rest of us. I do not mean to glorify war or dress up with pretty words the awful things war entails. But I do not also want to pretend that the good things we enjoy in this country are things that come to us without cost. It is not a sin to be moved by the playing of "Taps" or to weep over the message delivered by empty boots. Indeed, while we live, we are part of the church *militant* (which does not mean that we are the church obnoxious) and we should not be ashamed of that. I suspect that the meaning of the word, "sacrifice" has more to do with Christian discipleship than we sometimes let on. Maybe one of the reasons we are reluctant to talk about it is that we fear it might be required of us.

February 10, 2010

This morning I was on the phone with colleagues in Richmond, who found themselves this morning under several feet of snow. The reason for the phone conversation had to do with a planning discussion dealing with several events slated for the spring. During the course of the conversation, someone mentioned the picnic that was planned. The discussion moved quickly on but my thoughts lingered over the word, "picnic." Suddenly, the sun came out, butterflies were flitting about, children were running amok, and the soft drinks and potato salad were beckoning . . . .

Then a blast of cold wind hit me and I realized it was still February here, still winter, and our colleagues in Richmond were shoveling snow off their driveways and trying to stay warm, and we, though dealing with much less snow, were a long way from fried chicken and potato salad. But it was a nice moment, however brief, a vision of joy and warmth amidst a fairly bleak midwinter's day.

In a poem, entitled, "The Bright Field," R. S. Thomas describes seeing the sun break through to illuminate a small field, and how he walked past it as if it were merely another ordinary sight. "But," he writes, "that was the pearl of great price, the one field that had the treasure in it."[8]

Sometimes it takes a bleak midwinter day to give the word, "picnic," its due as something exotic, wonderful, a mysterious gift. I know that I am not a winter person and I know that winter possesses charms that the other seasons cannot match (e.g., a bare tree against a winter sky, the

8. Thomas, R.S. Thomas, *Collected Poems*, 302.

warmth of the fire in the hearth, the lovely silence that surrounds after a snow fall) but in truth, I have always thought that the best thing February has to offer is the fact that midway through it, pitchers and catchers report for spring training in Florida. That, for me, is a sign of hope and warmth and light. Sort of like the word, "picnic."

In any case, I hope the prospect of such picnics, baseball games, potato salads, and other "bright fields" cause us to turn aside for a moment, even in the dead of winter, and see the gifts that await, that are not that far off, that will come in due course. "The meaning," Thomas writes in another poem, "is in the waiting . . . ."[9]

November 16, 2011

This fall has been lovely in N. Carolina. One of the many things I have come to enjoy in this part of the world is the four seasons. I am not big on winter but winter is not all that fierce here, and the other three seasons more than make up for the few cold, icy days we have.

And this fall has been gorgeous. As I drive to work each morning I go down leaf-strewn streets with trees overarching, shedding their golden, brown, and red leaves all around me. Can anything that is dying be that lovely?

Gerard Manley Hopkins wrote a poem to a young girl who was sad to see all the leaves falling in the park. The first line of the poem reads: "Margaret are you grieving over Goldengrove unleaving?"[10] The poem is an extended meditation on the fragility of life and one's own mortality, which seems a heavy thing to lay on a young girl who is just sad over the falling leaves. Still, the old year is dying with the leaves, and even this term is gradually coming to an end. It all seems appropriate somehow. What seems odd is how beautiful it all is.

Last Saturday evening, I had the opportunity to visit with some retired folk at the Pines in Davidson. They had come to hear our President, Brian Blount, talk about the seminary. I watched as they listened raptly to him. Bent over, straining to catch each word, clearly interested in future of the church and in particular, the future of theological education in this part of the world, they were passionately engaged. As I watched them, I felt a bit like "Margaret" grieving that all these leaves, so beautiful, were

9. Thomas, *Ibid.*, 199.
10. Hopkins, *The Major Works*, 152.

gradually "unleaving." But they were not grieving. They were happy, intensely engaged, full of questions, eager to participate in what God was doing in their midst. I felt as if I were driving down Colony Rd. seeing the beautiful leaves swirling all around me. It was a gift.

January 4, 2012

Often after lunch, Pamela and Terry and I take a walk. We usually walk around the square block that constitutes Queens University's Myers Park campus. I look forward to these walks. One sees the seasons much more "up close and personal" when walking. In the spring the flowers in many of the yards jump out with beauty and life. In the summer, one hears the noise of neighborhood children playing chase or engaging in more daring games on the playground of the nearby school. In the fall, the leaves flame out in various colors. But in the winter, when it is cold and gray and brown, that is one of my favorite times.

Winter light is more gentle. The sun, even at noon, seems to be setting or at least angled to a much less fierce degree. Colors are subdued but just so the red of a cardinal or the bright yellow of a finch makes you catch your breath.

It is the "time being" as Auden noted, the time between Christmas joy and Easter passion, the time when winter light scarcely warms yet renders everything quiet and hard. "The Time Being is, in a sense, the most trying time of all . . . . There are bills to be paid, machines to keep in repair, irregular verbs to learn, the Time being to redeem from insignificance. The happy morning is over, the night of agony still to come; the time is noon: When the Spirit must practice his scales of rejoicing without even a hostile audience . . . ."[11]

So, in order to redeem the time being, we begin the spring term! There may well be some irregular verbs to learn. No doubt there will be new vocabulary terms to master, more papers to write, new books to read, ministry contexts to exegete. Now we "practice our scales of rejoicing," so that one day our singing may join with that of many others, in the praise and service of that One who has redeemed our time from insignificance. Winter light is a good time for learning and walking together and rejoicing.

---

11. Auden, *Collected Poems*, 399.

Chapter 14: Illness and Grief

January 14, 2004 (After colon surgery)

In one of Flannery O'Connor's letters she writes that an extended illness is more instructive than a trip to Europe. She suffered from lupus, which eventually did her in. Though I have not been nearly as sick as she, I have come to a deep appreciation of her insight.

One of the most instructive things about being ill and immobilized is how much simple expressions of kindness and good wishes come to mean. I suspect that having a low resistance to various bugs has a way of making life a bit more vivid and intense. For one thing, I find myself weeping more than I usually do. Silly, and somewhat embarrassing, I know, but there it is. On the other hand, a simple card, a call, a word of greeting has come to mean an enormous amount to me.

So, thank you for your good wishes, your prayers, your encouragement, and your support. I deeply appreciate all those expressions of good will and am happily in your debt.

For the record, I am feeling much better today and am looking forward to getting stronger each day.

November 17, 2005 (After the death of my father)

My last conversation with my father took place on the Saturday before he died on Monday. After my theology class, I returned to my office and called the hospital in Dallas, only to hear that my father had been told by his doctors that there was "no hope." My father related this matter-of-factly and without great emotion. I asked him, somewhat impertinently but also trying to be encouraging, "Well, what do the doctors know about hope?"

My father was silent for a while but he and I both knew that the doctors knew a great deal about what they had said, and the time for heroic impertinence had long since passed.

After a long while, my father told me to keep "revising" (his word— a strange one under the circumstances—perhaps the drugs were beginning to kick in, but perhaps he meant nothing more than attempting to do something in a new way) theological education. I told him that I didn't care about that at the moment; all I wanted him to know was that I loved him and was so grateful for all he had given me. My father seemed unimpressed with my words, and after a long silence, he repeated, "Keep revising theological education."

That was my last conversation with him. I took a plane that evening to Dallas and rented a car to drive to the hospital, but by the time I arrived, my father was unconscious and, a day later, he died.

But I think of those words he said and they now make me smile, not because I have any great plan for the revision of theological education, but because he thought what we were doing together here was pretty wonderful, something worth spending one's life on. And so, I am grateful, not only for my father (and his agenda for others!) but also for you with whom I get to collaborate each week in "revising theological education."

January 13, 2010

You have read already, I am sure, of the devastation in Haiti. There is a story in today's *Charlotte Observer* about Pam Carter, who with her husband, Ken, and many saints from Providence United Methodist Church (where Ken is pastor), have rebuilt an orphanage and school in Haiti. Ken took Pam to the airport on Sunday to fly down there for her latest mission effort. He received word last night that she was okay, but that the devastation was massive.

It seems cosmically unfair that a nation that has suffered as much misery as Haiti has should have to suffer even more from this natural disaster. But perhaps my sense of what is fair is simply a way that I have found to comfort myself or even turn away from such enormous suffering. I do not believe God turns away. Rather, I think God turns toward it and hears the voices of those who cry out in desperation for help. We often emphasize the Word of God and the way in which God speaks, but nothing is more certain than the fact that God hears the cries of God's children. "When they cry to me, I will surely heed their cry." (Exod 22:23) "Then they cried to the Lord in their trouble, and he saved them from their distress." (Ps 107:19)

But what happens if we do not overhear such cries? Then our deafness is more miserable than their misery. I am sure that you will be given opportunities through your church or in other ways to contribute to relief efforts. President Obama has encouraged all Americans to help. I received word today from Charlotte Presbytery that they are collecting funds for relief efforts.

We should also keep our brothers and sisters in Haiti in our prayers. That is a not a small or ineffective thing to do, nor is it merely pious wishing. I suspect that prayers would be appreciated very much. But do not misunderstand me. I do not mean to hector you or add to the list of obligations you already have. I would simply acknowledge with you that at this moment many people in Haiti are crying out for help and God has put us in a position to overhear that cry and to join with him in turning toward that misery in love and compassion.

February 24, 2010

Last week Sue Setzer led our faculty/staff devotions. The day was Ash Wednesday and she shared with us a meditation on the cross, whose grace, she noted, comprehends the ashes of our failures and loss, even as it makes painfully clear the radical nature of our resurrection hope. Hers was a helpful meditation and all who were there drew strength from her words.

Still, no one who was there that day thought that her words would be rendered so severely vivid in her life or ours so soon. Early this morning, as you may know, Sue's 39 year-old son, David, suffered a heart attack which has left him on life support in a local hospital. Sue and her husband, Peter, and their family are at the hospital doing what people do in that situation: watching and waiting, hoping for a word from the doctors or nurses, hosting visitors and waiting and praying and waiting and praying.

Sometimes, foolishly, I think, people ask how the gospel can be made "relevant" to our world. Sue's meditation on Ash Wednesday, with its word about the cross, seems to me almost more relevant to us than we can bear. The gospel is like that. When life crashes in, the gospel is the only thing that adequately describes our grief and sorrow, the only thing that holds on to us when we have lost our purchase on what we call "normal" life. The gospel is the only thing that speaks to our hearts and combats our fears when all that can be done is to wait and pray.

I know that you are keeping Sue and her son, David, in your prayers. In visiting with her this afternoon, she told me more than once how much those prayers have meant to her. The extent of her son's injury will not be known for at least 48 hours, and Sue and Peter will need all the strength they can muster to be where they need to be. It would probably not be a good idea to visit at the moment, but I know they would appreciate your prayers and letters. I do, however, want to note one gift that meant a lot to Sue and it is emblematic of the life we share together here.

One of our students, upon hearing of this news, went to visit Sue this morning at the hospital. He has been working under Sue's direction in his supervised ministry course. "I was doing okay," she told me, "until he walked into the room. I saw him, my student, offering me pastoral care, and I kind of lost it. He was such a gift at that moment."

Sue teaches "Group Process and Leadership Development" here and one of the books she has her students read is Dietrich Bonhoeffer's *Life Together*. In the section of that book on "community," Bonhoeffer writes:

> The physical presence of other Christians is a source of incomparable joy and strength to the believer . . . . The believer need not feel any shame when yearning for the physical presence of other Christians, as if one were still living too much in the flesh. A human being is created as a body; the Son of God appeared on earth in the body for our sake and was raised in the body. In the sacrament the believer receives the Lord Christ in the body, and the resurrection of the dead will bring about the perfected community of God's spiritual-physical creatures . . . . The prisoner, the sick person, the Christian living in the diaspora recognizes in the nearness of a fellow Christian a physical sign of the gracious presence of the triune God . . . . But if there is so much happiness and joy even in a single encounter of one Christian with another, what inexhaustible riches must invariably open up for those who by God's will are privileged to live in the daily community life with other Christians![1]

In the midst of deep trouble, the life together Christ shares with us is a gift, a gift that is sustaining Sue and her family during this time. She has been a good teacher in helping us see that gift, and now, she is in need of

1. Bonhoeffer, *Life Together*, 29.

our best thoughts and prayers as this gift holds on to her and to her son and to us all.

December 12, 2011

As some of you may know, I have been having problems recently with my innards, and have been hospitalized three times. I am out now and am working from home (grading papers!) but am scheduled for gall bladder surgery Wednesday morning. Thank you for your many expressions of concern and for your prayers. I hope you keep the prayers going up; they have been of benefit to me.

I think I should be a much nicer person after losing so much bile, but as a subscriber to the doctrine of total depravity, I am not optimistic. In any case, I will try not to let any of this affect my grading. Please accept this quite inadequate note expressing my hope that you all have a very merry Christmas. I look forward to seeing you in the new year—without gall or bile!

Chapter 15: Dying Well

February 9, 2005

Today is Ash Wednesday. The Roman Catholic liturgy beseeches Mary to "pray for us sinners now and at the hour of our death." Most of us hope for a quick death, I suspect, preferably a painless one, and in any case, one that will not render us a burden to others. That, I sometimes think, is the goal of modern life, i.e., "not to be a burden to others."

William May, a Presbyterian minister and widely respected ethicist, reminds us that in the Middle Ages sudden death was thought to be a great tragedy because one would not have had the time to confess one's sins to God and be forgiven. With the Protestant emphasis on our being justified once and for all in Jesus Christ, the fear of sudden death receded, even as the focus on one's death as an occasion for reflecting on one's life became less and less important.

In the Middle Ages death was ever present. Today one rarely sees a dead person. In fact we go to considerable lengths—cosmetically, commercially, culturally—to hide death from ourselves. The mortician's art is displayed in some ways to keep the ugliness and finality of death from ever offending us with its presence.

Yet on Ash Wednesday we are invited to remember that we too shall die. One day, as Karl Barth has noted, everyone will go to the cemetery but one will not come back. What are we to make of this invitation to remember that we shall die? Why do we have ashes imposed on us? To display our pretended or hard-won wisdom?

In T. S. Eliot's poem, "Ash Wednesday," he writes: "Teach us to care and not to care. Teach us to sit still."[1] We should care—about our lives, our families, our work, our callings. Life will end one day and we should indeed "work while it is day." But it is possible to care too much, just as it

---

1. Eliot, "*Ash Wednesday*" in *Selected Poems*, 84.

is possible to worry too much about one's own mortality. It may be that numbering our days leads to a heart of wisdom but unless such wisdom is informed by the foolishness of the cross, the numbering of our days will be just another form of self-centeredness. It is the cross that comprehends the arithmetic of our days, which is why we are baptized into the death of Christ so to be raised with him.

Perhaps the cross that is imposed on our foreheads this day is not only then a sign of our mortality, but even more a sign of the One to whom we belong. In him we are called to live and, like lilies of the field and birds of the air, to live happily in his praise and service, should our days be many or few.

"So, we do not lose heart. Even though our outer nature is wasting away, our inner nature is being renewed day by day. For this slight momentary affliction is preparing us for an eternal weight of glory beyond all measure . . . ." (2 Cor 4:16,17)

Dying we live.

March 30, 2006

A subdivision of theology is eschatology, the doctrine of last things. In some ways that may seem a strange category in which to discover God's grace at work. Philosophy, insofar as I understand that field of human endeavor, does not have such a category. Histories, novels, plays, poems all come to an end but not all of them find in their end the meaning of the stories they tell. Indeed, often they just end inconclusively.

Only in the Christian faith do we insist that life has a graceful ending, an ending appropriate to its purpose in creation, an ending of a particular story which, however sad or brief or even fragmentary it is, is read in the light of its true end in Jesus Christ. That is why the New Testament's attitude toward death is both antagonistic ("The last enemy to be destroyed is death." 1 Cor 15:26) and welcoming ("As for me, I am already being poured out as a libation, and the time of my departure has come. I have fought the good fight, I have finished the race, I have kept the faith. From now on there is reserved for me the crown of righteousness . . . .") (2 Tim 4:6–8)

So this spring term is coming to its end. I suspect that during the course of it, and perhaps especially at its end, there will be no lack of struggle, anxiety, even regret. And I certainly hope and expect that there has also been and will be even more a joy and satisfaction at the completion of good work, a kind of happy tiredness that comes at the end of the day when you know that you have worked hard and accomplished something important. But most of all, I hope that the end of this term will have proven to be a gift to you, a reminder that life, with all its inconclusiveness and fragmentary disjunctions, does not just go on forever without ever reaching a goal or achieving its end. The Christian life has an end. Its end is in him who gathers the strands of all our inconclusive efforts and fragmentary ways and binds them to his cross, where he tells us, among other things, "It is finished."

Those words are a gift, whether they come to us on Good Friday or at the end of the term or at the end of our lives. And because he said them and said them also for us, we can commit our unfinished work and our lives to his care and keeping. This end is the blessing of all our ends.

September 27, 2006

Last night Allen Brindisi, the pastor of Davidson College Presbyterian Church died, after a short but intense struggle with liver cancer. Allen moved to the Davidson congregation about the same time the seminary in Charlotte was getting started, and he befriended us from the beginning. Two of our students are from the congregation he pastored, and one of them, Julie Hill, has been carrying a heavy load while serving on the staff of the church. This would be a good time to remember Allen's family and the Davidson congregation, and the important work our students are doing there.

Also last night, Fleming Rutledge preached a sermon that might have been crafted to speak to those who were grieving Allen's death. She spoke on God's calling into existence "the things that do not exist." Death is ruthless in its efforts to make us not exist, and to have that be the end of our story. But the Lord we worship is the one "who gives life to the dead and calls into existence the things that do not exist," (Rom 4:17) which Fleming Rutledge reminded us was Abraham's story, and the story of our risen Lord, and by his grace is our story as well. This story is not a story of human potential, but of God's acting to deliver us from the clutches of death. His love writes the end to this story, not death, something not so easily asserted when death takes one whom you love. But that is the bold claim of the gospel, and the claim that you are here to learn how to make. May the knowledge of that end comfort those in Davidson who are mourning and giving thanks for Allen Brindisi's life.

October 4, 2006

October is one of my favorite months: the leaves are beginning to turn but the light at dusk lasts long enough still to be enjoyed; the weather is cool but not cold; the football games are getting interesting; the World Series is about to begin; and sometimes in the evening you can smell woodsmoke and burning leaves. Lovely.

But also classes are reaching the point that soon things like midterms and papers and tests will remind us that the semester is getting on and our progress along the way is beginning to be measured.

"People of the Way" is what Christians were first called, a phrase that is picked up in the Latin for traveler, or one who is on a journey: *viator*. The Way is a journey. Last week, Will Willimon was preaching here in Charlotte and said that the truth of the Christian faith is like a journey one takes, where at the end of the journey, one is not the same person one was when one set out. His point was that the truth of the faith is more like a journey than it is a sum or clinching argument, and the truth we come to know changes us in ways we could have never foreseen or imagined.

My hope is that the seminary journey upon which you have embarked is changing you. I hope you are learning and being stretched in some new ways. But I hope even more, that at the end of your time here, you will be not just smarter or more clever or even more skilled but a person of "The Way," a *Viator* being shaped in the way of Jesus Christ. Do not mistake this hope as a mere expression of administrative or educational piety. The Way is hard and the changes that occur are not always welcome. But all our ways, however disparate, are gathered into his way, and so in his company we learn the truth and find our way home in him.

This past week I had occasion to be reminded of the way of the *Viator* at Allen Brindisi's memorial service. John Kuykendall referred us to Isaac Watts' great hymn, "My Shepherd Will Supply My Need," calling our attention to its last verse that speaks of the way home.

> The sure provisions of my God
> Attend me all my days:
> O may Your House by my abode
> And all my works be praise.

There would I find a settled rest,
While others go and come;
No more a stranger or a guest,
But like a child at home."

His way is the way home.

January 24, 2007

As many of you know one of our students, Jan Parler, has been diagnosed
with cancer in her brain, liver, and spine. Jan has finished her course of
study here and will graduate in April. She is receiving treatment at Presbyterian Hospital, and is now awaiting further test results. I know that
she and her family are surrounded by your prayers and the prayers of
many others.

A friend asked me today what one might appropriately pray for giv-
en Jan's diagnosis. I struggle with the answer to that question. There have
been lots of tears shed around here, as you might guess, and perhaps you
have shed some as well. If Jan had not made us laugh so much, punctured
so many of our balloons, pious and otherwise, sung so beautifully, sacrificed so much to study here and offered herself for ministry, we wouldn't
have wept nearly so much. She has told me that she is not ready to throw
in the towel and give up. But her diagnosis is not easily dismissed.

I am grateful that she is receiving good care and has excellent doctors
and nurses looking after her. I am grateful also for her husband, Rick, and
their three boys, Sam, Clay, and Reid. A friend and fellow-student of Jan's,
who had come to see me this afternoon after visiting Jan in the hospital,
told me that she was glad to see Jan was still Jan. That is no small gift.

So, perhaps one prays most faithfully that God will ever keep Jan
who she is, which is, in fact, what we affirm when we confess what is our
"only comfort in life and in death." For we are most truly ourselves not
when we cling to our victimhood or think we are immune to the suffering and death that afflict others, but when we know that we belong, body
and soul, in life and in death, not to ourselves but to the One who alone
is faithful and able to keep us who we really are. I think we pray for Jan's
healing, not as desperate people without hope or silly people who ignore
the seriousness of this assault, but as people of faith who belong to Jesus
Christ. He does not invite us to pray timidly.

So, say a prayer for Jan Parler tonight, and for her husband and sons. The light shines in the darkness and the darkness, as powerful as it is, has not and will not overcome the light. That is the gospel. Death, despite its great power, does not get to define who we are. It does not even get to define our end. That is what it wants to do, but it cannot, because there is One who will not let us go or let us cease to be who he created and redeemed us to be. We belong to him.

That's why we study here, right?

February 21, 2007

Today is Ash Wednesday and at noon some of us trooped over to Covenant Presbyterian Church to hear that "from dust we have come and to dust we shall return."

Which got me to thinking. What is the purpose of remembering that we are dust? One answer might simply be that remembering one's own mortality (*memento mori*) puts things in perspective and offers a healthy corrective to our more limitless notions of self. Recalling one's own mortality, in other words, can lead to an appropriate humility.

But I am not sure that is what is going on here. "Dust" is what God made us out of. "Dust" is what God takes on in the flesh of Jesus Christ. God seems to love "dust." "For he knows how we were made; he remembers that we are dust," sings the psalmist (Ps 103:14). Even the "dust" and those who go down to the "dust" offer praise to God, claims the otherwise more somber words of Psalm 22 (vs.29).

To remember that we are dust and to dust we shall return is to remember that we belong to God who is not ashamed of dust. For this God dust is not a barrier or blockage or some transcendent limit. It is what this God embraces and redeems and uses to commune with us. Rather than offering a corrective to our outlandish ambitions, this business of remembering that we are dust makes a bold claim, not about us but about the radical, expansive, outlandish, exuberant love of God. This God makes treasures out of earthen vessels. He does not call angels or spiritually elite athletes to be his people, but "dusty" men and women who are busily engaged in the details and frustrations of life, sending them to announce the glad good news of this God's love for all his "frail children of dust."

I know we are all supposed to be made penitent and seriously reflective by Ash Wednesday, and I do not object to that. But I think when we affirm that we are dust and to dust we shall return, we should remember also that the God whom we worship is well-acquainted with dust, is able to make dry bones offer praise, is able to lift up from stones glad witness to God's grace, and from dust itself to render perfect praise.

I think God loves dust. And I think Ash Wednesday ought to call us to the joyful and unashamed embrace of our own "dustiness," which seems to be just the right stuff to offer praise and thanksgiving to God, and to offer care and love for other "dusty" sinners in need of bodily healing and soul redemption.

Perhaps it is inappropriate to wish one a "Happy Ash Wednesday"; it sounds either vaguely sacrilegious or full of that smiley-faced American optimism. But I do wish you the joy of this day, even as you remember that you are dust.

February 6, 2008

Today is Ash Wednesday. As it happens I have received two emails this morning, one arguing that Reformed-type people have no business celebrating Lent or marking this day as particularly noteworthy, and the other arguing that Ash Wednesday signifies a sinful world's return to reality, the mirror in which we can all see ourselves most clearly, warts and all, and so come most authentically into God's presence.

In this morning's paper there was an article about Protestants' "returning" to Lent. What is one to make of all this?

It is true that Calvin says some very negative things about Lenten practices and argues against observing it as a special time of repentance. In part his objections have to do with what he regarded as the hypocritical and self-justifying religious apparatus erected by the Roman Catholic church of his day to justify its own penitential system. He also does not think that Jesus' fasting in the wilderness is meant to be exemplary for Christians. (Calvin was not interested in asking "What would Jesus do?" as if we, who are not Jesus, were able to do what he does.) Rather he thinks that Jesus' fasting is best understood as redemptive, as part of his atoning work on our behalf.

However, his real objection to the practice of Lent has to do with the trivialization of repentance and forgiveness, making both seem like human possibilities and achievements which we can manage and practice when we set our mind to do so (e.g., during Lent). Calvin thought we do better to attend to Christ's repentance and forgiveness, which he gives to us daily as his gracious gifts. We are to live our whole lives in every season in gratitude for such gifts and in sincere commitment to make the best use of these gifts in following him.

Perhaps because I was brought up in a Calvinist home, I find myself persuaded by Calvin's arguments and am a bit uneasy with our church's enthusiastic embrace of Lent and its practices. And yet, just as the religious effort to justify ourselves through some ascetic practice can trivialize grace, so too can our timid refusal to identify ourselves with the church's witness become a cover for a privatized faith. The mark of ashes on one's forehead, the daily reminder of some comfort denied or given up, trivial as that might seem, can be a way of being brought more deeply into Christ's own life. Getting better acquainted with "not having" or "not consuming" might give us a taste of what many of Christ's brothers and sisters regularly experience. Such a practice might even make us more generous. For example, I read this week of Haitian children eating "dirt cookies" because they had no food. A Lenten practice can serve to reveal the countercultural dimensions of our faith and the call to be a sharing people.

It is a false modesty to be unwilling to claim the name Christian, even if our actions and our faith make painfully clear how imperfect and flawed we are. Giving up something small might train us to make larger and more meaningful sacrifices, or rather, to live larger and more generous, Christ-centered lives.

What Calvin objected to was not the ascetic nature of Lenten practices. No one was more ready to talk about self-denial or the cost of discipleship than he. Rather, he rejected the notion that such a life could be reduced to a "season," as if we belonged to ourselves the rest of the time. What he objected to was the placing of ourselves at the center of the Christian life. The drama of the gospel was not ours to reduce to temporary or even more habitual religious achievements. He knew that was wrong and did not want the church to add to that distortion.

But to the extent that Lent can become a time, not of religious self-justification of "me" but a deeper journey into Christ's life, then identifying with Christ, through the sign of the cross can mark a blessed occasion for a lifetime of following.

October 1, 2008

Last summer, in preparation for a course in Christian Ethics, I read a book by Stanley Hauerwas entitled, *God, Medicine, and Suffering* (Eerdmans, 1990), a new edition of a book previously published under the title, *Naming the Silences*. I thought this might be a book that would stimulate conversation with area pastors and care-givers, so I invited several in this area to come to the seminary for a conversation. They came and we met all morning and then broke for lunch. The conversation was so rich and full I did not want it to end. It finally did end with worship and with the singing of the hymn, "Now Thank We All Our God."

Just as I was congratulating myself on what a great occasion this turned out to be, I was tapped on the shoulder by a colleague here telling me that the husband of one of our recent graduates had called to say that she was probably in her last labors of life, and if her seminary colleagues wanted to come by, now would be a good time.

Several of us drove over to the house to be with her. She had been struggling with cancer for some time, both while she was a student and while she worked part-time in our Advancement office. Now the end had finally come. Suddenly our conversation became quite unacademic and terribly concrete. We gathered around her bed, a hospital bed placed in the middle of the living room. We prayed. We wept. We blessed her and her husband and her family. We waited and simply touched her arm and hand, and sat for a while on the mourner's bench.

Her pastor was there also, and he suggested we sing a hymn. So surrounding her bed, and with her husband and our group, we sang the first verse of "Now Thank We All Our God." The morning's worship had become the afternoon's labor, or rather, gift. I am not sure what to call it. The time was so full of tears and love and sadness and joy. Sometimes what you do in seminary seems theoretical or even abstract but when it comes into focus, this matter becomes almost blindingly intense.

> Now thank we all our God
> With heart and hands and voices,
> Who wondrous things hath done
> In whom this world rejoices;
> Who from our mother's arms
> Hath blessed us on our way
> With countless gifts of love,
> And still is ours today.

I left this last encounter not with a peaceful heart or an untroubled spirit but with a deep, deep sense of gratitude for this woman's life and for the faith that calls us to sing such a song at such a time. On the way home, I remembered the second verse of that great hymn, which I wish we had sung too and which I would like to leave with you now:

> O may this bounteous God
> Through all our life be near us,
> With ever joyful hearts
> And blessed peace to cheer us;
> And keep us in God's grace
> And guide us when perplexed,
> And free us from all ills
> In this world and the next.

I am grateful for the gift of sharing in this work and this life together with you. School work has its own intensities and its own joys but even here, especially here, life sometimes crashes in, and when it does, the importance of what we have studied and learned and taught becomes almost unbearably clear.

October 7, 2008

"After great pain a formal feeling comes"[2]—or so, Emily Dickinson. Last Sunday, many of us worshipped with the family and friends of Jan Parler, giving thanks for her life and bearing witness to the promise that is ours in the risen Lord. This morning at staff meeting, our devotionals recalled Jan again, and her love of music and her courage in the face of a relentless enemy. That devotional service "cleaned" me out. I don't mean that it left me exhausted or weary. There were tears shed and tender thoughts expressed and great hymns sung, but at the end of the service, I sensed something of that "formal feeling" the poet speaks of.

We talk today of "moving on" and we smile knowingly at our Victorian forebears who made such a big deal out of grief. They wore black arm bands or put on heavy, dark dresses, almost as if they were parading their sorrows and celebrating their loss. But maybe they were right in a way we find difficult to understand. Maybe this was the way they "moved on," a way that recognized much more faithfully, even honorably, the very real loss death inflicts.

2. Dickinson, *Collected Poems*, 372.

For us, it is rare for a "formal feeling" to come at all. Indeed, we celebrate the casual as if it were the most authentic of virtues. Which may be why we have such a hard time understanding both the laments of the psalms or their expressions of joy, why we miss so easily scripture's griefs and glories. Yet acknowledging "great pain" can be exactly what "cleans out" all the casualness with which we attempt to navigate life, replacing it not with blimpish seriousness, but with that "formal feeling" that knows a strange contentment, a feeling that is through with grieving because it has *not* gone around it but cried its way through it.

This contentment is not merely "formal" nor is it merely a quiet resignation, but is instead a deep confidence that there is One who will wipe away every tear from our eyes, One to whom we belong in life and in death.

Toward the end of his life, Karl Barth was in and out of the hospital. At one point, after a series of surgeries, he wrote the following to a friend: "Somewhere within me there lives a bacillus with the name *proteus mirabilis*, which has an inclination to enter my kidneys—which would mean my finish. I am certain that this monstrosity does not belong to God's good creation, but rather has first come in as a result of the Fall. It has in common with sin and with the demons also that it cannot simply be done away with but can only be despised, combatted, and suppressed . . . . But the main thing is the knowledge that God makes no mistakes and that *proteus mirabilis* has no chance against him."[3]

Cancer may be powerful enough to cause great pain, and it can take from us those whom we would never wish to be without. It is powerful. But it has no chance against God, and by God's grace, we belong in life and in death, not to cancer or worse, to our griefs, but to Jesus Christ. Jesus is Victor! That confession is the way "a formal feeling comes" and the way, the only way, one "moves on."

October 22, 2008

A prayer I often pray before sleep is one that is attributed to John Henry Newman, of Oxford Movement fame, who left his Anglican communion and became a Roman Catholic in 1845. He was a gifted theologian and controversialist, who wrote this prayer that is now included in our *Book of Common Worship*. It reads: "O Lord, support us all the day long, until the

---

3. Barth, *How I Changed My Mind*, 86.

shadows lengthen and the evening comes and the busy world is hushed, and the fever of life is over, and our work is done. Then, in thy mercy, grant us a safe lodging and a holy rest and peace at the last, through Jesus Christ our Lord. Amen."[4]

When I was a pastor, I prayed that prayer at many a graveside, and its words always brought deep comfort. Recently, I prayed this prayer at Jan Parler's memorial service. The words seemed to stick with me and I kept hearing their rhythm and tone in my mind's ear. One morning, I heard them again in my mind, but this time to the tune, "*Sursum Corda* (Smith), which tune is in our hymnbook. The first verse came to me as I was driving to work and then, with Susan Hickok's help, I framed that verse, and worked on three others, trying to make a hymn out of the prayer.

You did not ask for this, but I am going to share the words with you here, and later, with Joe Sandoval's help, invite you to sing this hymn at one of our evening services. I have entitled this prayer-poem, "Evensong" and it goes like this:

> O Lord, support us while the day is long,
> 'Til shadows lengthen and the evening comes;
> Then in your mercy grant us lodging safe,
> And peace at last through our Lord Jesus Christ.
>
> O Lord, be with us as the darkness falls.
> The darkness is not dark to your great light.
> Be with us as the busy world is hushed,
> When work is done and day slips into night.
>
> O Lord, you give to your beloved sleep,
> And when our fevered life comes to its close,
> You make of rest a holy night of praise,
> And wake us fresh with your new day in Christ.
>
> All praise to Father, Son, and Holy Ghost,
> Whose triune dance enfolds our life's employ.
> All praise to Jesus Christ the risen Lord,
> Whose lowly cross lifts all to heaven's joy.

Well, there it is, such as it is. In any case, I believe there to be a deep connection between theology and doxology, between knowing God

4. *Book of Common Worship*, 942.

and singing to God. In some ways, the most appropriate response to the Easter news is to burst forth in song. What else can one do?

I hope you found some rest over fall break. Still, a part of me wants most of all for you, that while studying here you learn to . . . . sing.

April 20, 2011

For some years now I have been a fan of Emmylou Harris. This morning at staff devotionals, I played several cuts from her album of some years ago, entitled, "Angel Band," a collection of several gospel songs. Most of the songs on this album have to do with death, not in the abstract or as a philosophical problem, but as the familiar enemy and at times welcome friend of every believer.

One might consider these gospel songs as merely sentimental, but it is surprising how often and how clearly their lyrics speak of dying, a subject that tends to embarrass more affluent and well-educated Christians in the 21st century. And what these songs fear about death is not "the end" or "the futility of it all" but the power of death to pull us apart, to separate us from one another, to make us eternally lonely.

These songs sing of an "angel band" that gathers us to One who will not let us go; they sing of Jesus, who, when he is lifted up, becomes "our father, our mother, our sister, and our brother," the one who brings "joy to our soul." Their vision of heaven is not a private one celebrating great achievement, but "a beautiful shore," where we are gathered with all those whom we have loved and join with them in singing "the melodious songs of the blest." Many of these lyrics sound as if they came from folk who know what hard labor is, what loneliness feels like, what it might mean to be orphaned. And the hope buried in these songs is the hope of deep fellowship, of being gathered into a family, of being given space for life together, of receiving the joy of good companions.

Tomorrow is Maundy Thursday, and in John's Gospel, at least, Jesus speaks there of "good companions," even "friends," in the face of death. He does not hesitate to speak of death, and is not embarrassed by it. Instead, he speaks of life together, specifically, of his being the vine and the disciples being the branches, of his abiding in them and they in him. He calls them "friends," as if friendship were a weapon of the Spirit, whose love is stronger than death. He bids his own to love as they have been loved.

How striking that on the night of his betrayal, a night of darkness and deceit, Jesus longs for that life together that his own life makes possible, and which soon, when he is lifted up on the cross, will "draw all people to himself." (John 12:32)

All people. Recently, on a very different note, I have been reading a biography of Mickey Mantle, a marvelous ballplayer, if deeply troubled soul. Toward the end of his life, he was asked what he missed most about the game. Was it the home runs? The World Series wins? The Triple Crown he won in 1956? No, what he missed was the clubhouse, the laughter, the sharpened wit of good friends and close companions.

On Maundy Thursday eve, I wonder if that is not something we might recognize, not only in the Passion narratives but in our own lives. We complain so easily about the church and its grunge work of committees and failures large and small. But when I look back at my own ministry, even here at the seminary where there have been more than a few meetings, what has given me the most joy is the good companions with whom it has been my privilege to study, to share in learning and teaching, in dealing with the ups and downs, the tears and laughter of our life together.

The shared joy of that *koinonia* is what sustains one in the face of death, and surely it is a foretaste of that deeper life together to be shared around the banquet feast in heaven. Heaven is not a lonely place.

> There is a land that is fairer than day
> And by faith we can see it afar;
> For the Father waits over the way,
> To prepare us a dwelling place there.
>
> We shall sing on that beautiful shore
> The melodious songs of the blest,
> And our spirits shall sorrow no more,
> Not a sigh for the blessing of rest.
>
> In the sweet by and by
> We shall meet on that beautiful shore;
> In the sweet by and by,
> We shall meet on that beautiful shore.

April 27, 2011

Recently, my wife and I went to see the movie, "Of Gods and Men," the story of 7 Trappist monks in Algeria, who were murdered in 1996 by terrorists. I remember reading about this tragic event shortly after it happened, and learning something about the Prior of the abbey, Father Christian de Cherge. His last testament—a letter he wrote to his sister before he was executed—is a theologically profound document, not least in its expression of love for the Algerian people and its generosity toward his Islamic executioners.

The question that confronts the monks as the terrorists close in is whether to leave or to stay. They know that they could be (as in fact they were) pawns in a power game fought out between Islamic terrorists and the Algerian government. The village where the abbey is located is almost entirely Islamic but the villagers are united in their desire for the monks to stay. The monks are not clear in their own minds what to do, with some wanting to stay and others wanting to return to France. Their leader, Christian de Cherge, attempts to build consensus slowly. He lets each monk have his say. Eventually, through much prayer and struggle, they decide to stay, knowing that it might mean forfeiting their lives.

Their situation reminded me of Bonhoeffer's when he was in New York in the summer of 1939, and was struggling with the decision as to whether or not to return to Germany. How much easier it would have been to stay in New York, lionized as a brilliant young German theologian, but the way of faithfulness was more narrow than that and harder. The way of faithfulness for these French monks was to practice the Benedictine virtue of "stability" and to stay put, tend to their bees, market their honey, care for the sick and poor in the village, and to love that piece of the Kingdom that was at the foot of the Atlas Mountains in Algeria.

The most moving scenes in the picture are of the monks worshipping together. They often stand in a circle or in two lines facing each other, singing their prayers at night or early in the morning in their sanctuary. Their worship is beautiful. And their love for that particular part of the world is portrayed as remarkably unsentimental yet entirely gracious. One can fall in love with these people.

Which makes me think that ministry is not always about going some place else or far away or to another call. More often the way of faithfulness is loving the people and the places that seem all too familiar, that are quite unromantic, that are, in the best sense of the word, mundane.

Such places are not always easy to go to and they are even more difficult to remain at. These monks stayed. As the gospel says of Jesus, "Having loved his own who were in the world, he loved them to the end." (John 13:1) So did they.

A portion of Father de Cherge's letter reads as follows:

> My life has no more value than any other. Nor any less value. In any case, it has not the innocence of childhood. I have lived long enough to know that I share in the evil which seems, alas, to prevail in the world, even in that which would strike me blindly. I should like, when the time comes, to have a clear space which would allow me to beg forgiveness of God and of all my fellow human beings, and at the same time to forgive with all my heart the one who would strike me down. I could not desire such a death. It seems important to state this. I do not see, in fact, how I could rejoice if this people I love were to be accused too dearly for what will, perhaps, be called 'the grace of martyrdom,' to owe it to an Algerian, whoever he may be, especially if he says he is acting in fidelity to what he believes to be Islam . . . . My death, clearly, will appear to justify those who hastily judged me naive or idealistic . . . . But these people must realize that my most avid curiosity will then be satisfied. This is what I shall be able to do, if God wills—immerse my gaze in that of the Father, to contemplate with him the children of Islam just as he sees them, all shining with the glory of Christ, the fruit of his Passion, filled with the gift of his Spirit, whose secret joy will always be to establish communion and to refashion the likeness, delighting in the differences . . . . (And then, Father de Cherge, addressing his executioner, writes:) "And you also, the friend of my final moment, who would not be aware of what you are doing. Yes, for you also, I wish this 'thank you'—and this 'adieu'—to commend you to the God whose face I see in yours. And may we find each other, happy 'good thieves' in Paradise, if it pleases God, the Father of us both. Amen.[5]

One prays to become such a "happy, good thief," in this work of ministry and in our life together.

5. de Cherge, *First Things*, August-Septermber 1996.

July 6, 2011

This morning, we were reminded during our devotionals that today is the 596th anniversary of the martyrdom of John Huss, who was burned at the stake on July 6, 1415 in Constance (Konstanz), in what is now Germany (on Lake Constance, near Switzerland). Huss was, like John Wycliffe, a morning star of the Reformation. A Czech-Bohemian, Huss emphasized the importance of scripture as an authority for the church, and opposed such papal-endorsed practices as the selling of indulgences.

Religion in those days, as today, was bound up with politics, and the ebb and flow of Huss' career followed very much who was in power in Bohemia and elsewhere. A scholar at the University of Prague, Huss was promised safe passage to the Council of Constance, but the safe passage was withdrawn when he was convicted of heresy.

My point in rehearsing all of this for you is not to give a mini-report on the life and death of John Huss, but to recall that we are very much the people whose stories we remember and tell. John Huss died for the faith. He was given several opportunities to recant, and he refused. He was not the only martyr and not all the martyrs were Protestant (Cf. Edward Campion). But by remembering his day, we are reminded that the faith we hold, however poorly or casually we hold it, is not a trivial thing, not merely a cultural way of life, but an affirmation of the truth of God's redeeming grace in Jesus Christ.

People die in service to the faith. And they do so not as sanctimonious, passive-aggressive "martyrs" but as voices telling the story of what is life-giving, what is joyful, what is true. We apologize too quickly for the outrageous claims of the Christian life; they seem to clash so embarrassingly with the smallness of our fast-paced lives. But John Huss, Christian de Cherge, and so many others remind us that this life of ours has been delivered from such tedious smallness by the outrageous claim of Jesus Christ that we, and all those with whom we disagree, belong to him.

Could that be why we are trying to learn Hebrew this summer? Could that be why we tarry over some creedal text? To know something of what John Huss knew? Does that seem too big?

Well, here is something smaller. The other day, I was reading Will Willimon's book, *Pastor*, in which he tells of an encounter with a young Duke student, who refused to participate in some fraternity shenanigans, and was belittled for his prudish, "Christian" sensibilities. The student confessed to having been hurt by this rejection and even having wept at being ostracized by his so-called "friends." Willimon's reply to the student is instructive: "I told him, 'That's amazing. You are not the greatest Christian in the world, are you? You don't know the Bible that well. Don't know much theology.' The student admitted that all of that was true. 'And yet,' Willimon continued, 'even a Christian like you, in the right environment, can be recognized as a threat, can be persecuted . . . . You are young. You don't know much about Church History. There was a time when to be a martyr, a witness, you had to be good at preaching, had to be some sort of saint. These days, even a guy like you can be a witness, in the right hands.'"[6]

I don't know about you but I find Willimon's story strangely comforting. Even believers like us, who are not John Huss, not even remotely like John Huss, can, "in the right hands," bear our witness today. That is a story worth remembering.

June 13, 2012

When I was in graduate school, my uncle died. He was my father's youngest brother, and he was 53 when he suffered a cerebral hemorrhage playing handball. I was studying in Scotland when he died, but I remember talking to another uncle later, who told me only somewhat in jest, that it was just like his younger brother to get promoted first.

Up until then, I had not thought of dying as a promotion, but since then I have had occasion to reflect on the idea. The Apostle Paul, in his letter to the Philippians, confesses that he is hard pressed to decide which is better: living in the flesh or departing the body to be with Christ. "For me to live is Christ and to die is gain." (Phil 1:21) Perhaps because I am a sinner or maybe because I just enjoy a glass of Chilean red wine so much but in any case, I have never quite believed Paul at this point. I love this life and am not eager to leave it. And I suspect many might say the same, especially those who grieve the loss of one who has been "promoted."

And yet, Paul is right that one can love this life too much, clinging to it as if it were our own possession, fearful always of being robbed of it. The gift is to receive life as a gift, never denigrating the sweet pleasures of the flesh but never making an idol out of them either, expecting, rather, that the God who made such good things for his children will have even better things to offer in the life to come.

6. Willimon, *Pastor*, 260.

I once heard a theologian from Cambridge University, Janet Soskice, say that she was sure that there would be skiing in heaven. "Why," she was asked. "Because," she replied, "I think heaven will be a place where God will enable us to be fully alive, and when I ski, I feel fully alive." I am not sure her conclusion would satisfy the Standard Ordination readers, but I think I understand what she was talking about.

We (i.e., preachers) often speak so glibly about death not having the last word that we sometimes forget or at least, overlook, how powerful its word is. I remember when I was a pastor sometimes feeling, as I led a memorial service, that I was like a man inside of a comfortable shelter talking to people who were standing outside in the rain. We find it so easy to offer cheap comfort when we are ourselves are well-insulated.

Yet the gospel's word about "promotion" offers neither cheap comfort nor merely spiritual counsel. Its "promotion" is the vindication of the Crucified ("And I, when I am lifted up from the earth, will draw all people to myself." John 12:3), a fact that came as a surprise to all, and most especially to Jesus' disciples, who were quite willing to accept the easy comfort of sad wisdom or spiritual resignation (Cf. Luke 24:13) No. Easter does speak of "promotion" and does so without apology. This "promotion," like all of God's gifts, comes not as a reward or possession or afterthought but as the unexpected and, in any case, undeserved gift. This "promotion" does not obliterate this life or reduce it, but expands and deepens it. In this respect, Thomas Aquinas, not a Reformed theologian, is right to claim that grace does not destroy nature but perfects it.

So our "promotion" is a kind of perfection, a completing of our baptism, coming to us, not as a destroyer of what was sweet and good in this life, but as the sweetness and goodness we can glimpse only dimly here but one day will enjoy in fullness.

April 24, 2013

This morning Terry Johns and I were trying to hang a banner that will welcome our graduates and their families on Saturday. We wanted to see if we could hang it on the brick wall near our entrance. As we were measuring and stretching, Terry noticed that at the bottom of a brick bench near our new cross, right where the stone walk abuts the brick, two little green clover shoots were trying to eke their way out to the sunlight. There couldn't have been more than a grain or two of sand down there, but whatever there was, was enough for this little green leaf to take root and unfold upward.

As I was walking down the gravel road that runs along the west side of our building, I noticed the weeds and grass and various kind of flora poking up through the hard gravel and dark stones.

All of which makes me wonder about the urgency of life, the implacable, almost unstoppable urge towards life. Concrete cannot seem to crush it. Stones are unable to keep it down. Bricks are even split by its green shoots of life.

This past week has been full of death, whether in West, Texas (a small community in central Texas near Waco, where Czech immigrants farm and where they make the best kolaches this side of Prague) or Boston or Pakistan, that it can seem that death is all-pervasive.

Bret Stephens, who writes a Pulitzer-prize winning column for the *Wall St. Journal,* reminds us that no words, no admiration for the first-responders, no appreciation for the toughness of the citizens of Boston, no beautiful memorial service can suffice to "justify" or explain, much less heal or overcome the horror that death deals out. What happened in Boston was, however one slices it, a manifestation of evil, of that part of the world (and no doubt that part of ourselves) that insists Jesus is not really Lord; that seeks to undermine or lie about his Kingdom; that worships Death as Lord. Terrorism is not the only form of that worship but it is one. And to that extent, it seeks to offer a kind of witness that Death is in control of things. The pain it inflicts is massive and persuasive. And we find it easy to believe that Death is more powerful than the gospel. And given our comforts and affluence, we might be tempted to resign ourselves to Death's rule, picking our spots, hoping we are not the ones stricken next, not the ones harmed.

That comfortable resignation describes very well the grimness and smallness of our quiet despair today.

But then, I start thinking about that concrete, those embedded stones, that brick bench, that hard gravel—so impenetrable, so tough, so strong, and yet a little cloverleaf can pop through, a weed can split the stone. "What is all this juice and all this joy?"[7] asks the poet. What right does that little green cloverleaf have to insist on living in the face of the crushing power of concrete and brick? What right indeed, except

7. Hopkins, Gerard Manley Hopkins: *The Major Works,* 130.

the terrible urgency of life, the unquenchable grace that regularly defies gravity, yielding itself only to the rays of the sun.

Such a cloverleaf is not enough. Stephens is right about that. It will not make the hurt go away or even mount much of an argument against the power of Death. Still, in its own way, in its simple refusal to stay put, in its joy of living, it gives a quite adequate witness against the power of death, and testifies that for all the hurt, not even Death can speak the last word.

Chapter 16: Advent, Christmas, and Easter

November 2, 2005

Recently, I have been reading Kallistos Ware's classic interpretation of Orthodoxy, entitled, *The Orthodox Way*. The book begins by discussing what Jesus meant when he said, "I am the way, the truth, and the life." In the Prologue, Ware tells of a 4th century Desert Father who made his way to Rome on a pilgrimage, where he found a celebrated recluse, an old woman who lived in one room, never going out. Skeptical about such a "witness," the Desert pilgrim asked her, "Why are you just sitting there?" To this she replied, "I am not sitting; I am on a journey."[1]

So are we on a journey this term, even when we are sitting studying Church History or Ethics or New Testament, or even when we are just "sitting." Christian discipleship has sometimes been called, "The Way," and is often described as a journey upon which we do not travel alone, or without maps and guides, but always in the company of One whose steps overtake us and whose life becomes for us "the Way." It is not just any journey, much less is it a religious journey of self-discovery. Rather, it is a journey that leads us into the truth of this particular life.

It is a long journey for most of us, a marathon not a sprint. And on this leg of the journey (i.e., this term at seminary), we are but a little more than halfway home. Our journey this fall ends in Advent, the point where the church's calendar begins. It will take us to Christmas, where we will join with those journeying Magi as they make their way to Bethlehem. Later, we will follow our Lord through his baptism and public ministry, and his long, slow walk to Jerusalem.

Our journey here has a fixed term, but the journey of discipleship is both more mysterious and more surprising. I am glad to be walking toward Advent and beyond with you.

1. Ware, *The Orthodox Way*, 1.

December 16, 2005

I have been asked to teach a Sunday School class at a nearby church on the topic, "Advent Hope." The text I will be looking at is Matthew 25, the parable of the Delayed Bridegroom and the Wise and Foolish Maidens. That parable ends with the words, "Keep awake, therefore, for you know neither the day nor the hour."

Concerning which, Robert F. Capon has this to say:

> When all is said and done—when we have scared ourselves silly with the now-or-never urgency of faith and one-and-always finality of judgment—we need to take a deep breath and let it out with a laugh. Because we know we are watching a party. And that party is not just down the street making up its mind when to come to us. It is already hiding in our basement, banging on the steam pipes, and laughing its way up our cellar stairs. The unknown day and hour of its finally bursting into the kitchen and roistering its way through the whole house is not dreadful; it is all part of the divine lark of grace. God is not our mother-in-law (forgive the sexist connotations), coming to see whether her wedding present china has been chipped. He is a funny Old Uncle with a salami under one arm and a bottle of wine under the other. We do indeed need to watch for him; but only because it would be such a pity to miss all the fun.[2]

Could our Advent hope take such a surprising form? Could we be waiting for a party to begin? Capon may not have it all right, but his interpretation of this text has the virtue of reminding us that whatever else Advent hope is about, it is not something boring. It may even surprise us with unexpected joy. Or would we rather be seriously wise, strategically cautious, managing our resources? I suspect Advent hope is more reckless than that and in truth, much more of a spendthrift of God's abundant grace.

November 30, 2006

I have always been fond of the Collect for the 2nd Sunday in Advent as it appears in *The Book of Common Prayer*. It reads: "Blessed Lord, who hast caused all holy Scriptures to be written for our learning: Grant that we may in such wise hear them, read, mark, learn, and inwardly digest them,

2. Capon, *The Parables of Judgment*, 166.

that by patience, and comfort of thy Holy Word, we may embrace and ever hold fast the blessed hope of everlasting life, which thou hast given us in our Savior Jesus Christ."[3]

In reading this Advent prayer, I have been struck how apt it is for those of us engaged in theological studies. Many of you are in the New Testament course, in which you have come to know firsthand what it means to "read, mark, learn, and inwardly digest," the words of the gospel. All of us face the same task in other courses, either directly or indirectly. One of those courses is the "Theology of Dietrich Bonhoeffer," in whose life, for example, we see what it means to "read, mark, learn, and inwardly digest" the word of Jesus Christ. As we enter the Advent season, and as we come to the end of this term, I commend this prayer to you, and especially the slow, steady pace of its words, almost a kind of walk into the path of discipleship.

December 21, 2006

Many years ago, when I was in college, I had an English professor who drew my attention to a line in *Hamlet*, a play we were studying right before the Christmas break. It is a description of Christmas and its gifts, a description that points to that "peaceable Kingdom" for which we long. It reads: "Some say that ever 'gainst that season comes, wherein our Savior's birth is celebrated, the bird of dawning singeth all night long; and then, they say, no spirit can walk abroad; the nights are wholesome; then no planets strike, no fairy takes, nor witch hath power to charm, so hallowed and so gracious is the time."[4] Merry Christmas!

December 17, 2008

This year has been difficult for many in our country, and for a number of students here. A "bleak, mid-winter," indeed. Speaking for myself, I will not be sad to see 2008 come to an end. The Christmas story, at least as Luke tells it, though full of angels and their singing, takes place in the midst of the ordinary, mundane, and even tiresome things like taxes, governmental forms, and journeys that end with a "No Vacancy" sign. There is very little "Hallmarkish" about this story. Yet, where animals feed

3. *Book of Common Prayer,* 92.
4. Shakespeare, *Hamlet,* Act I, scene 1.

and gather, Christmas sneaks into our world. In one of his poems, G. K. Chesterton captures something of the homelessness of this child, whose gift is to make a home for us. I leave these last verses with you.

> A Child in a foul stable,
> Where the beasts feed and foam;
> Only where he was homeless
> Are you and I at home;
> We have hands that fashion and heads that know,
> But our hearts were lost—how long ago!
> In a place no chart nor ship can show
> Under the sky's dome.
>
> To an open house in the evening
> Home shall men come,
> To an older place than Eden
> And a taller town than Rome.
> To the end of the way of the wandering star,
> To the things that cannot be and that are,
> To the place where God was homeless
> And all men are at home.[5]

December 8, 2010

My wife loves to decorate our home for Christmas. She buys the tree, enlists my help in putting it in an acceptable corner of our house, she pulls out the Christmas ornaments, puts on "I'll Be Home for Christmas" and other holiday classics, and serves up hot apple cider and embraces the season. Not me. I have be dragged kicking and screaming into this annual ritual. My wife has learned to anticipate my Scrooge-like attitude, but she does not let my grumpiness mar her enjoyment of the festivities.

I have sometimes wondered why I am made so irritable by all of this. I have wondered, for example, if it is a "guy thing" not to want to enter into all these activities, but I know, to my shame, that there are many guys who do this and do it gladly.

Maybe it is vanity. Christopher Lasch has famously noted that one of the characteristics of the narcissistic personality is his reluctance, if not refusal, to look at the past with any sense of gratitude and joy. A year older, a lower horizon of possibilities, a worrying sense of the unfulfilled

---

5. Chesterton, "*The House of Christmas,*" in *Selected Poems*, 129.

promises of life, and now even less time and strength to push on—Christmas ornaments, nostalgic songs, rituals of the season can only serve to remind us of all of that: the passing of time, the loss of youth, and the distance that exists between life then and life now. Sigh.

Which is why Christmas, like everything else the gospel has to teach us, requires a miracle to happen.

Last week, I had occasion to remember with my theology class John of Damascus' interpretation of how Christians are made. His model is Mary, the mother of Jesus, and he asks what was the organ by which the Son of God was conceived in her. Most people might say, "the uterus." But, John of Damascus, the last great theologian of the Orthodox church before Islam blanketed the eastern Mediterranean, taught that it was her ear. He thought that Christ is conceived in us, i.e., Christmas comes to us in the same way that it came to Mary. The word of the Lord is spoken to Mary and Mary hears it and responds, "Let it be to me according to your word." (Luke 1:38) The word is conveyed to Mary's ear by the Holy Spirit and takes root in her heart, and so she becomes pregnant with Jesus.

Which is what happens to us. The word comes to us, and we hear it by the power of the Holy Spirit, and it takes root in our heart, and the miracle happens. Jesus is born in our lives.

Advent is like getting pregnant. Clearly, I have little experience with that phenomenon, but its effect on me is to make me grouchy, irritable, self-pitying, and gloomier than usual. I also eat too much. But then, the child kicks; that is, the Holy Spirit seizes my ear and bears the word to my heart, and Christ is born, kicking and screaming, to my astonishment and wonder and baffled joy.

He comes as he always promises to do, interrupting the serious business of my life and yours, making a nest for himself within us. And when he comes, there really is Christmas wonder. All our gifts and presents to each other have something of that as their aim. Their muchness is not to be denigrated as distractions or dismissed as merely "material" things. They are that, of course, but their aim is to reflect the wonder of the real gift and to remind us that Christmas, far from being yet another chore, is a gift that brings us together and showers us with love. What happens is a miracle, a time when, as Auden put it, 'for once in our lives, everything became a You and nothing was an it."[6]

Merry Christmas!

6. Auden, *"For the Time Being,"* in *Collected Poems,* 399.

December 5, 2012

In Joseph Bottum's little book, *The Christmas Plains*, he re-tells a fable first told by William Dean Howells in the 1890's. The fable concerns a little girl who liked Christmas so much that she wanted it to be Christmas every day. This is sometimes a thoughtlessly but popularly expressed sentiment, but in this case the little girl got her wish. So Christmas came on December 25th, and then again on December 26th, and then again, on the 27th, and then again on the 28th, and on and on. After about three or four months of this, the little girl grew weary of the routine of Christmas, finding the gaily-wrapped presents and the shimmering tree and loaded stockings depressing. One day, she simply sat down and cried. In six months she was worn out by Christmas. By the next fall, "people didn't carry presents around nicely anymore. They flung them over the fence or through the window, shouting, 'Take this stuff, you horrid old thing!'"[7]

Bottum goes on to note that these days this fable has almost come true, with Christmas shopping and decorations beginning around Labor Day, until the constant scream of it all is only extinguished by the day itself, after which we are exhaustedly grateful for the sheer relief that "Christmas" is over.

Bottum does not think this is the way we ought to keep Christmas, adding: "This is what Advent, rightly kept, would halt—the thing, in fact, Advent is designed to prevent ... " By slowing us down, making us count, making us wait, "Advent keeps Christmas on Christmas Day: a fulfillment, a perfection and completion of what had gone before."[8]

The Advent texts, often terrifying in their judgment, remind us that preparing our hearts to come into the presence of God in the flesh is no easy or casual task; that the words, "sore afraid," rightly belong to the vocabulary of the season; that what Christmas brings is a remedy for something deeply, deeply wrong within us, something that needs healing and hope. Just as Advent needs Christmas to bring the light that will overcome our darkness, so Christmas needs Advent to keep us from trivializing it into something that is simply captive to our own wants and wishes. No, only in Bethlehem are "the hopes and fears of all the years met," and it takes a journey, just as it did of old, to get there.

7. Bottum, *The Christmas Plains*, 123.
8. *Ibid.,*125.

November 20, 2013

When our seminary was located at Queens University of Charlotte, but before we found our present location, we were invited to look at a possible site that was owned by a Seventh Day Adventist Church and school. One day, Susan Hickok and I trooped over to the church and were met by a member, who gave us a very thorough tour of the facilities. The last stop on the tour was the sanctuary, which we thought, might serve as our chapel. In the foyer of the sanctuary there was a not very well-executed painting of Christ returning to earth. This was an Adventist church, after all. I looked at the painting and thought it a bit crude and shabby. But the fellow who was showing us around was proud of it, and pointed out some of its features to us, making sure we noticed it. For him, the painting represented the heart of his faith, the very real expectation that Jesus was coming, and coming soon to heal this world and reclaim his own, an Advent hope that seemed to him to be good news.

My mental (Calvinist) snickerings silently objected to the notion that our job was to sit on our hands waiting for Jesus to come, instead of getting busy doing good works so that should he show up, he would at least find us doing his work. But my smart-alecky thoughts were stopped in their tracks by the sincerity and genuine hopefulness of this person's faith. He really expected Jesus to show up. Maybe today or tomorrow, but in any case, soon.

I began to ask myself, "What about you, buddy? Do you really expect Jesus to show up in this world?" I was ashamed that I did not have a very good answer to my own question. "Christ plays in ten thousand places," the poet tells us, "lovely in limbs, and lovely in eyes not his . . . ."[9]

This year Thanksgiving is crammed even more closely than usual to Advent, making the season a wild mix of turkey and dressing and candles and song, leading up to the mad rush to Christmas. Will you forgive me when I say that all of this has come to seem almost hopeless to me? The last thing one might expect in all this holiday rush is that Jesus would show up. But might he not? Perhaps in a student's face or a parishioner's or a friend's. Or perhaps in ways even more troubling and more joyful, and in any case, less metaphorical.

In my office there is a print by Breughel, entitled, "The Numbering at Bethlehem." It depicts a portion of the Lukan account of the Christmas story. The scene is Bethlehem (portrayed as a 16th century north

9. Hopkins, *Collected Poems*, 129.

Flemish village), and there is a large crowd lining up to be "registered" in a temporary shed. The mass of people are not paying any attention to the couple that have just arrived. She is riding on a donkey, he is carrying their worldly goods. In fact, no one is paying much attention to them. The scene is a winter day, the pond is iced over, people are going about their work, children are playing in the snow and ice skating. Nobody is expecting that something special is about to take place in their midst.

But the child is coming, without asking permission, and coming into their world of busyness, weariness, silliness, games, labors, buying and selling, and paying taxes. Into that world he comes, almost unnoticed, the way hope silently seeps into our lives despite our best efforts to keep it a bay. He does indeed "play in ten thousand places, lovely in limbs, and lovely in eyes not his." That hope has a way of shutting up our smart-alecky snickerings, inviting us to see what we had not seen before. He may not be where we think he ought to be or where we would expect him to be, but he comes. He thinks this world is worth coming to, worth an Advent and even a Second Advent. Maybe we should be so hopeful about this world as well

December 11, 2013

I have tried to write a poem to celebrate the end of our fall term, but what I have written seems something of a mess. It doesn't always rhyme and the meter often goes haywire. Still, I send it to you with Advent and Christmas greetings.

A Sort of Poem for Students at Advent and Christmas

> Fall term's over and exams are done.
> Final papers graded and the winter sun
> Insists on shining despite the cold
> As if to remind us the year's grown old.
>
> The place seems quiet with no students here,
> Almost too quiet, as the old Westerns made clear:
> No students, a few meetings, and a slow slouch
>   toward Bethlehem,
> Which suddenly seems now, all too near.
>
> The term started in September with convocation crowd
> Snug in our chapel, happy and loud.

Anxious beginners wondering if biting this apple
Might be too much, as they sang in chapel.
But soon immersed in Church History and Christian life,
    they learned a new song
Sung on Saturdays, full of councils, heresies and saints
        gone wrong.

What followed were readings, readings, and more readings,
    and occasional quizzes,
And papers and tests with some hits and some misses.
But with the perseverance of the saints, and the bread of life
    at noon,
And table fellowship after, good eats and laughter, and soon
We were able to inwardly digest the gifts large and small,
        word and tune.

Which is where Advent should find us, as it found Mary of old,
Preparing for the birth of Christ to be conceived within
        each of us.
What do men know of conceiving or giving birth
        without a uterus?
Perhaps as much as a Virgin, whose conception was, in
        any case, by *Sancti Spiritus.*
And receiving the Word, Mary humbly obeyed
As we should do in the very same way,
Through hearing the word of scripture and attending
    that angelic song,
Impregnating Spirit leading us on
To manger and stall, where all our journeys find their end.
There to discover that he has been expecting us for a long time,
As if we were late for class, as if he were drawing us throughout
        the year
Through book and lecture, worship and question, laughter
    and tear,
As if we were meant to find him just there. Just here.

March 16, 2005

Thomas Hardy, a gloomy soul who wrote novels and some quite good
poems at the end of the 19th century and beginning of the 20th, has a
poem entitled "The Darkling Thrush" that in an odd way speaks of Good

Friday. The poem tells of a late spring day still trapped by "winter's dregs," which makes the day itself seem weak and colorless.

> The ancient pulse of germ and birth
> Was shrunken hard and dry
> And every spirit upon earth
> Seemed fervorless as I.

So, he's walking along on a cold gray day, depressed in spirit, his mood matching the dreary weather, when he hears a bird sing.

> At once a voice burst forth among
> The bleak twigs overhead
> In a full-hearted evensong
> Of joy unlimited
> An aged thrush, frail, gaunt and small
> In blast-beruffled plume
> Had chosen to fling his soul
> Upon the growing gloom.

Cheered by this bird's voice, the poet concludes that the bird sang of

> Some blessed hope
> whereof he knew
> And I was unaware.[10]

The poem makes me think: why should an "aged thrush, frail, gaunt and small," sing so happily, flinging his soul "in full-hearted evensong"? Doesn't he know how dreary things are? Such songs are useless against the darkness. Yet he sings, "of joy unlimited" that is forever useless even as it is forever true and full of grace. Useless songs are always the most important ones. We die without them. Which is why the real "darkling thrush" flings his soul in an evensong on Good Friday, where is voiced that blessed hope, of which he knows, and we, so often, are unaware.

Martin Luther called the cross our true hope, precisely because we cannot "use" it but must receive it as a gift, a song sung under the bleakest of circumstances that heals our souls. For all its "frail, gaunt and small" voice, this song sounds the notes that Easter will render audible even to our ears, and will one day make us want to sing as well.

---

10. Hardy, "*The Darkling Thrush,*" in *The Collected Poems of Thomas Hardy,* 134.

April 13, 2006

As we enter the final days of Holy Week, we witness together the Passion narrative's most agonizing and moving scenes. Here is where the battle was fought and won. I think it is important to remember that Christ's victory took place on Good Friday. We are sometimes tempted to think that Good Friday was the tragic loss, which a glorious Easter, surprisingly transforms into a victory. Not so. What Easter does is reveal the Crucified as Victor. The defeat of the power of evil and death took place on Friday. That is why it is called, quite un-ironically, "Good Friday."

We should remember that because the Passion narrative is not a story of a caterpillar becoming a butterfly. It is not a "success" story about the re-invention of self. No, it tells of death and resurrection, of the power of death being overcome by the life and death of this one man. As the creed reminds us, he "died." He was "buried." But just so was death buried and defeated. Just so, the crown of thorns bears true witness to the King. Just so the cross becomes his throne. Just so the tomb is revealed to be empty because death can no longer contain him. Just so, Jesus is Victor! Easter does not add to this victory. It merely (!) reveals it and points to the extent of his glory. The Crucified is the Risen Lord. Easter is to be found in the rejoicing of that reality.

So, I wish you the blessings of this Eastertide. Especially, I hope that Easter brings you joy. Despite the terrors of war, the miseries of hunger, disease, poverty, and the defeated but not powerless threat of death, Jesus is Victor. Even in the face of our own weak witness to that reality, still, Jesus is Victor. That is why, Karl Barth can say of the Easter witness that it always remains, "obstinately joyful."[11]

And so must we remain "obstinately joyful," not because things look so great or we are so smart, but because the faithfulness of God is so relentlessly gracious.

May 14, 2014

In a recent article in *Journal for Preachers* (Easter 2014), Will Willimon notes how easy it is for ministers of the gospel to despair. The distance between the word the gospel proclaims and the world we so often encounter can make us wonder if that eschatological gap can ever be bridged. Of

---

11. Barth, *The Humanity of God*, 60.

course, the easy way out is to give up the preaching of the gospel. It is that task that causes all the trouble. In Barth's *Church Dogmatics* he claims that the source of Job's problem is not his sores or his loss or his sufferings, but the fact that he believes in God. "Surely all ancient and modern skeptics, pessimists, scoffers and atheists are innocuous and well-meaning folk compared with this man Job. They do not know against whom they direct their disdain and doubt and scorn and rejection. Job does."[12] Job's problem would go away if he simply gave up his faith. If he would cease believing in God, then the world's evils and sufferings would become quite explicable. That's just the way it is. Stuff, to put it more politely, happens. But Job believes in God and in God's goodness. And because he does not curse God, because he persists in believing in God's faithfulness even when that faithfulness seems quite heavily disguised, his life becomes a struggle, an agony.

And just so is the Christian life, and by extension the preaching life, a struggle and even an agony. Do not misunderstand me. I am not trying to over-dramatize the work of preaching. I am just pointing out that regular and serious engagement with the gospel will cause one to ask hard questions, most especially of one's ministry. Apart from that engagement with the gospel, our sermons are merely silly or boring.

This world would be so much easier to write off as a bad job if we could just turn loose of this story that claims us. Then we could be 'smart' or skilled virtuosos and not have to rely on something as elusive and as unprovable as the empty tomb or the risen Lord. Then we could despair and be thought wise in our despair. Much of our world is already there, and quite content with whatever wisdom it can generate on its own. Such despair need not struggle; the world is simply the way it is. One need only try to navigate things the way they are and make one's own life as comfortable as possible. It is the gospel that is troublesome. It is the gospel that makes us struggle. It is the gospel that refuses to let us despair. Knowing all the "facts," the gospel persists in singing.

Willimon concludes: "Because of Easter, we preachers are not permitted to despair. There is certainly enough failure and disappointment in the preaching life to understand why depression, disillusionment, and despair could be considered three curses of preaching ministry. Despair is most understandable among some of our most conscientious and dedicated preachers. Any pastor who is not tempted to despair has

12. Barth, *Church Dogmatics*, IV/3/1, 404.

probably given into the world too soon, expecting little of the preached word. Weekly confrontation with the gap between what God dares to say and what we are able to hear leads many of our best and brightest to despondency."[13]

Yet, for those who preach and who study to preach this gospel, despair can never be an option—not because we are such skillful preachers but because our hope is in Christ, who quite without our help or wisdom, God raised from the dead. That little seed, that bothersome story, that intrusive and insistent note of joy is what causes all our trouble. It pierces our despairing wisdom and grants us a vision that thrusts us into a life-long struggle, a happy, self-forgetting effort to bear witness to the risen Lord whose Kingdom shall have no end. We are not lumbered with a message of some good person who met a tragic end, but we are invited instead to share the feast which is the life the risen Lord insists on giving us. Easter will always bother us that way. This Lord will not stay put in his tomb where he belongs. He never stays put where we think he belongs. No, he insists on meeting us in places of his choosing: in a garden cemetery, in a locked upper room, along the road, in the midst of our despair. And there he reveals himself in his own words, breaking bread with us and feeding us with the bread of life. His life is a feast. He bothers us like that. And so should our preaching bother those who hear this gospel, and perhaps bother us who preach it most of all. It is that bother, even that struggle, that makes of preaching such a joyful gift.

"The Lord is risen; he is risen indeed."

13. Willimon, *"Preaching as Demonstration of Resurrection," Journal For Preachers, Easter 2014,* 15,16.

Chapter 17: Seeking a Home

May 22, 2003

I have been out of town recently and am glad to be back home! I think of "home" as a biblical-theological category, beginning at least with the promise to Abraham for a homeland, a promise fulfilled in the liberation of Israel from Egypt, and their wanderings in the wilderness taking them on the long way "home". But I know "home" can be a problematic category as well. One can become comfortable and "at ease in Zion." Israel can even be exiled from home and find it difficult to "sing the Lord's song in a foreign land." (Ps 137:4) And Jesus tells us: "Foxes have holes, and birds of the air nests; but the Son of Man has nowhere to lay his head." (Luke 9:58) Which may be why the most vividly described home in the New Testament is not one that we possess or build but a future home, a new Jerusalem "coming down out of heaven from God, prepared as a bride adorned for her husband." (Rev 21:2)

Still, I believe that "home," with its many gifts, can bear witness to our true home. Loving our homes is not to be dismissed as a bourgeois virtue unrelated to the word of scripture. Listen, for example, to Father Alexander Schmemann as he reflects on coming home after a long trip.

> I love my home, and to leave home and be away overnight is always like dying—returning seems so very far away! I am always full of joy when I think about home. All homes, with lit windows behind which people live, give me infinite pleasure. I would love to enter each of them, to feel its uniqueness, the quality of its warmth. Each time I see a man or a woman walking with shopping bags, that is, going home, I think about them: they are going home, to real life, and I feel good, and they become somehow close and dear. I am always intrigued: What do people do when they do not "do" anything, when they just live? That's when their life becomes important, when their fate

is determined. Simple bourgeois happiness is often despised by activists of all sorts who quite often do not realize the depth of life itself; who think that life is an accumulation of activities. God gives us His Life, not ideas, doctrines, rules. At home, when all is done, life itself begins. Christ was homeless not because he despised simple happiness—He did have a childhood, family, home—but because He was at home everywhere in the world, which His Father created as the 'home' of man. 'Peace be with this house.' We have our home and God's home, the Church, and the deepest experience of the Church is that of a home. Always the same and, above anything else, life itself—the Liturgy, every morning, a feast—and not an activity.[1]

It is good to be home.

April 21, 2010

This last week I was in Texas lecturing and preaching at the church where I served prior to coming to Charlotte. I enjoyed the time and tried to represent the seminary well, but in truth it was a kind of weird experience. Everything was recognizable but everything had changed. A famous N. Carolinian once opined that "you can't go home again," and I guess he was right. You can't go home again not only because "home" has changed but because you have changed as well. "Home" is not the same place.

Nostalgia may be a form of homesickness but what it really indicates is a deeper longing not so much for the past but for the future. The home we miss is not just the home we remember but the home we are seeking, the home we are longing for, the home we pray for.

The author of Hebrews writes of those who have died in the faith, that they "who speak in this way make it clear that they are seeking a homeland. If they had been thinking of the land they had left behind, they would have had opportunity to return. But as it is, they desire a better country, that is a heavenly one." (Heb 11:14,15)

We are nearing our graduation and those who are graduating are in fact, "seeking a homeland." They have been here 4, 5, even more years preparing for the future. Given the amount of time the students have spent here, they might grow nostalgic about their lengthy sojourn at the seminary. But whatever else commencement means, it has little to do with the past. These graduates are looking toward the future.

1. Schmemann, *The Journals of Father Alexander Schmemann*, 23.

The other day, I talked with a recent graduate, whose "home" today is an urban ministry site during the week and a small country church on the weekend. She did not see this "home" while she was studying here, but in longing for that "homeland," that "better country," she found this combined ministry, where God has called her, and it is the place where she is happily serving.

That is another strange thing about "home." We rarely see it coming, until one day we discover that we are "home," that our labors, our hopes, our loves are bound up with the place and the people we are serving. My prayer for those who are graduating, is that they will not look back, or if they do, they will do so only momentarily and with gratitude, but that they will focus their eyes and their convictions on the future "homeland" where they have been called to serve.

There is nothing wrong with "longing for home." Such homesickness is, in fact, a longing for heaven. And that should make us attentive to all the places heaven touches earth, places where Jesus is already at work, bidding us to come and join him there. Some of those places don't look so wonderful, much less like "home," but that is only the way Jesus hides himself from us in order that we might discover him there, and in the company of others, discover the joy of life in him.

January 11, 2012

Recently I received a letter from a friend in Texas whose husband was a Presbyterian minister for many years. He died long before we moved to Charlotte but she wrote me this past week to tell me that she had saved all his sermons and letters, asking if I wanted them for our library. She is in a nursing home now and she and her daughter are trying to shed some of the "stuff" that has accumulated over the past 85 years. It is a big job.

I don't know that I was all that helpful in my reply but her letter got me to thinking. I have a lot of "stuff" too. Old sermons, old papers, old chapters from unpublished books, old books, old periodicals, letters, etc. What am I to do with all this material? I hope my widow and/or my children do not have to sort through it all.

Sermons have a very short shelf-life. No one, including me, is really interested in papers I wrote in college or seminary, but I still have them. Do I think all of this will have historical or archival value? No. Like barnacles, these things have stuck to me as I have sailed through the seas of life, and in truth, I probably need to be put up and scraped clean.

But my books, my books are something else. They are old friends. My office is a mess, something that is readily apparent to those daring enough to enter it, but I feel at home here in no small measure because I am surrounded by books. Some of them are old, some more recent, some are thick, others thin, but all—in some measure—telling the story of Jesus and his people.

Does that sound too pious? Well, in any case, it is true. And listening to the story of Jesus told by so many various commentators, theologians, novelists, poets, historians, scholars, preachers and teachers, makes me smile, fills me with good cheer, and makes me not worry about the many barnacles affixed to my hull. I am a fellow-traveler who has fallen into company with the most remarkable group of people, who have the most amazing stories to tell.

In my living room is a print of all the characters in Chaucer's *Canterbury Tales*, lurching their various ways toward the shrine of the "holy, blissful martyr." Their journey begins with an agreement that each pilgrim is supposed to tell a story along the way, and whoever tells the best story will win a "supper" at the inn in Southwark. And some of the stories are funny, some sad, some ribald, some moving. But it is clear that in going to Canterbury, this company of sinners will be sustained by a deeper story, one that is drawing them to a table where the "supper" will be provided by that gracious host whose story is the best one of all. (For a better and more complete account of this narrative, see David Lyle Jeffrey's, *People of the Book*, Eerdmans 1996.)

To live and work and study together in seminary as we move toward the goal of ministry is to be caught up in this story, and to find ourselves, daily, surrounded by old friends and good companions. They remind us of the best story that encompasses all our own, and invites us to share in a meal with him at his table.

January 25, 2012

When I was in college, I was invited to read Oscar Handlin's *The Uprooted* (Little Brown and Company, 1973), a history of immigration in this country. Handlin's book recounts the remarkable stories of uprooted people from eastern and southern Europe who sought a better life in

America. One of the points Handlin makes is that the first generation of immigrants, i.e., those adults who choose to leave their native country and venture into a new land, that group always loses. They lose the home that, however pitiful, they still remember fondly. They lose family and friends. They even lose some of their history, since no one is interested in that in their new country. They have a harder time mastering the new language and customs of the strange new world into which they have brought themselves and their family. They often work humbler jobs, and because of the language, find themselves in lower positions than they might have in their 'old country.' They can't help always feeling a bit awkward, as if they don't quite fit in their new surroundings.

Their children, the second generation, get on well, however. They have less to remember of the old and seem to master the new with little difficulty. They learn the idioms, the customs, the folkways very quickly and before long, they begin to look on their parents as something of an embarrassment: clueless, old people speaking with a funny accent. America is about the future, the young, the lack of tradition, etc.

The point of all this? Well, recently I have begun to feel a bit like an immigrant. Age will do that to you. The world I remember is, in so many ways, "the old country." So many of the things I have loved (admittedly not a random sample)—a church where good theology was not only valued but seen as critically important, where good preaching was unapologetic and hope-filled, where there were good neighborhoods where people knew each other, where there were good public schools, good newspapers that everyone read and followed, good sports teams where players stayed on the same team for several years, where there were good jobs for those who did not go to college and lifelong careers with one company or one field of endeavor for others—no longer seem to exist. I miss that world.

What I find difficult and awkward in "the new world" are churches that are either hip or angry or both, but in any case, no longer interested in the ministry of either word or sacrament; neighborhoods that are, in many cases, filled with "nice" people, none of whom know each other and many of whom live in a vast desert of loneliness; public schools where the cost of educating children is not taken seriously into account, either by those who simply want to spend more money or those who do not want to spend any at all; sports that have become idolatrously big, where money talks and only money; where society seems increasingly divided, and not just politically, but socially and economically.

Maybe this is just the rant of an old man and maybe things are not nearly so bad as outlined here. But I keep thinking of those first generation immigrants and how tempted they must have been at times to go back, to have done with this strange, new world, even to despair. No doubt some of them did. No doubt others would have if there had not been a costly ocean voyage to be paid for. But for the most part, those immigrants' courage and refusal to give in or give up is what made your world and mine a better place.

Scripture knows something about being a stranger, an exile, a pilgrim. Indeed, such is the characteristic feature of people of faith ("aliens and exiles" 1 Pet. 2:11), whether we find ourselves with Abraham, who was told to go from his own country to "the land I will show you," (Gen 12:1) or with the psalmist who wonders how to sing the Lord's song in a foreign land (Ps 137:4), or with the exiles returning to their own land only to discover that "home" is no longer home (Ezra 3:12,13).

The danger is not really trying to cope with the awkwardness we feel upon entering a strange land. The danger is feeling so rich, so comfortable, so settled that we no longer remember what it is like to be an immigrant. Discomfort may be the way we are reminded of who we are, as the author of Hebrews so well describes in outlining this journey of faith: "They (i.e., all the saints who died in faith) confessed that they were seeking a homeland. If they had been thinking of the land that they had left behind, they would have had opportunity to return. But as it is, they desire a better country, that is a heavenly one. Therefore God is not ashamed to be called their God; indeed, he has prepared a city for them." (Heb 11:13b-16)

Being a first generation immigrant may be exactly what the Christian life really feels like. When we think of faith, we don't often think of it in terms of courage, but immigrants know, or rather they quickly learn, how much hope it takes to press on.

September 11, 2012

I am sitting in my new office at a temporary desk, with unpacked boxes on the floor, writing you this note. As you may surmise, I am very happy. We have the loveliest, "smartest," pedagogically well-equipped building in town, which also makes its own faithful witness to the gospel. I hope you bring your friends "to come and see".

A building can easily become an idol. I know. And, indeed, there are many aspects of this building that tempt me to do just that. But a building does not make a seminary anymore than it does a church. We Calvinists have a deep suspicion embedded in our DNA of lifting anything in the created order to divine status.

But sometimes I think our fear of idolatry is greater than our trust in God's incarnate grace. In scripture, there are no words that are not embodied in some piece of the created order: a burning bush, a courageous prophet, the bread and wine of Christ's own body and blood. Buildings can make a witness too, pointing to realities greater than themselves, convictions that speak through brick and mortar. This building speaks. Its very location tells of a strong relation to the church and the faith that church proclaims. Through library and classroom, this building reminds us that authentic faith always seeks understanding—not pat answers, not formulas or strategies for fixing other people's problems, not the sheer accumulation of information—but the understanding of what faith believes and which enables faith to embrace and love the world.

This building also speaks of that faith. Our "worship space" (chapel/ gathering space/ dining hall) unapologetically yet simply and clearly declares that Jesus is Lord. It is the place where we are fed, with word and sacrament, but also with more daily bread. Here is where we eat. In a way that architect and contractor and theologian sometimes forget, this building is built to inspire and delight. It does.

Finally, and no less important, this building seeks to enable the gift of human fellowship, the gift of life together. This gift is made manifest in the shaping of offices and hallways, in the welcoming space as one enters, in reading rooms, in hearth and kitchen. Students come from some distance to study here; this building welcomes them and as they say around here, makes them feel "at home."

There are "joys" of home ownership that will temper my enthusiasm, I know. Things will break, water fountains will leak, complicated security systems will require learning and mastery. But at the moment, I can only be glad to enter this house with you and to find here the joy of learning and studying and worshipping that will serve to prepare us for the even longer journey ahead.

September 25, 2013

The other day I had a meeting with a friend in Chester, S. Carolina. We are sharing in a joint presentation before Trinity Presbytery, and we thought it a good idea to get our story straight before the presbytery met. We had agreed to meet at a little restaurant near the highway, around noon.

He was late so I had some time to people watch. The restaurant appeared to be family-owned and operated. And most of the customers seemed to be familiar faces to the waitresses. These folks would often just order "the regular" and the waitress would know what that was and write it down on her pad.

The talk varied from the economy to the weather but the most animated conversations were about last Friday's football game and the prospects for the local high school eleven this weekend. Those conversations soon expanded to include memories of previous teams and games, heroic triumphs under the "Friday night lights." There was much laughter and hoo-rahing. The waitresses were not young, but were kind and solicitous. It seemed a happy place.

When my friend arrived, we ordered, and our orders came with cornbread and iced tea, and for a moment I thought about staying there for the rest of the afternoon. Most of my ministry was in small towns. I know they are not perfect places. I grew up in a large city and learned from reading Sinclair Lewis' novel, *Main Street*, what vicious and hypocritical places small towns could be. But I think Mr. Lewis got some things wrong, and not all the liberations available in big cities are all that liberating. Small towns contain their distinctive parts of God's varied grace.

What impressed me in this little, clean, well-lit restaurant was the palpable sense of community. The men were dressed in overalls and wore work shoes; the women were in print dresses and wore flip flops. One elderly couple brought their even more elderly relative, who used a walker to get to her table. Nobody paid attention. An African American couple ate with their two little boys, both of whom listened intently to the 'football talk.'

I came back to Charlotte and there was, and is, plenty of work to do around here. But that lunch reminded me of how important our own sense of community is, and what a delight it is simply to break bread with one another in this place. We have that opportunity each Saturday, and in truth, I cherish it. We too have a clean, well-lighted place to be together.

The deepest human community is to be found in such nourishing settings, which may be part of the reason why the sacrament of the Lord's Supper is such a gift. So many of the 'homecomings' in scripture involve meals or banquets or simple celebrations of God's goodness. And I believe that it is not wrong to think of heaven as a place where our homecoming nourishes us in just such a way. I found a little bit of that in Chester, S. Carolina, on Tuesday, and I look forward to discovering some more with you on Saturday.

December 4, 2013

As this term comes to an end, I find myself feeling almost sad. Partly, this is because I have enjoyed teaching the courses I have been assigned to teach, and partly because I have enjoyed the fellowship with students and faculty and staff this term. The problem is not just that time has flown—one term is pretty much like another in that respect—but that the conversations have been so rich, the readings so stimulating, the time together such a delight. I am sorry to see all that come to an end.

When I was a child, I used to be invited occasionally to play at a friend's house. He lived in a house bigger than ours. His older brother was much more interesting than my older sisters. His parents would often take us to eat ice cream. And when, at the end of the day, his father would drive me home, I remember feeling a bit let down that the day was coming to an end, and that I was having to return to my boring old home and family and chores. That night, my family would gather around the table for the supper my mother had lovingly prepared, and I would sit there glumly sharing in a meal with my three sisters and little brother, wondering where all the zest in life had gone. I never thought that what seemed boring and tedious to me was in fact very heaven; that the life that was being shared with me around that table on a daily basis was in fact a rather large gift of grace.

Adventures, we are tempted to think, are elsewhere, concerned with more impressive people, doing more interesting things. But I think adventures of the Advent kind are more ordinary than that, and are easily overlooked.

I often grow weary with the efforts to make the church's worship more "dramatic," as if the gospel's narrative has to be juiced up to make it interesting. When we do that, we are like children sitting around a plentiful table complaining about how boring and pedestrian such a gift seems. Or, we are like a child that is sad because he has to go "home."

In truth, Advent is about just that: going home. There is no reason to be sad here. Even though I had so much fun "playing" with all of you this term, I know that it is time to go home. Home is not finally the classroom or the paper or the exam. Home is to be found in the life of that child who was homeless in Bethlehem. His life and company are not boring. And to follow him is not tedious. To quote a great poet and man of faith,

> He is the Way.
> Follow him through the Land of Unlikeness;
> You will see rare beasts, and have unique adventures.
>
> He is the Truth.
> Seek Him in the Kingdom of Anxiety;
> You will come to a great city that expected your return for years.
>
> He is the Life.
> Love Him in the world of the Flesh;
> And at your marriage all its occasions shall dance for joy.[2]

Going home is the greatest adventure available to us. I send you off with Advent hopes that your journey takes you, wherever you go, closer to home.

March 5, 2014

When I was in college, I majored in History. When I was a little boy, my mother would take me and my sisters to look at old family gravestones in cemeteries throughout the South. When I was 9 years old, my family moved from a very stable church in a well-established neighborhood to a large city where my father was to organize a new church in a growing but featureless suburb. This uprooting had the effect of making me instantly nostalgic for the past, especially for my more settled existence in our previous home. The point is that I have always found it easier to look backward rather than forward. I am not sure that this attitude is all that helpful in ministry, and I doubt that it is warranted by scripture, which, while it does enjoin us "to look from the rock from which we were hewn," (Isa 51:1) seems more interested in the future and what God will

---

2. Auden, "*The Christmas Oratorio*" in *Collected Poems*, 400.

do with Israel ("Behold, I am doing a new thing, do you not perceive it?" Isa 43:19) and with Jesus' disciples ("No one who puts his hand to the plow and looks back is fit for the Kingdom of God." Luke 9:62), and finally, what the risen Lord will himself do with the whole creation ("Then I saw a new heaven and a new earth . . . ." Rev 21:1).

What strikes me about these passages of scripture is the way they turn us toward the future but do so without offering us a strategic plan. I know we need strategic plans; our seminary is engaged in just that important work right now. But thinking about the future, rather than reflecting on the more pleasant, and in my case, selfish consideration of the past, is not about envisioning a clever plan or espying what other dullards miss, or even being prepared for foreseen and unforeseen events. No, thinking about the future is to hope.

Hoping is hard work. Yet for people of faith it is essential. Sentimental longing for the past is the opposite of hope, which is why it is so easy.

When my father retired, he served on his presbytery's "Committee on Preparation for Ministry" and attended every presbytery meeting. At the time, and I must confess even now, I thought he was, not to put too fine a point on it, nuts to do that. I would have thought the prospect of being "honorably retired" would be a kind of "get out of jail free" card with respect to the councils of the church. But he saw it differently. The last year of his life, he was raising money to send a Cuban refugee to seminary so that this young man could seek ordination in the Presbyterian Church. My father hoped. And his hope took concrete form. It did not encompass a grandiose plan for the future but instead invested time, money, and energy in the most simple and near-to-hand witness to Christ and his church.

The other day in preparing for my theology class, I was doing some reading in Calvin on the Christian life, and my eye fell on a page that dealt with what scripture means when it talks about our "treasure in heaven." A refugee himself, Calvin writes:

> We ought, then, to imitate what people do who determine to migrate to another place, where they have chosen a lasting abode. They send before them all their resources and do not grieve over lacking them for a long time. But if we believe heaven is our country, it is better to transmit our possessions thither than to keep them here where upon our sudden migration they would be lost to us. But how shall we transmit them? [Here you might expect Calvin to say something pious like being prayerful or

casting our cares upon God or reflecting on the spiritual life
among the blessed. But he does not. Listen:] Surely by providing
for the needs of the poor; whatever is paid out to them, the Lord
reckons as given to himself.[3]

Hope is acting as if heaven were our country, a place where the
wealth of God's grace in Jesus Christ reveals our solidarity with every
beggar looking for bread. You want to know what heaven is like, what
it means to hope for the future? "Give alms," the poet Hopkins advised
his friend, Robert Bridges, who asked him a similar question. And do
so, not as charity, not as a downpayment on some future reward, but as
the appropriate witness to the One to whom every needy person on this
planet belongs. In him is our hope. Nostalgia, for Christians, is always a·
false luxury, available only to those who think themselves "wealthy." It
is a lie, inviting us to believe in the myth of our own self-sufficiency, to
which we are only too ready to cling. Hope, on the other hand, migrates.
Like Abraham, like the people of Israel, like the disciples, hope looks for
a better country up ahead. "If they had been thinking of the land that
they had left behind, they would have had opportunity to return. But as
it is, they desire a better country, that is a heavenly one." (Heb 11:15,16)
As migrants of hope, we are disciplined against nostalgia and taught to
look toward the future. We do not see everything nor is our vision com-
prehensively clear. Hope reveals just enough light for us to take the next
step. Just so do we learn to invest ourselves in what matters, acting as if
heaven really were our country.

3. Calvin, *The Institutes*, Bk.III,xviii,6.

Chapter 18: The Sin of Boredom

January 4, 2006

Last week, my wife and I went to see the movie, *The Chronicles of Narnia*, which we enjoyed. Despite some quibbles, we thought the Disney people did a creditable job of portraying that narrative. Perhaps it was all the snow or the cold majesty of the evil Queen of Narnia, but I was struck with what it might mean to live in a world where "it was always winter but never Christmas."

In some ways, that is a description of a modernity that thinks it has no access to heaven's grace, that lives in a bottom-line world in which there are no mysteries or wonders but only the boredom of getting and spending. And as a result, I have come to think that another name for "always winter but never Christmas" is that deep, soul-destroying boredom, against which the monks struggled, naming it *acedia*. That word is sometimes translated as "sloth," though that seems too weak and colorless a term to cover the matter.

In any case, sloth is one of the things the gospel liberates us from. The risen Lord's triumph over death is a victory also over boredom, particularly that self-absorbed "darkness that wastes at noonday" that would seek to blot out the joy that is ours in Christ.

The study of theology and the preparation for ministry are the most un-boring of undertakings. Which does not mean that they are easy or alway euphoric undertakings. But God has given us "weapons of the Spirit" to contend with all that might assault us on this path. Not least of these "weapons" is the life we share together in worship and praise. There we discover again and again and ever again, that Christmas does come, melting the tedious snows of winter, and unsettling the boring tedium of tyrants within and without.

January 29, 2006

Arthur McGill taught for several years at Harvard Divinity School before he died in 1980. McGill was a keen observer of American life and a good theologian. One thing he noticed about life in modern, affluent, technologically hip America was how bored people were, a fact that he connected to a loss of faith.

He writes:

> The human spirit cannot be satisfied and exalted by the glory, say, of human thought or national sovereignty, of utopian visions or muscular athletics, or even of sacrificing love. These have a kind of glory; they elicit praise; they elicit that sense of the wonderful . . . . But in each case, they are a limited glory. We cannot worship any of these with all our intellectual and moral passion . . . . Somewhere we will be bothered by inadequacy. More important, however, when people live by [such inadequate] glories, they are threatened by worship, by glories and magnitudes which utterly surpass them . . . . I often think that many people go into the ministry of loving the unworthy neighbor as a way of running from themselves . . . . Most people who live and who try to be real by holding onto themselves do not want glory—hence the intolerable boredom into which they become so easily locked . . . . . To be joyful in the worship of the living God is to be redeemed from all boredom . . . [1]

To be joyful in the worship of God is to be redeemed from all boredom. What a gift! And indeed, what a gift it is to be redeemed from so desperately holding on to ourselves, which is, perhaps, the most boring undertaking of all. The promise of worship is the joy of being lifted up, beyond self, to what is truly glorious. Which is why worship regularly invites us to lift up our hearts.

October 29, 2008

I believe it was Eugene Peterson who drew a distinction between a tourist and a pilgrim. Much of American life is designed to make us feel like tourists. The tourist's life is not a bad life; it is, for the most part, a comfortable way to see the world. To be sure, it is a consumerist life, a life which is waited upon, shown around, welcomed and received, all for a

---

1. McGill, *Death and Life: An American Theology,* 70.

price, and most often for an affordable price. Though people who go on tours often find and make good friends, more often tourists maintain a certain distance from each other, not wanting to get involved with or be burdened by the claims of others. One comes back from a tour tired, perhaps, but not usually lumbered with additional concerns or obligations. "It was fun," we say. "I enjoyed visiting the place. I wouldn't want to live there but it made for a nice visit."

Tourists go on trips that are occasional, not enduring, trips that are full of sights and sounds but are soon over. Pilgrims, on the other hand, know themselves to be on a long journey, one on which they may be burdened with claims that last a lifetime. Pilgrims have left home behind and are looking for a home they have not yet found. Pilgrims are not in a rush—not trying to see 16 cities in 14 days in order to get the biggest bang for their buck. Pilgrims are slow, often having to retrace their steps or even begin again at the beginning. C. S. Lewis, entitled the book about his conversion, *Pilgrim's Regress* (Eerdmans, 2014).

A pilgrimage makes little sense in a consumerist world that can only understand it as a form of "seeking," which is hardly distinguishable from "shopping." But pilgrims rarely seek. That is why they are often misunderstood. They know something already and are following One whom they believe to have sought them.

Several years ago, I was traveling with my wife in England over Christmas and we decided to go to Canterbury between Christmas and New Year's. On December 29th, we took the train from London to Canterbury to see the cathedral and look around. We were tourists.

Canterbury Cathedral is a lovely place, and when we arrived, we were joined by hordes of other tourists, who had come, like us, to see the sights. As we walked into the cathedral, I was drawn to the chancel area, and found myself looking down on a roped-off area below, where I noticed folk kneeling and praying. "What's going on here?" I asked one of the guides. She replied, "Today, is the feast day of Thomas Becket. These people are pilgrims who have come to offer their prayers in his memory." "Oh," I thought. "These folks are not tourists. They are pilgrims. They have come to bear witness to a saint and martyr to the faith."

Next Saturday is All Saints Day, an occasion to remind ourselves that we are not studying here as tourists but as pilgrims. One of the gifts of being a pilgrim is finding that there are others walking the same path as you, and that all of us together make a strange company that Jesus Christ is drawing to himself. There is no need to rush here. Seminary is not about taking 16 courses in 14 weeks. This pilgrimage is not about checking things off a list or being credentialed. It is about a longer and more mysterious journey, a pilgrimage whose joys are found in the walking, in the discipleship, in the company of that One who has called us to come and follow.

June 13, 2013

For several years I have attended a summer conference sponsored by the Center for Catholic and Evangelical Theology. In the past this group of Lutherans, Roman Catholics, Episcopalians, Baptists, and some Presbyterians have met to discuss such topics as Christian unity, the role of scripture and tradition in the life of the church, Jesus Christ, the sacraments, social ethics, holiness, church conflict, and other topics rooted in and stimulated by the call to bear faithful witness in our day and time.

I have enjoyed these conferences in part because they rarely seek to be "relevant." Often I have found, however, that in digging more deeply into seemingly unrelated matters of the church's faith, this conference has shed a flood of light on the way we attempt to live faithfully now. This year's topic was "Heaven, Hell, and Purgatory?" Lest you think this topic either too celestial or too diabolical to offer much substance for Christians today, let me simply note what a gift it was to hear theologians speak of God and God's purpose for creation, for our humanity, its end, and the life we share together. Thinking faithfully about heaven, or what it might mean that we live under the judgment of God, or whether universal salvation is the intended message of the gospel, or why Jesus spoke so often about hell, or what constitutes Christian hope, or where the idea of Purgatory came from, and what theological significance it might have, if any—these matters were unfolded for those gathered to think about and reflect upon. The experience was delightful, a joy, not least because the lectures and discussions were framed by worship.

Theology is not a parlor game. Thinking faithfully about "man's chief end" compels us to probe into the very depths of what it means to be human, and how "glorifying and enjoying God" describes the very height of human flourishing.

I think people come to worship hoping to hear (even if they have given up the expectation of hearing) the word of God, the story that is at once bigger than what the culture, or we ourselves, will allow, and smaller and more narrow than our grandiose dreams of self. This word encompasses heaven and hell. This word refuses to leave us alone. This word throws us into the company of others, in whose midst we discover new thoughts, new ways of being faithful, new questions to ask.

Dororthy L. Sayers insisted that there is more drama in the dogma, more heaven in the ordinary confession of the faith, more real struggle with the "principalities and powers" than we can imagine when we dare to think and speak faithfully of the gospel.[2] Ministry is dramatic in that sense, and in any case, like theology, is never boring but full of surprises and delight.

September 18, 2013

I suspect that by the time you read this note, you will have read a number of opinion pieces and editorials reflecting upon the latest shooting tragedy in Washington, D.C. I do not mean in this missive to offer my own prescriptions or my cry of rage. But there have been so many of these incidents, so many killings, so many deaths. What can one say? What must one say? That we should have stronger laws to keep firearms out of the hands of mentally disturbed individuals? I would support that. That we should summon the political will to examine the whole business of guns and their place in our society? I would be for that too.

After the young Australian ballplayer was shot dead in Oklahoma this past summer by some apparently "bored" teenagers, I began to wonder if our problems aren't deeper than what political solutions could bring about. I do not write this note to offer a solution, nor am I merely lamenting a lamentable situation. If I am tired of reading such stories, how must the parent of a child shot at school feel, or the spouse of someone who went to work on Monday but did not come home, or a parent who sent a child off to America to play baseball, only to have him gunned down while he was out for a run? It is enough to make one sick.

And that is what I want to call to your attention today: this sick feeling. There have been so many of these "incidents" that I am afraid we are becoming inured to them, dismissing them while waiting for the 24 hour news cycle to bring us another fresh catastrophe. When one loses the gift of being ashamed, the grace to be sickened by what human beings can do to each other, one loses a vital piece of one's soul.

2. Sayers, *Letters to a Diminished Church*, 21.

I remember reading once that the opposite of this was precisely what Heinrich Himmler worried about. His great fear was that his SS troops might develop some residual form of human compassion, rendering them useless in the killing of Jews and others.

So, before we seek a political solution, before we write our congressperson or organize our interest groups, I wonder if we don't have some shame to learn, some sorrow to confess to God, some silence to cultivate in the face of such terrible pain. Do not misunderstand me: I am not arguing for a form of self-flagellation or another "woe is us" sermon, both of which can be excellent ways of avoiding the pain we face. No, what I believe is that a healthy sense of shame is rooted in Jesus Christ and his victory over sin and death. Only there do we learn of a power greater than the comfortable nihilism that continues to lacerate and seduce us.

Being "bored" enough to kill someone, being angry enough to strike out at little children, being contemptuous enough to fire away at colleagues, all of that is nourished by the resentment that modern day nihilism so plentifully provides. And worse, all of that wears us down to the point where after a while we don't care. After a while, we don't get sick anymore. After a while we learn to look the other way. Unless our well-cultivated insulation is pierced by the story of One who did not look away, who did not get worn down by death, who rather wore death down in providing us with the gift of life, unless that miracle happens, we remain in deep peril.

Pardon if this seems like preaching. I don't think that I am solving anything in sharing these thoughts with you. Rather, I am trying to hold on to the sick feeling inside me that does not know what to do with itself and is suspicious of adding to the anger and resentment that is already so plentiful. I am hoping this sick feeling is, in its way, a sign of faith, and perhaps pointing in a direction toward more responsible action. In any case, I commend it to you. Maybe that is, in part, why we are studying here, to learn something of what the gospel discloses of our own illness.

Chapter 19: Texas Independence Day

February 28, 2007

Six years ago, I left my native state of Texas to come to N. Carolina to serve in this work. You might think that 6 years would have been long enough to put some things away and, as they say these days, "move on." People from Texas can be annoying enough in Texas but take them out of the state, and they can become obnoxious. I cite Stanley Hauerwas as but one example, which might suffice for the whole.

Anyway, try as I might, I cannot seem to make being Texan a theological category. Indeed, its loudness, bigness, swaggering pride, etc., seem to exemplify more what the Lord regularly "scatters in the imagination of their hearts," bringing down "the powerful" while "raising up those of low degree." All of which is why the gospel is so baffling to Texans, especially the out of state ones, and why it requires a miracle for them to make much headway in its call to discipleship.

Before he died, my uncle taught New Testament at a seminary in Texas. He told me once that he had discovered that the Apostle Paul was not from Texas. "What do you mean?" I asked. He replied, "Paul told the Philippians that he had learned to be content in whatever state he was in. No Texan could ever utter such words."

Dumb joke. Still, you have to say this for my fellow Texans: they know good barbecue and they can make good ice cream. Which counts for something in this vale of tears, and demonstrates, if nothing else does, the mysterious providence of God and the goodness of creation. And that is something worth celebrating, as well as the goodness of the life that is ours together in Jesus Christ, in whatever state we find ourselves. He sets us free to enjoy the gifts he so richly provides, even when they come from the land of bluebonnets, blue jeans, and Blue Bell Ice Cream.

The chief feast of the church is often inaugurated with the words, "Come, for all is now ready." Well, I hope you will come on Friday night to eat some beef barbecue, taste some ice cream, and listen to the happy tunes of a bluegrass band in which one of our students plays the mandolin. I have invited some homesick Texans to come so you may see some of them. So, come, for all is now ready.

February 27, 2008

Recently I have been thinking about food. This usually happens around noon when I debate between going to get a smoothie or a cup of soup. Most of my life I have thought of food as a kind of fuel to keep the metabolism kicking over, but in recent years I have altered my thinking somewhat.

For one thing, scripture pays an enormous amount of attention to food. And not only food, but its proper preparation and appropriate diet. The one miracle that occurs in all four gospels is Jesus' feeding of the 5,000. He regularly is engaged by Pharisees over the matter of food. Luke tells us that he welcomed sinners and ate with them. And on the night of his betrayal, he shared a meal with his disciples.

Marcel Proust maintained that merely biting into a cookie could launch him into a journey of memory, its taste bringing back as nothing else could, the sadness and joys of other times and other places. Texas barbecue does that for me. I'll admit its taste is not as subtle as whatever Proust was chewing on, but it serves very well as a kind of "soul food" that recalls for me happy times with family and friends.

Each of us has our own "cookie," I suspect. I am assured by some natives of N. Carolina that Brunswick stew and shredded pork fulfills this role. When I am not longing for beef brisket, I feel the same about what we call, erroneously, "Mexican food," another commodity difficult to find in these parts.

The point is that food can become sacramental in that it carries in its flavors and preparation memories of the past that tell our story and remind us who we are and to whom we belong. Perhaps that is why Jesus chose bread and wine to feed us with his own body and blood, identifying us as his own, and calling us to eat and share in his life. Just as we are sometimes tempted to think of food as merely utilitarian, so are we surprised to learn that eating can be a form of discipleship. Who would have thought? Service, giving, praying, all of these things we are ready to believe Jesus wants us to do, but eating? How can that make us more faithful?

I know that our theology tells us that it is the Holy Spirit that unites us to Christ, but the Spirit also seems remarkably interested in food, and is quite unashamed to make the gift of food, bread and wine, the means by which we are united to Christ.

We will not be celebrating communion this Friday night, but we will be celebrating the joy of our life together and the joy that is ours in Christ's service. It is Christ who feeds us, daily, and it is Christ who bids us to give the world something to eat. So much of ministry is simply obeying Jesus' words, "You give them something to eat."(Luke 9:13) Indeed, I think that is what seminary is about: learning how to cook and prepare nourishing meals for God's people to feed upon. We are a "cooking" school in some respects. So, as scripture invites us to say, "Come, rejoice with me!" The fatted calf has been slain, the barbecue is ready, and Blue Bell is on its way. Come, rejoice with me!

Chapter 20: Technology

July 16, 2008

Yesterday, my colleagues and I attended an all day seminar on Microsoft Word 2007, an upgrade to our current word processing and email capabilities. The teacher was a delightful, persistently cheerful soul, and led us at the end of the day to a deeper understanding of the usefulness of this new system. A long day but a good one.

During the course of our time together, Gilbert, our instructor, expressed some concern about our lack of back-up drives to preserve our data in Charlotte. He urged us to purchase an external disc drive to save all of our files. So a couple of us did just that. Uncharacteristically, before attaching this external drive to the computer, I read the manual, whose first chapter was entitled as follows: "How to Save Your Own Life." It continued: "Follow the three simple steps for getting started, and let the saving begin." At the end of step 3, which I eventually reached, the manual concluded with these words: "Your installation is complete. You are now ready to save your life."

Well. Apart from the redemptive language employed in the service of this particular piece of technology, I find it disconcerting how easy it is for us to identify the work that we do with our "life." To be sure, life may be more than computer files and email notes but were such to disappear, I would find it difficult to accept such a loss with equanimity. Still, the Sermon on the Mount is a sermon in no small part because it tells us that such is not our life. And to the extent that we believe that it is, to that extent we become as boring and tedious as the little manuals that assure us that we are able to save our own lives. The lilies of the field and the birds of the air know that is a lie, and also they know that the joy of being a lily of the field and bird of the air has a good deal to do with not being concerned with saving one's life. Which is to say, they know the *joie de vivre* which is the gift not of an external hard drive but of One whom we cannot manipulate but who is more faithful than any redundant technology.

I am still struggling with my external hard drive; I may have installed it incorrectly (though I did reach and complete "step 3"!). Perhaps "my life" then is "un-saved," a condition that for perverse reasons gives me much pleasure. Learning what the lilies of the fields and birds of the air know is not easy, harder even than installing an external disc drive. No doubt both have their place in God's economy, and I do want my files saved. Beyond that, however, I suspect an even bigger miracle must come into play.

February 16, 2011

A few Sundays ago, I attended worship at a self-styled "mega-church" here in Charlotte. I am still trying to "process" what I experienced there. My wife was out of town, so I went by myself, intending to study the goings on, much as a cultural anthropologist might. I attempted to keep an open mind, something that is very hard for me to do, especially in regard to worship. Let me try to relate some of what I experienced on this day.

This particular campus—it is one of several and not, in any case, the main one—was located in a high school auditorium. All the campuses of this church are connected by very sophisticated and, I would guess, very expensive technology, that allows the preacher to be "beamed in" during the worship. I found the parking area ample. As I walked from my car toward the auditorium, I was greeted about every 15 feet by a smiling person, welcoming me to the church and pointing the way toward the entrance. In a way, that was nice. Who could complain about such friendliness? But after the 5th or 6th greeting, I found it a bit creepy.

Entering the foyer of the auditorium, I discovered on the right a "store" where one could purchase this mega-church's branded items: t-shirts, CDs, DVDs, scarves, license plate holders, decals, etc. On the left side of the foyer, I was ushered into the large, dark, movie-theater-style room, where I was individually taken to a seat. The room was dark but the stage was well-lit, and on it a rock band was playing loud music, whose lyrics were voiced by a comely, young blonde woman dressed all in black, wearing long black boots. We watched her sing. Some who knew the words, sang along. The screens behind her and beside her projected her image even though she was singing directly in front of us.

There were lots of people there. Most of them were young; more women than men, some families but more singles; few children. I had to keep reminding myself that we were all praising Jesus because I could not take my eyes off this singer. She sang and the band played for another 10 minutes or so, then the band and the singer disappeared and there was nothing on the stage but the screens.

Okay, I thought, we will have a call to worship now. And we did, sort of. There was a 2 minute commercial for the church. It was very interesting. It was aimed at young people, especially young women, and featured a young woman asking those in the audience if they had been on drugs, or were coming off a bad high, or had had an abortion, or had just lost a boyfriend, or were alienated from their families, or were lonely. If any of this was the case, then this church was for you. And I believe that the church really believes that and deserves credit for identifying and addressing some of the wreckage that afflicts human relationships today.

The service then began and its theme was taken from the Beatles' song from some years ago, "Get Back!" The Beatles' theme continued as the comely, young lass in the black boots reappeared to sing, "Yesterday," as the opening call to worship.

The first act of worship that involved all the campuses was to congratulate one of the usher-greeter people and award him or her with a gift, acknowledging that person to be the outstanding usher-greeter that month. The gift was an Ipod containing the complete works of the Beatles. It also contained some sermons by the pastor. The best usher-greeter was actually an elderly (i.e., my age) couple, who seemed pleased and surprised to win this "award."

We sang another song, or rather the singer and rock band did, and the preacher, who was beamed in by closed circuit TV, preached on "Getting Your Edge Back," using a text from 2 Kings 6, concerning the prophet Elisha and a floating ax head, whose sharpness provided the "spiritual" edge the preacher wanted to talk about. Most of what "getting one's edge back" consisted of was following the 14 rules the pastor saw as "spiritual essentials."

I stayed through the sermon but left during what I assumed was the final song.

As I have indicated, I am still reflecting on what I experienced, wondering what the rationale was behind each part of the 'liturgy,' who was the target audience, why this experience was so attractive to so many, and on what basis did I really find it lacking. Despite my reservations about it all, this experience has got me to thinking.

About H. Richard Niebuhr, among others. His book, *Christ and Culture*, describes several paradigms for the way the church has engaged with the world. My experience on this Sunday, led me to believe that the model this church represented was that of "Christ of Culture." This church enthusiastically embraced popular culture, particularly the culture of technology. Most of the sermon illustrations were taken from the field of technology or social media. The language of worship seemed to validate the culture of technology. Indeed, the world of technology and social media is the world in which this church swims, and swims happily.

As you may have guessed, I found the theological content of the worship "thin." I suspect that the folks who worshipped there and their worship leaders would find the worship which makes sense to me, "thick," if not dense. I was surprised at how small a role Jesus played in this service of worship. It seemed to me that there was a desire to avoid any creedal or explicitly theological claims, a desire to be free from such baggage. I did not see a cross anywhere. The only "cost" that was mentioned in connection with the faith was the pastor's admonition that believers should "work out" regularly, in the exercise of faith. There was no offering taken.

I left the worship feeling empty. And my ears hurt. But I don't think others felt that way. Most people seemed happy, upbeat, enthusiastic. They were not troubled by the "baggage" that was weighing me down. They seemed glad to be traveling so light. May God bless them.

I know that it is possible to engage in interminable debates, as our denomination has, and feel very weighed down by theological claims and counter-claims. Still, I wonder if Christian discipleship can ever really be so thin as to do without baggage altogether. In American culture, the happy face, can so easily become iconic, not just replacing the cross but depriving us of the joy of the Crucified's victory. And if we seek to travel so lightly, there may come a day when some of that confessional baggage is exactly what we need to help us bear witness to his victory. One thinks of Barmen, for example, which certainly divided the church, slowed it down, even weighed it down, at a time when many were enthusiastically embracing the reigning cultural paradigms.

I know we are not living in such tumultuous times, despite our attempts to dramatize the urgency of our witness. But I suspect that even the small witness we are called upon to make to Jesus Christ will involve more difficult things than facility with technology, celebration of the culture, and embracing the consumerist in us all.

One of the reasons we look back at the Civil Rights struggle is not just that its moral claims were, by comparison with today, so much clearer, but also because they were so much more significant, heavier, more full of theological baggage, and more costly. I would not want to go back to those days. However, I am grateful for those whose costly witness and whose theological baggage made a better world for all of us.

I worry about a church that so embraces the culture that all it has to offer to its disciples is an Ipod with a complete set of the Beatles' songs. One of the reasons we are in seminary is to ask whether giving that kind of gift as a mark of Christian discipleship reflects the story that has claimed us. If we no longer ask what kind of church God is calling us to be, then giving that kind of gift and even less costly ones will do just fine. We will not need much theological baggage in that case. But if we think God has something more for us to do, then we might have to ask more difficult questions and what is even harder, listen more attentively to the questions God insists on putting to us.

June 1, 2011

Do you think Jesus would have been on Facebook if such had been around in Galilee during the first century? Maybe so. He seemed to draw large crowds of people to him, some of whom, no doubt, "liked" him. At one point, at least, he called his disciples, "friends," and he seemed eager to engage with a variety of folks, from Pharisee to publican, women and men, children and their teachers. Moreover, Jesus used the means of communication available to him at the time, speaking to crowds from a boat, from a mountaintop, in the temple, through prophetic symbols (e.g., riding on a donkey into Jerusalem), etc. He had a message, indeed, was the message, which message he did not hide under a bushel basket.

And yet . . . . The gospels do not portray Jesus as a chatty person. His reticence is noticeable, not just when he chooses to go to a quiet place to pray, but even more in his silences (e.g., in the wilderness for 40 days being tempted by Satan and dealing with wild beasts, a kind of combat that does not lend itself to small talk), his refusals to explain "what he really meant," and in his abrupt responses to those who were all too willing to chat about the gospel (e.g., to the one who vowed to follow him anywhere, the response: "Foxes have holes and birds of the air nests; but the Son of Man has nowhere to lay his head.") (Luke 9: 58) How does one respond to that?

I don't think Jesus was an easy guy to chat up. As the Pharisees, not to mention the disciples might remind us, this guy was a little bit scary. And maybe that is why I have difficulty imagining him on Facebook. Facebook is designed to take the scary out of relationships, to provide a place where one can chat, keep up with friends, share news, offer support and encouragement, or occasionally share the silly or inane or catty or simply funny comment or picture. What strikes me as odd, and here I am sure I betray my generational obsolescence, is how willing we are to fill the space with chatter, sometimes about the most personal matters. We think that the virtual nature of this reality insulates us from the risk of real friendship.

I know I am leaving myself open to accusations of being a pig-headed Luddite. Complaining about the effects of technology on us is a bit like King Canute commanding the waves to cease. Good luck with that. And perhaps people like me said the same thing about papyrus or the printing press or telephone. I know. I know. I just wonder if virtual friendship is a means of filling the empty spaces that characterize so much of contemporary life with a kind of chatter designed to reassure us that we exist.

My wife tells me to hush, that my melancholy reflection on these matters are best reserved for inner conversations. She is probably right. Still, I persist in thinking that real friendship can never be virtual, that being Jesus' friend has always been a scary proposition, that learning to live with the silences is one of the ways we are drawn into Christ's life.

February 29, 2012

Things have changed since I was in seminary. I suspect this will not come as news to you, but every once in a while I kind of gulp at how different our world has become.

How so? I remember delving into card catalogs to find books in the library, or picking up a huge volume of a periodical index to locate a particular article. We used note cards, which could be arranged in such a way as to help us in writing research papers. Information, while not scarce, was not readily available, and had, in any case, to be searched out and found.

Recently, I read the following from a book review in the *Wall St. Journal*:

> If every image made and every word written from the earliest
> stirring of civilization to the year 2003 were converted to digital
> information, the total would come to five exabytes. An exabyte
> is one quintillion bytes, or one billion gigabytes—or just think
> of it as the number one followed by 18 zeros. That's a lot of digi-
> tal data, but it is nothing compared with what happened from
> 2003 to 2010: We created five exabytes of digital information
> every *two days*. Get ready for what's coming: By next year, we
> will be producing five exabytes every 10 minutes. How much
> information is that? The total for 2010 of 912 exabytes is the
> equivalent of 18 times the amount of information contained in
> all the books ever written. The world is not just changing, and
> the change is not just accelerating; the rate of acceleration of
> change is itself accelerating.[1]

All of which makes me very tired to think about. We don't have
much choice about changing. As one might say, it happens. And there
is no point in standing athwart this change and telling the world to stop.
King Canute tried that and Luddites in their day with about equal success. And yet there is something about this flood of information that
makes me wonder if any of us will be able to survive this tsunami intact.
Indeed, I wonder if this unceasing flow of information will not just make
us smaller, narrower, with each person trying to somehow manage his
or her trickle of information. They will become "Experts" no doubt, but
their expertise will be so narrowly focused as to render it trivial.

400 years ago, long before the "Information Age," the French
mathematician and philosopher, Blaise Pascal, wrote of the then bur-
geoning field of astronomy: "The eternal silences of these infinite spaces
terrifies me."[2] That's kind of how I feel after reading about exabytes.
Overwhelmed.

The psalmist knew something also about being overwhelmed.
"When I look at your heavens, the work of your fingers, the moon and
the stars that you have established; what are human beings that you are
mindful of them, mortals that you care for them?" (Ps 8:3) Yet even
amid the abysses, even in the face of the flood of information, even while

---

1. Shermer, *"Defying the Doomsayers," Wall St. Journal*, Feb. 22, 2012.
2. Pascal, *Pascal's Pensees*, 61.

looking into the terrifying "infinite spaces," there is One who cares for us, who made us "a little lower than God." (vs.5)

The good news is that God does not abandon us to the flood, but enables us to navigate in new ways (an ark, a mouse, a cursor, what else?) to bring about a measure of space and peace and hope to build and to plant. The important thing is not to "lose heart," not to be so overwhelmed as to fall into paralysis or despair. Floods can do that to you, just as the "eternal silences of infinite spaces" can as well. Or the flood of things you need to do today: writing papers, preparing for tests, completing a myriad of other tasks.

In the New Testament, it is clear that Jesus was besieged by folk needing help. (Cf. Mark 4–6, for example), which he provided. Yet Jesus in those gospel stories never seems to be in a hurry, never seems eager to please or to check something off his list. He works. He goes from town to town. He teaches and heals and feeds people, and the flood of human need never seems to overwhelm him, anymore than a raging storm on the lake. We may cry, "Teacher, do you not care that we are perishing?" (Mark 4:38) But his "Peace, be still," is able to calm the wind and the sea, and even render the flood of information heading our way into fruitful channels of witness in our world.

Chapter 21: Coming to the End

March 31, 2004

I have been invited to preach a sermon next week for the students at Queens University of Charlotte. The topic I was asked to address was the sin of sloth. I am not going to do that. Instead, I thought I would talk about joy. Joy is the gift of the gospel and only in its light can we discern the shadowy distortion of that which would prevent us from receiving it. The shadow can be seen only in the light of the gift. Joy's great gift is to take us outside of ourselves into a realm where, for the sake of its beauty, we gladly lay aside our self-absorption, and find ourselves "lost in wonder, love, and praise."

The reason I mention all of this to you, who are otherwise very busy people, is that I know this has been a long and difficult term. It began with snow and ice, cancelled classes and then make-up classes, various health concerns, in some cases, loss of family members, all of which has made this term a long, hard slog. On such a long march, one can grow tired, even slothful—not lazy, but despairingly trudging along, just hoping it will all be over soon.

Well, the end is nigh. The even better news is that our end as revealed in the Easter story is also nigh and that is great, good news. What defeats sloth is Easter, the joy that can say with gladness, "He is risen! He is risen indeed." That fact undermines our grim determination simply to finish and tie up loose ends, and instead, surprises us with the unexpected laughter of the empty tomb. He is not where we thought he should be. "He is not here." (Mark 16:6) "Why look for the living among the dead?" (Luke 24:5) Why miss the joy of the gospel for the sake of merely "finishing"?

I drive to work every day through a tunnel of Bradford pears, blossoming cherry trees, redbuds, and other trees and shrubs that are proclaiming the glory of God. I am sometimes struck at how easy it is for me to miss their created glory in thinking about all of the things I have to do that day, all the chores that must be finished. By the time I get to work, I am grimly serious about the unfolding day, so full am I of self.

Sloth is being weighed down by one's gravity; joy is being lifted up by Christ's levity. In any case, the end is coming and it is, despite our dead seriousness, happy.

I thought I might share a verse or two from Coleridge's *The Rime of the Ancient Mariner*, with the college students. That poem knows a good deal about sloth and how it can turn us so far into ourselves that we become like a ship that is dead in the water. There is no wind propelling our sails. Then, only a miracle of the Spirit can liberate us from the clutches of our despair, and enable us to bless the gifts with which God has so richly blessed us.

> He prayeth best, who loveth best
> All things both great and small;
> For the dear God who loveth us,
> He made and loveth all.

The end is coming and it is a surprising gift, even for those studying for exams. Fear not and work hard. This end always surprises us with its joy, whether on the road to Emmaus or in the garden of an empty tomb, or at the conclusion of a difficult term.

November 30, 2005

Father Alexander Schmemann wrote the following in his journal:

> The source of false religion is the inability to rejoice, or rather, the refusal of joy, whereas joy is absolutely essential because it is without any doubt the fruit of God's presence. One cannot know that God exists and not rejoice. Only in relation to joy are the fear of God and humility correct, genuine, fruitful. Outside of joy, they become demonic, the deepest distortion of any religious experience . . . . Somehow 'religious' people often look on joy with suspicion.[1]

Skepticism about joy (and even the reasons to be joyful) is part of what it means to live in the modern world. At best joy seems an ornamental emotion, at worst a kind of empty 'happy face'—both of which imply a desire to look away from the harsh realities of suffering and injustice

---

1. Schmemann, *The Journals of Father Alexander Schmemann*, 129.

so pervasive in our world. And indeed, if joy were a human emotion or something we had to contrive, then the skeptics would be right. But at the heart of the gospel is this unexpected, often unwanted, unprofessional, uncredentialed, unmanageable gift that seeks us out—at the grave of one's parent or in the nursing home of an ancient relative or amidst preparation for a final exam at seminary—a gift that blurts out the open secret that there is a reason to smile, even to laugh, because Jesus is Lord, the Crucified is the Victor.

Idols, whether ancient or modern, are much more solemn than a babe wrapped in swaddling clothes, and they demand a much grimmer seriousness than does this child.

So, as we approach the end of this term, and with it, the prospect of Christmas, I hope you sense the joy of the pilgrimage, and discover the laughter that always surrounds those who dare to undertake the ridiculous, impossible, yet joyful work of ministry.

March 21, 2007

The end is nigh. The end of the spring term, that is.

As will no doubt be the case at the Grand Assize at the end of time, there will always be certain souls who will request an "extension." I can easily see myself in this company, pleading, "Lord, when did we see thee hungry or thirsty or naked or in prison?" Matthew 25 does not depict a Jesus who is very big on "extensions."

Or to take another parable, this time from Luke 16, the parable of the rich man, "who dressed in purple and fine linen and who feasted sumptuously every day," and Lazarus, a poor man covered with sores, who sat at his gate longing to eat "what fell from the rich man's table." As you will remember, both the rich man and Lazarus die, and the rest of the parable concerns the rich man's request for an "extension." If he was given one, he could at least warn his brothers of the fate that will await them if they do not show mercy in this life.

The rich man's request for an "extension," you will recall, receives a negative, with Father Abraham telling him that if those who remain are unable to find mercy in the gospel Moses and the prophets proclaimed, they will not find mercy, "even if someone rises from the dead."

Americans, Scott Fitzgerald wrote, always believe in the "green light," which is one of the reasons it is so difficult for us to understand the gospel. We don't really believe in "the end," even for ourselves. *Memento mori*, remembering that we are going to die, so important to the ancients, seems to us almost un-American. Terms, however, like lives, eventually run their courses, and the end comes with the inevitability of judgment.

Because our faith in "the green light" is so strong, we don't like to talk much about judgment, though scripture is embarrassingly full of such talk. The only thing more sure than judgment, scripture insists, is the identity of the Judge. He is mysteriously more gracious than any "green light," and more certainly our Judge than any contrived self-condemnation. He is our end, the end for rich and poor, virtuous and failure, the wise and the foolish. And his end, his judgment is a gift, the surpassing gift of his presence.

When the last curtain truly falls, this One, we are told, will wipe away every tear from our eyes. Who would want to avoid this end? Who, in the face of this Judge, would want to ask for an "extension"? Do we have a field to buy? Some cows to round up? A wedding to attend to? No. Disciples of this Lord have long since lost their fear of the end, and have even welcomed its arrival, knowing that there is no better place to be than to be found in the presence of this Judge who is also our Redeemer.

So, remember Father Abraham, the sheep and the goats, the thief in the night, even the withered fig tree, and stay as far away from "extensions" as you possibly can. You will be glad you did. You will be able to welcome the end and embrace it as the gift it is.

As a very old goat, as a rich man who often has had second thoughts, as one who is constantly surprised by deadlines obvious to others, I will have mercy on those for whom an "extension" is necessary (i.e., those who have suffered a broken leg, the loss of an immediate family member, shipwreck, etc.) and who request it, but I take seriously scripture's dire warnings about asking for the same. And I hope you do too.

March 28, 2007

A hymn that is not sung so much anymore, except at the occasional funeral, but used to be sung a good deal, is, "Abide With Me." This hymn's lyrics offer an extended meditation on the transience of the created order and the abiding presence of God's eternal faithfulness. One of its verses reads as follows:

Swift to its close ebbs out life's little day,

Earth's joys grow dim, its glories pass away.
Change and decay in all around I see.
O Thou who changest not, abide with me.

All of which sounds to me more like a paean of praise to Aristotle's
Unmoved Mover than to the God of Jesus Christ. Still, the hymn does
possess a very strong sense that life, work, even a spring term, all come
to an end. Indeed, the hymn's sense of an ending indicates in some ways
how un-modern it is, which is, perhaps, why I like it so.

We are approaching not only the end of this term but also, for a few
of our students, the end of their time here. Commencement will take
place at Selwyn Ave. Presbyterian Church at 10 a.m. on April 21st. That
"end" will mark the "beginning" for those graduates, as they scatter to
undertake ministries of various sorts.

But I keep coming back to the hymn. It takes our ends seriously,
and construes God's eternity not in terms of timelessness but in terms of
God's faithfulness and presence. Implicitly the hymn asks, "Is God faithful even in the face of the changes in life? In the scattering that scatters us
from each other at the end of term? In the face of death that scatters us
all? Will that end define who we are?"

This hymn does not deny death or seek to avoid it but confesses that
we have another end. Easter, the hymn insists, has written a resurrection
ending that is the true meaning of God's faithfulness. That is what Ezekiel
found in the valley of dry bones, seeing an Israel scattered and defeated
and left for dead, only to be rattled together by the Spirit of God. That is
what the post-resurrection narratives tell us of the risen Lord, who interrupts our despair and reveals himself to us in the breaking of bread. That
God is faithful means that death cannot do the one thing it seeks to do,
namely, separate us from God and, in Jesus Christ, from each other. Our
ending is written by Another, not death.

So, at this end of term, we can rejoice that our end is not finally one
of loneliness or being scattered to the winds but sharing in the life Jesus
Christ has made for us in his service. That is our end in this life and in the
life to come. The last verse of the hymn sings:

Hold Thou the cross before my closing eyes;
Shine through the gloom and point me to the skies;
Heaven's morning breaks, and earth's vain shadows flee;
In life, in death, O Lord, abide with me.

April 23, 2008

When I served congregations as a pastor, I never paid much attention to academic occasions. I don't mean to imply that I thought they were unimportant, but only to note that they were at the margins of my consciousness.

Since moving to Charlotte, I have participated in enough of these services to feel maybe not quite a veteran of them, but at least a happy participant. I enjoy seeing, for example, the various robes and hoods that people wear. I take pleasure in my job of "hooding" our accomplished graduates. The group pictures, the academic processions, the worship and music, all lift my heart. I like the whole "show."

The Reformed tradition is not big on the "show." If we wear robes, they are usually black, and we try not to draw attention to ourselves. (I remember once hearing John Leith wickedly observe that in his experience of listening to many sermons, a preacher's profundity was inversely proportional to the colorfulness of his or her robe.)

But at commencement, the academy tends to let itself go: beautiful colors and lots of them, much processing and recessing, joyful singing and celebrating, moments of 'hooding" and proudly wearing the colors of a new degree. And that is as it should be.

Commencement bears some resemblance to the final celebrations found in the book of Revelation, when at the end of all things, St. John the Divine sees a new heaven and a new earth, none of which seems to be dressed in Puritan simplicity but rather is described as a riot of colors. The New Jerusalem possesses a radiance like jasper; its walls are encrusted with jewels—sapphire, agate, emerald, onyx, carnelia, chrysolite, topaz, chrysoprase, jacinth, and amethyst. The gates of this city are constructed of pearls and its streets are gold. Is this the kind of city a Calvinist could possibly dwell in? Happily?

Well, we may have to learn how to do that, however difficult it might be, but perhaps commencement here can help teach us what to expect there in terms of joy and gratitude and exuberantly colorful celebrations.

November 12, 2008

Karl Barth died on Monday evening, December 9, 1968. He had been working on a lecture dealing with the unity of the church, when he was interrupted that evening by two phone calls. The first was from his godson,

Ulrich Barth, who was discouraged and to whom Barth quoted a verse from a hymn about Christian hope. Later that same evening, about 9 p.m. he received a call from his old friend and colleague of some 60 years, Eduard Thurneysen. He had called Barth to chat and discuss with him the gloomy world situation. At the end of their conversation, Barth is reported to have said, "But keep your chin up! Never mind! He will reign!"[2]

He will reign. The phrase came from Christoph Blumhardt, a kind of Pentecostal-Socialist, who had impressed Barth in the early 20th century with his unapologetic faith in the power of Jesus Christ. "Jesus is Victor" was one of Blumhardt's favorite affirmations.

Barth had been working on an essay about the importance of the church and the gifts of its own witnesses, even from the past. "God is not a God of the dead but of the living," he noted, and "in him they all live—from the apostles down to the fathers [and mothers!] of the day before yesterday and of yesterday."[3] After the phone call, Barth did not return to his study, but went to bed, where he died peacefully that night. His wife, Nelly, found him the next morning when she came into his room to put on a Mozart record to waken him to a new day.

Barth was 82 years old when he died. The point of my rehearsing all of this for you is, simply, to be reminded of and draw strength from an 82 year old man, who in 1968 (a tumultuous year in Europe and in America and elsewhere), affirmed to his old and trusted and equally weary friend, "Jesus is Victor. He will reign."

This term is rapidly drawing to a close. I know you have much to do. In some ways, the temptation is not that you won't get it all done. You will. The temptation is that it will become so much of a burden that you begin to lose hope. There is gloom enough in our world of 2008, but perhaps we too could stand being reminded that the darkness does not have the last word, even at the end of this term. "Keep your chin up! Jesus is Victor!" Also for us.

March 31, 2009

In my theology class, the end of the course readings center on the doctrine of "last things," or more formally, "eschatology." This subject always

2. Busch, *Karl Barth*, 498.

3. *Ibid.*, 498.

seems to me to come too soon, i.e., before we have learned all we really need to know.

Since it deals with the end, we tend to think of the eschaton as a kind of blank finality that declares, as old movies used to do, "The End." However, the end of a term, even a difficult term, is not really about completion, nor is it about the fact that 12 weeks have passed or that an exam or paper has been written, and thus can be checked off the list. One hopes, indeed, that we are different people at the end of a term than we were at the beginning, but in truth the end of which scripture speaks has less to do with our completing something than it does with our longing, amidst the incompleteness of our lives, for that One who is our "Author and Finisher." He is the One who completes our baptism.

The truth is we will never finish our work; it will always remain incomplete. One of the great sins of our time is the conviction that we can organize ourselves into the Kingdom of Heaven, check off all our tasks, present ourselves as completed human beings before our Maker. Such a view strikes me as utterly hopeless, completely turned in on itself, denying, even fleeing from any sense of our neediness before God.

One of the readings for this past week's discussion was from the Heidelberg Catechism, Question 52, which asks, "What comfort does the return of Christ 'to judge the living and the dead' give you?" Here is a notion of the end that offers not a blank finality but a word of comfort. And what is the source of that comfort? "A. That in all affliction and persecution, I may await with head held high the very Judge from heaven, who has already submitted himself to the judgment of God for me and has removed all the curse from me . . . ."

How does one manage "ends" when one's work is never done? According to this confession, one does so with one's head held high, not out of pride or bravado, but out of gratitude for Jesus Christ, who suffered the end none of us will ever have to face, and whose grace completes our unfinished lives (and academic terms) with joy and confidence. The end has everything to do with this Lord, does it not? And not just the end of this term, but also the end of our lives.

December 9, 2009

Last week in theology class we read in the *Church Dogmatics* I/2 the section on "The Miracle of Christmas." There Barth is dealing with that part of the creed that confesses that Jesus was "conceived by the Holy Spirit, born of the Virgin Mary . . . ."

Barth does not think that belief in the Virgin Birth is a requirement for salvific faith but he does think the Virgin Birth means something and cannot simply be dismissed as the mythic fantasy of a more primitive age. The Virgin Birth, he thinks, is a sign, and works like all of Jesus' signs (miracles) to bear witness to the presence of God in our midst. In this respect, the function of the Virgin Birth is like that of the empty tomb, which far from proving Jesus' resurrection, nevertheless, bears witness to his triumph over death and the grave. The Virgin Birth and the empty tomb form, he says, "bookends" for the gospel account. They belong together and frame the story.

So what does the Virgin Birth denote? "The Virgin birth denotes particularly the mystery of revelation. It denotes the fact that God stands at the start where real revelation takes place—God and not the arbitrary cleverness, capability, or piety of man."[4]

I think that it is interesting that a theologian as prolix as Barth does not think theology is about clever explanations of biblical concepts. He attends, rather, to the miracle, which, he thinks, points to the mystery of Christmas. Children recognize this mystery better than the rest of us, who have learned to trust more in our cleverness and capabilities and piety than in the gifts God puts right before us.

As this term winds its way toward its end right in the middle of Advent and leaning pretty heavily toward Christmas, I hope that the Christmas miracle will be born anew in you. Further, I hope that you discover that the great gift of theological training is not to be found in our clever explanations or fervent piety, but in something as scandalously out of place in our world as a child placed in the manger by a mother, who, however baffled in her ponderings, obeyed God's word and received this mysterious gift.

Sometimes I hear students (and faculty too!) complain about how hard it is to understand certain scriptural texts. Was it supposed to be easy? Is the gospel self-evident? Is our Reformed passion for clarity and intelligibility not an obstacle at times to seeing the mystery of God's grace? A false faith can too easily multiply mysteries and become not so much child-like but simply childish. But the birth of Jesus Christ to the Virgin Mary is meant, I believe, to shut us up long enough to learn

4. Barth, *Church Dogmatics* I/2, 182.

how to kneel before that mysterious goodness we cannot contrive or give ourselves, but which has, nevertheless, become incarnate in our world, blessing us in the form of this miraculous child.

March 31, 2010

Some denominations and churches (e.g., many Episcopalians, the Orthodox Church, and others) baptize new believers on the Saturday night before Easter, Holy Saturday. Leading the rather sheltered life of a Southern Presbyterian, I found this to be a "new" practice, though, in fact, it has been the practice of the church for centuries. Such a celebration of the sacrament is deeply scriptural (i.e., Rom. 6!) and altogether liturgically descriptive of what baptism is about. We are baptized into Christ's death, Paul tells us, in order to be raised in him (on Easter Sunday) to newness of life.

This year, because of the snows, our 'spring term' will "die" on Holy Saturday, April 3rd. This has been a long term, and for some a very long term, full of snow and delays and make-ups, and other heavier burdens. To reach the end of anything can be a gift, but to reach the end of this term seems a particular blessing.

Yet, as I write this, I can look out my window and see dogwoods and redbuds blooming, and nearby hyacinths, tulips, daffodils, and little purple flowers whose name I do not know. Such a lovely sight. And I am tempted, as perhaps you are, to rejoice in all of that beauty and simply be glad the snows are past.

But the term *dies* on Holy Saturday. Our work here is not just interrupted by a beautiful spring but in fact our work leads us to Holy Saturday, to that tomb where, if there is to be new life at all, it will have to come from beyond the grave. Here too we are saved by grace. That is what it means to be baptized into Christ's death. We have to wait and do nothing and let him do his work on us. Which is hard for us to do. When Paul preached such a gospel, he was asked if this meant that we could just sin that grace might abound, a question, which, when it is really asked, always makes me think that the gospel has really been heard.

I am not suggesting that we should sin like that or that we should cease to study or read or engage with the world. But I think the only way to Easter is through Good Friday and the terrible silence of the grave, a place where we can do nothing but trust in that One whose death conquers death, and whose life is at work in ours even when we cannot see it. Much of Christ's work is done underground. Holy Saturday should remind us of that.

A final note. Like Jeremiah's buying a plot of land in Anathoth, being baptized into Christ's death on Holy Saturday is a sign of hope. Both scenes look like dead places. But God is at work in places where we have long since given up expecting much. That is why Holy Saturday has much to give our church, why there is reason to hope, also for us.

Blessings on you as you enter this Passion week.

December 1, 2010

Academic terms do not saunter to an end, I have found; they rush to the finish line. In any case, I have been panting lately. And of course, the fall term ends with the beginning of Advent, when everything else is ramped up to warp speed and life itself seem to be a mad race toward Christmas and the end of the calendar year.

Recently, I have been reading a little book of essays by Alan Jacobs, entitled, *Wayfaring*. The last essay in the book is really a call to faithfulness. Jacobs thinks that whatever good the Christian church has ever brought into the world is a fruit of its faithfulness to Jesus Christ. Yet he knows that faithfulness is never directly achieved. It always comes as a gift from the One who alone is faithful. Pursuing something abstract like "faithfulness," strangely does not yield the desired result.

He notes, for example, that C. S. Lewis wasted years of his life seeking the peculiar stab of longing he called "joy"—only to discover in the end that, like a stray cat, it declined to come when called, but appeared when it was least looked for.

Faithfulness, Jacobs argues, is not so much a task or a state, as it is clarity of focus. He writes:

> Last Christmas Day my pastor, Martin Johnson, spoke of his youthful habit of walking in the forests of British Columbia at night, guided only by moonlight. It was remarkable how far he could see by that meager illumination, how delicately beautiful the landscape was. The only problem was that he couldn't see where to put his foot for his next step, and as a result he took plenty of tumbles. The light of Christ, said Martin—the light that is Christ—is just the opposite: it illuminates with perfect clarity your next step, but blots out the surrounding territory. Christ is the Word of God, and the psalmist tells us that that

word is a lamp unto our feet and a light unto our path: it shows us where to place one trembling foot, but it does not make us authoritative cartographers of the whole territory. It's worth remembering that when people ask Jesus the cartographic kinds of questions—'Will many be saved or only a few?'—Jesus tells them to mind their own spiritual business . . . . 'What is that to you? Follow me. One step at a time.[5]

Jacobs then goes on to tell a story about Pope John Paul II, who was asked in an interview how he felt when faced with the reality that by the year 2000, there would be more Muslims in the world than Catholics. The question was meant to be provocative. But to this inquiry the Pope replied placidly that Jesus Christ proposed a still more frightening question, namely, "When the Son of Man comes, will he find faith on earth?" That is, "Will there be any faithful believers at all?" And yet the same Jesus, John Paul reminded [the reporter], had already given this word to his fretful and anxious disciples: 'Fear not, little flock, for it is your father's good pleasure to give you the kingdom.' [This is the same verse (Luke 12:32) that Karl Barth found apt in addressing a frightened church facing the onslaught of Naziism, a word he quotes at the conclusion of the preface to the Barmen Declaration.] The whole business of counting the adherents of religions in order to find out which of them 'has a future' is a process at best distracting from, at worst hostile to, true faith."[6]

So, as we come to the end of this term and the beginning of Advent, what are we afraid of? Final exams? Final papers? Presentations? No doubt all of us have anxieties about many things. The good news is that God is faithful, and though we might be afraid of all the things we can see, the whole cartography of anxiety, our faithfulness consists in simply not being afraid to take the next step. There is light enough to do that. "Fear not, little flock, for it is your Father's good pleasure to give you the Kingdom."(Luke 12:32)

March 28, 2012

When I was a little boy, my father used to travel some. He would come home on the train in the evening. I can remember longing for evening to come so I could see my father again. In our neighborhood there was a

5. Jacobs, *Wayfaring*, 150.
6. *Ibid.*, 151.

string of sycamore trees lining both sides of the street. I would climb the tallest one in front of our house, as high as I could go, from which perch I could see the Dallas skyline, and pretend to see Union Station, where my father would soon be arriving.

I can still remember the smell of the end of a summer's day on the south side of Dallas. It was a strange mixture of creosote, sweat, heat, and a kind of burnt up dryness that seemed to match my longing for my father to be home. I always associate the end of the day with my father coming home. Everything would be all right then. We would be family again around the supper table. I would be safe at home.

There was a good tiredness about the end of those days, a tiredness that did not seem to be quarrelsome or anxious but a tiredness that was strangely content even in weariness itself and glad for the gift of the end of the day. So, at the end of this term and at the end of this day, I wish you quiet contentment, good rest, and refreshment.

March 20, 2013

I remember reading a story about Martin Luther, perhaps apocryphal, who was asked once what he would do if he knew the world was going to end the next day. He replied that he would plant a tree. His point being that whatever else the future holds for us, it should never paralyze us with its anxieties or distract us from our tasks of faithful service. Jesus is still Lord, even if the world ends. He is Lord over every end, even The End.

Last Saturday, after class, my wife and I caught a flight to San Antonio in order to help our 2 year-old granddaughter, Birdie Carey, celebrate her birthday. As grandfathers go, I am not much, but my wife, on the other hand, is a world champion grandmother. In any case, I enjoyed watching Birdie celebrate her special day. She liked the balloons and she had no problem putting away the cupcakes, but she seemed baffled and embarrassed when we stood around and sang "Happy Birthday" to her. She did not know what to make of that and began to tear up, so reluctant was she to be the center of attention for all those people. Of course, at that exact moment, she won my heart. Which is not to say that she didn't have it before, but her modesty was so appealing.

What she loved best was playing with her grandmother, listening to her read stories, trying on her grandmother's shoes and walking around the bedroom in them, and serenading us with songs she had learned in nursery school. (e.g., "Itsy Bitsy Spider" and "Farmer in the Dell," songs that I am glad to know are still in the nursery school repertoire.)

One day, I watched as she sat in a big chair listening to her grandmother read. Her neck was arched and she was hanging on every word. She looked so beautiful. As I watched and listened, I thought how good God is, how lovely are the creatures God has made, and what a gift are such brief, happy, moments.

I worry about the world into which this child will enter, and if I am not careful, I can make of my worries quite an idol. In theology class, as we come to the end of our spring term, we have been studying the doctrine of "Last Things," and more particularly, the nature of Christian hope. What are we to hope for? The Christian hopes, Barth writes, by looking toward the future, armed with certain weapons of the Spirit, which he calls "*alacritas, hilaritas,* and (following Calvin), *laetitia spiritualis*": cheerful readiness to serve, confidence in the victory of Jesus Christ, and spiritual joy or joy in the Holy Spirit.[7]

One can learn a certain amount of alacrity, hilarity, and spiritual joy from watching a two year-old play with her grandmother, which is, perhaps, the best way to learn to hope. "See what love the father has given us, that we should be called children of God; and that is what we are." (1 John 3:1)

July 24, 2013

Not too long ago, my wife and I went to the movies, where we saw a number of previews of movies I will probably not go to see. I would say there were about 10 of these and of the 10 at least half of them dealt with some version of the end of the world. The other half dealt either with vampires or zombies. The end of the world previews depicted the destruction of well-known symbols of "the world as we know it," like the White House, the Capitol building, New York skyscrapers, Los Angeles freeways, etc.

As I sat through these previews, I began to wonder why our culture, or at least Hollywood, seemed focused on such lavish displays of destruction and terror. Sometimes I think it has to do with the pointlessness of so much of American life, a life so secularized that no transcendent reference is possible. Such a life almost longs for "the end" if only to relieve the tedium of trying to live without one. A life centered simply on one's

7. Barth, *Evangelical Theology,* 155.

career or success or self is finally a deeply boring thing, and eventually one grows tired of one's self. Wholesale destruction might at least put an end to all of this, and maybe, if violent and destructive enough, pierce our numbness and allow us to feel something again.

At other times I have wondered if this fascination with the destruction of symbols of American life might not bespeak a kind of guilt, perhaps even shame over the affluent emptiness of our culture. Fundamentalist preachers used to do this sort of thing, pointing out the manifest failures all around us ("You got trouble, right here in River City.") in order to drive us toward repentance or some more material goal. Maybe these movies seek to remind us that in a world of vast suffering, we do not deserve the comfort or affluent lifestyle so many enjoy. We deserve a bit of destruction. A little bit of karma going round, so to speak.

But whatever theory accounts for these displays of massive destruction, I think they all reflect a deep hopelessness about our world and its future that is troubling. A couple of weeks ago, I had a conversation with a woman (not a student) who wanted to talk "theology" with me. I am always nervous about such encounters, knowing that in the past I have been asked to supply 'answers' to questions I cannot answer, and so inevitably, disappoint. In any case, this woman had been told by family members and friends that we were living in the final dispensation and soon the end would come and the good people would be going to heaven to watch the bad people get their just deserts in a fiery catastrophic end. (As Dave Barry might say, "I am not making this up.")

As I listened, I kept thinking of those movie previews on the silver screen. What could be more hopeless than resting at ease in Zion while watching other sinners be consumed by flames? Is that the gospel? Is that the end toward which we are all headed?

One of the reasons people are tempted to believe these versions of the end is because we do not talk much about the end ourselves. We have left the field to others. I don't mean that we need to come up with an equally dramatic scenario that will compete with the fireworks and destruction that the cinema or more religious types seem to purvey. Jesus, in fact, warns against that. What I mean is that we need to do a better job talking about Christian hope. What is our end? What is our chief end? What is the meaning of our lives, and our world, both of which will one day come to an end?

In medieval times, preparing for a good end made sense precisely because such preparation could testify to the whole purpose of one's life.

We don't worry about such matters today, and in fact, are concerned far more with living 'too long' than with being cut off before making adequate preparation.

Well, we are coming to the end of our summer term. It has been a long one for many of you, but perhaps not long enough for others. The end of this term is Saturday, but its "end" is to prepare you for service in the ministry of the hope of the world, even Jesus Christ. He is our end, indeed, he is our 'chief end.' He is our hope. He is the one who "welcomes sinners and eats with them," in this life and in the life to come. To come to this "End" is not a catastrophe anymore than it is a vindication of our self-righteousness. The good news of the gospel is that everyone gets to come to this End. He is unavoidable, just as his grace is relentless. To hope in him is to be confident that neither our despair nor our guilt, neither our self-righteousness nor our boredom can separate us from the piercing love of this End who has determined to be our End as well.

So, rejoice and be glad! The End is nigh, as is our end this term.

March 19, 2014

In my office there is a print of a Pieter Bruegel (1525–1569) painting depicting laborers in the field on a hot summer day, harvesting wheat. Some are taking a lunch break and relaxing under the spread of a tree. Others are resting in the shadows, finishing off their bread and cheese. Still others have already gone back to work and are cutting the wheat with their scythes, stacking and binding it in sheaves. There are two things that strike me about this print: 1) The sun is shining and everything looks warm and vibrant and full of life. On a cold, gray day, like today, one can almost feel the heat coming off that field where these laborers are at work. All of which I find strangely encouraging. 2) What these folks are doing is "bringing in the sheaves."

We don't have that song in our hymnbook, which is more the pity, but the other day I had occasion to look again at the verses. I had always thought the hymn sentimental and vaguely revivalistic but it is neither. It sings of the labors of one's life and finally, of offering those labors and that life to God. It is true that the idiom is agricultural but the words are not treacly or sweet. The song sings about the end: the end of one's labors, the end of one's life, and the One who makes of our ends an occasion for rejoicing. Listen:

Sowing in the morning, sowing seeds of kindness,
Sowing in the noontide and the dewy eve;
Waiting for the harvest and the time of reaping,
We shall come rejoicing, bringing in the sheaves.

Sowing in the sunshine, sowing in the shadows,
Fearing neither clouds nor winter's chilling breeze,
By and by the harvest and the labor ended,
We shall come rejoicing, bringing in the sheaves.

Going forth with weeping, sowing for the Master,
Tho' the loss sustained our spirit often grieves;
When our weeping's over, He will bid us welcome,
We shall come rejoicing, bringing in the sheaves.

There is a harvest coming for all of us. The song knows this, but the harvest is not an occasion for sadness or despair but rather joy. "We shall come rejoicing, bringing in the sheaves." What is hard is "winter's chilling breeze," those losses which cause our spirits to grieve. But winter does not last forever, nor do our tears. The end is happy, a time of rejoicing.

I am thinking about all of this for two reasons: 1) I am approaching the end of my time of work here. I am about to bring my sheaves in for the harvest. With only two more classes to teach, I am apprehensive, somewhat nervous about what lies ahead, but not sad. The work in the fields has been a joy from day one here. Here, it has always been summer. And at the end, there can only be rejoicing, and not just for what has been done or even for the ending, but even more for what is yet to come. He will bid us welcome and we shall come rejoicing bringing whatever sheaves we have. 2) The second reason is much more mundane but no less theological. It has to do with the fact that you will be much more happy in bringing in this term's sheaves by not asking for an extension. Endings are gifts. Don't spoil them by asking for an extension. There are no extensions (or at least that is the default position of the dean as he approaches his end here). So, if you want to come rejoicing, bring in your sheaves without asking for an extension! You too will then rejoice. I promise . . . .

June 24, 2014

Terry Teachout is a drama and art critic, who writes for various publications. Although I know little about art, I have found Mr. Teachout to be a trustworthy guide in these and other matters. Recently, he was given an award for commentary, and in response, he was called upon to say a few words. He spoke about the difference between art and propaganda, between the mystery (and complexity) of beauty and the false simplicity of ideology.

Though he was talking about art, I found myself thinking about theology and particularly, preaching. Mr. Teachout is suspicious of art that seeks "to persuade," art that puts itself in service to a "cause" that hopes "to change the world." He cites Oscar Wilde's observation that genuine art never tries to prove anything, an observation that applies to theology as well.[8] Instead, art, like a good sermon, seeks, as Flannery O'Connor has written of short stories, "to show and not to tell."

Do not think that what Teachout is arguing for is some notion of "art for art's sake," devoid of any moral content. There he would disagree with Oscar Wilde. The artist's commitment to reality, to its mysterious complexity and hard truths, is, Teachout maintains, profoundly moral, particularly in its refusal to alter reality, or offer a false picture that however beautiful is less costly or true.

I am aware that the New Testament employs language of transformation, and one of the promises of the Gospel is that those who follow Jesus Christ will, in fact, be transformed. The Gospel does not leave people the way they are. But neither does the Gospel reduce the mystery of being human to something formulaic or falsely simple. Faith always makes things more difficult, a fact that Job knew only too well and his "friends" completely overlooked. And it is surprising how little Jesus exhorts his disciples to undertake this cause or that. Rather, he tells them to follow him.

And he tells them parables, stories. These parables, like a work of art, do not prove things. Instead, they open a window in which Kingdom reality is disclosed. Those listening to these stories soon find themselves in a world that at first glance looks familiar but is soon strangely unsettling. This is a world the listeners can recognize but precisely so, come to understand that they did not make, a world which they inhabit but in the company of others they did not select. The stories can both baffle and unnerve, shock and trouble those who have ears to hear. These parables complicate things. Yet, they give us, to borrow a phrase from Teachout, "a glimpse of the transcendently true."

---

8. Teachout, *"Acceptance Remarks"* on receiving the Bradley Prize, June, 2014.

Which is what a good sermon always does. No one, the Fourth Gospel reminds us, "has ever seen God." There are no proofs that a sermon can offer. None. Rather, "it is God the only Son, who is close to the Father's heart, who has made him known." (John 1:18) Sermons point to him.

This is my last note as dean to be sent to you. I offer it as a kind of witness to the One who has so happily complicated my life for the past 38 years of ministry, and particularly, for the past 13 years of serving you as dean. There is nothing easy about his ministry, and there are no proofs or arguments or even causes that render such ministry self-evidently useful or easy or even clear. There is only the hard, unyielding grace of his love, the narrow path of his expansive calling, the indirect, often stumbling joy to be found in his service. I offer this witness to you in gratitude for the gift this work has been to me. There are no easier ways of ministry, even in service to what we might call our best causes. Transformation happens in the complicated, messy, unproven, and often unclear life of discipleship. But there it does happen, and in his company we become what we were not, and in his service, we find our true freedom.

May God bless and keep you, and most especially keep you from the sentimentalities of right and left that would reduce ministry to something easier, cheaper, boring and false. But that can only happen if the Holy Spirit intervenes and reveals to us the mysterious beauty of our life in Christ. I pray that gift will be yours in the coming days, weeks, and years, and that the church and the world will be blessed by your ministry and witness.

First Steps . . .

(Homily delivered to entering students,
September 8, 2010)

Let us pray: Before we knew you, O Lord, you knew us and loved us; before we ever took a single step toward you, you were with us, drawing us to yourself. We do not pretend that these steps here are important because we are taking them; only because you have called us do we dare to make this beginning. Be with us. Give us the freedom to be courageous, bold, even content with our own foolishness in setting out on this venture. Help us not to look back but only toward you, grasping your hand that is leading us. We pray in Christ's name. Amen.

"And immediately they left their nets and followed him."
Mark 1:17

It is presumptuous to think that these are really your first steps. Part of what so undermines the church's witness today is the conviction so easily held by contemporaries that faith begins only when it begins with me, only as I think it or feel it or affirm it. We are, we sometimes think, the authors of our own faith, and whatever it is we believe is only authentic to the extent that we create ourselves or the religious world we seek to enter.

Nothing is more inimical to scripture's witness than such a conviction, which is perhaps why we have such a hard time understanding scripture today. We live, as did Israel of old, in houses we did not build, drawing from cisterns we did not fill, benefitting from vineyards we did not plant. Most of us, or at least many of us, cannot even remember our baptism, our entrance into the Christian community. All of us can testify in ways large and small that we were loved before we ever knew what it meant to love, or even knew how to love, and that our journey of faith has been, for the most part, a journey not of our own creating but of stumbling, bumbling, and occasionally coordinated and surprisingly beautiful following, often dimly sometimes much too clearly seeing a step or two ahead.

Yet today we do take some serious steps together, some new steps, and make a beginning. The text is the familiar one of Jesus' call to discipleship of those who, we read, "immediately" left their nets and followed. I don't presume that this student orientation can stand by the sea of Galilee to make this parallel work, or that you or I find ourselves easily placed into this story. But I do suspect that there is something about going to seminary that suddenly makes one awkward, something that does require us to take a new step, perhaps even a first step on this long road of study.

Anytime one undertakes something new, one may well feel awkward and unsure at the moment. And in truth, there is a great danger that at some point we think we have gotten good at this walk, that we have mastered it and no longer feel it to be so strange. I hope today that you let its strangeness, the awkwardness of this moment, the scariness of what you are about to get into stay with you for a moment. Don't lose that or let it go by too quickly. This is a big step. What happens here will be different from what you are used to, though perhaps not so different from what Christian people always have faced. Still, I want to acknowledge with you today, the bigness of this step, the fact that you are leaving now some things behind. Perhaps not nets or fishing but time, and some forms of work, perhaps even some family responsibilities – none of which are small things. Whatever else you have gotten yourself into, it is not trivial.

Nor is it tedious. And that is the other point, I want to make. As awkward and scary as all this may seem, I hope you sense also that this is going to be a very exciting journey. Nets and fish can be left behind, not with sacrificial sadness for what has passed, but because the prospect of following Jesus Christ is so surpassingly consuming, interesting, fulfilling, something like a pearl of great price that is worth selling everything for to possess, something like a coin that you have lost for a long while, only to find and cannot wait to celebrate its finding with neighbors. I am here to tell you that whatever you have gotten yourself into, whether you are taking Hebrew or Church History or The Christian Life, will be for you the time of your life. Something that has been lost, something that you have been looking for for a long time is about to take your breath away.

And what is that? Those courses? Well, maybe, but in them, through them, through worship, through service, through the fellowship you have with each other, through our life together, you will engage with much more than those courses –as stimulating as they are and will be. We think you will not be following them or your professors or this school but Jesus Christ. It is his call to which you are responding and it is he you will be following. The first steps here are but steps along a journey you have been making with him for a long time, and are meant simply to prepare you to go a much longer distance in his company. He is the joy of the journey, the gift that makes all our awkwardness a kind of dance. Welcome to dance class. We are looking forward to learning how to dance with you and with the One who insists on bringing us to this dance. Amen.

The Joyful Feast

(A sermon preached before Charlotte Presbytery,
October 16, 2012)

Let us pray: In Jesus Christ we see, O Lord, that your ways are not our ways, or your thoughts our thoughts. Which is why we praise you and rejoice in the gift of your encompassing love. You are not the lonely god, who stands in silence far away and demands that we justify ourselves, but you are the God who talks to us, who feeds us, even when we have no money and our labor seems poor indeed. So speak to us now that we might see something of your beauty and rejoice in the gift of our life together in you. We ask this in the name of Jesus Christ our Lord. Amen.

"Ho, everyone who thirsts, come to the waters; and he who has no money, come, buy and eat!...For as the rain and snow come down from heaven, and return not thither but water the earth, making it bring forth and sprout, giving seed to the sower and bread to the eater, so shall my word be that goes forth from my mouth; it shall not return to me empty . . . " Isa. 55:10,11

"And the Pharisees and the scribes murmured, saying, 'This man receives sinners and eats with them.'" Luke 15:2

"On the last day of the festival, the great day, while Jesus was standing there, he cried out, "Let anyone who is thirsty come to me, and let the one who believes in me drink." John 7:37

The truth is I have always dreaded presbytery meetings. I say this without any pride, rather with some degree of shame but it is nevertheless true. I have tried to do better but like so many areas of my life, I have had little success in reforming or improving. Sanctification is hard, a hard gift to receive.

I have thought about why I am so poor at this. Maybe, it was what happened 39 years ago, when I was examined on the floor of what is now Grace Presbytery for 2 hours, with the fathers and brothers (there were very few mothers and sisters then) trying to determine if I was a universalist or just a poor theologian. They finally decided on the latter and let me in, but the experience was not a particularly happy one and ever since I have always felt a little bit like I needed to watch my step when I entered the councils of the church.

But "murmuring" against presbytery, despite its long and at times satisfying history, is really too cheap an answer and besides, one of the most important things a presbytery does is examine its candidates for ministry. Few things are more important. But when we do that what should our life together be like? What should these occasions be, for example, when a candidate is received into presbytery, what should we say to such a person and what should we remember and what should we affirm at such times?

At a recent meeting of Charlotte Presbytery discussing some painful issue – I forget which – I was struck by an aside one of the ministers almost casually let escape from his lips. He said, plaintively, "We don't know each other, really. We are a bit lonely. We don't know how to talk to each other." Maybe I paraphrase or embellish, but I think that is what he said, and it struck me as true.

I am an introvert and often have difficulty talking with others, and for this reason as well as for other better ones, I usually hate that part of the liturgy that requires me to "pass the peace" to my neighbor. I don't like to "pass the peace." I know it is hospitable and sort of friendly, and I am not opposed to it, but it always seems to me to be a bit of an artifice, as if worshipping the Almighty needed an ice-breaker or two to get started. But what if that pastor was right and we are a bit lonely, gathered here only for business, forced by polity to check this task off our list before doing the real work of ministry elsewhere? What is it that holds us together or even invites us to care for one another?

The text I have selected for today is one that offers a vision of plenty, not of scarcity; of exuberance not of timidity, a vision not of small things, but a robust, fullness of plenty. The prophet is preaching to folk who have had their fill of bad news, who are tired of losing, who are trying to digest what it means to be displaced persons, exiles, even scattered, lonely, struggling refugees. These folks don't much like themselves anymore and see only the things they have lost: their land, their temple, their king. It's not just that they are discouraged; it's worse than that. They just don't see the point anymore. And whatever future they can discern is one that has little to do with their past. That whole business is over. These folks, if they are to have any future at all, think they will have to reinvent themselves.

Which is lonely and in truth boring work. The temptation is to develop a new strategy, a new business model, as they say. But the vision that is offered by the prophet is entirely un-strategic, as un-strategic as a resurrection. "Ho, everyone who thirsts, come to the waters; and he who has no money, come, buy and eat!" This vision of plenty makes no strategic sense at all; it is so unsophisticated, so naïve a gift. Come and eat. If anything, it seems to be a kind of implicit critique of strategies, of church growth strategies, of getting hip to the culture strategies, even of transformative language strategies. "Why," the prophet asks, "why do you spend your money for that which is not bread, and your labor for that which does not satisfy?" Why indeed? The implication is that you are starving yourself to death on that stuff. The prophet thinks you will be bored to tears by your many reinventions. You will lose the only joy that brought us into this life and into this ministry in the first place. What is wanted is to "practice resurrection." But how does one do that?

So why did you enter the ministry? Why did you become an elder? Why do you worship? Why do we gather here? Is what we are doing here all that essential?

"Hearken diligently to me, and eat what is good, and delight yourselves in fatness . . . " I think that people who enter the ministry and dare to undertake such an errand in the modern wilderness, do so because they have fallen in love. They have seen something beautiful, something delightful, and that vision has fed their soul and they want, perhaps hesitantly, perhaps inarticulately, perhaps reluctantly to be a part of that. Does that sound too strange to you, too pious?

The other great Swiss theologian of the 20th century was the Roman Catholic, Hans Urs von Balthasar. He has noticed how often the prophets and apostles speak of being seduced by God, of falling in love with God's enterprise in this world, with its beauty, of how discipleship is rooted in a journey that goes out in joy and is led forth in peace, how the Lord is sought not where we want him to be but where the Lord gives himself to be found, and is called not as if this Lord were far away but because this Lord is nearer to us than we know.

The wisdom of this world, the wisdom of philosophers, particularly of theologians since the Enlightenment, tells us that the way to proceed is always first of all to discover the truth and then and only then, learn what is good, and finally, if there is time, discover the beautiful. But the beautiful is ornamental, perhaps something extra but not essential. It's the truth that matters and is, along with goodness, what we fight about most of the time. But von Balthasar thinks the gospel works just the other way around. Only someone who has been charmed by the beautiful, seen a vision that delights in the flourishing of human life, tasted and seen and eaten food that is "without money and without price," only such a one could have the daring to leave her nets and, in the gospel's word, "follow." We hear a word and sense the deep beauty of the Kingdom and it captures us. We are a bit like the police interrogator in the movie *The Lives of Others*, who is sent to spy on a subversive artist and hears the artist playing the piano and finds himself transported by the music into seeing another person, and suddenly, he knows, *he knows* the artist is a good man. God is sneaky that way, and as Jesus' parables so often indicate, this God does not play fair. We are drawn into his world by these words, absorbed into this story that slowly captures our hearts with its beauty and power. And the next thing we know, we risk following. We risk leaving our nets. We start eating this stuff, without money and without price. Perhaps worst of all, we start needing each other.

And then in the company of this Lord, whose ways are not our ways, and whose thoughts are not our thoughts, we begin to learn what is good. We begin to see things we had missed or so easily overlooked: the homeless person on the street, the prodigal son, the unbearably righteous elder brother, the hungry child, the boarded up school, the hopeless neighborhood, the church itself which we thought we knew, even the presbytery we thought we could do without. He opens the eyes of the blind – he still does that—which is how we learn most of the time to see what is good, how to see what we would have otherwise missed or even refused to see. And he gives us the strength to go into such places of the heart, of scripture and of our world and of the church, messy as they all are, and embrace what we find there. His word does not return to him empty. His word has captured your heart.

And we come, von Balthasar argues, last of all, to the truth. The truth is always last and takes a lifetime to discover. Only in the Enlightened West would we ever think that it would be easier than that, cheaper, more direct: a project, perhaps; a formula, some grand theory we could quickly master. No, the truth comes only in his company and only with a lifetime of following, of being trained by him (and others whom he has called) to look for wine and milk bought without money and without price. Such a truth, like grace itself, is a gift, never a possession, never a strategy, never a program, but a way, a following, and in Jesus Christ, a following in the company of others.

I don't know if von Balthasar is right or not but I suspect that most of our journeys of faith, most of the paths disciples have always trodden have been messy ones, often wandering and complicated, often full of struggle and at times, deep weariness. But God is perhaps most sneaky in not letting us wander such paths of discipleship alone. I have wondered at times, if it is that which is most offensive about presbytery – not the boring reports, the angry conflicts, the collection of egos, the financial struggles, but the fleshly, messy, life together that so offends me. How much cleaner things would be on my own. How much more agreeable things would be if I could dispense with what is going on in Rockingham or Steele Creek, with Sardis or Grier Heights. But the God who invites us to "come, buy and eat, without money and without price," is the God who insists on our coming together to this feast, to this joyful feast.

I am not sure that I will ever love presbytery as it deserves to be loved, but it does seem to me that the most crucial theological question that is before us today is this: Can we love the church? Not the church of our dreams. Those dreams kill the church. Can we come to the feast of the church that is given to us? Are we hungry for this wine and milk?

I suspect we are hungry for other things and often view presbytery and the church itself as a necessary evil that exists only to help us support this cause or that. This mission or that. This movement or that. And I suspect that the church, not to mention presbytery often fails and fails miserably to meet our expectations. It brings so much baggage with it. But the Giver of this feast does not really ask us if we can love a cause or if we have a church that meets our high standards. Rather, this joyful feast is set for those whom he has gathered around his word and sacrament, and those folk may not be the ones we would have chosen. "Those who love their dream of a Christian community more than the Christian community itself become destroyers of that Christian community even though their personal intentions may be ever so honest, earnest, and sacrificial."[1]

I believe the church to be at the heart of the gospel. There is simply no Jesus Christ without those sluggards whom Jesus has drawn to

---

1. Bonhoeffer, *Life Together*, 36.

himself. The question before us is whether we can love the church today, or whether we love other agendas, even I will say, other missions, more. I know that in the heavenly city there will be no temple because its temple is the Lord God the Almighty and the Lamb. But the Lord God Almighty and the Lamb is the feast, the joyful feast, to which even presbytery is called to bear witness and in its own way reflect in our messy, frustrating, and at times, even happy life together. Maybe this is one of those truths that becomes clear only after a lifetime of struggle. I hope so. I want to affirm it. Even more, I want to celebrate the feast of our life together with you. "Ho, everyone who thirsts, come to the waters; and he who has no money, come, buy and eat!"

Bibliography

Akst, Daniel. "Say It As If You Mean It," a review of *Sincerity* by Jay Magill." In *The Wall Street Journal*. New York: July 8, 2012.

Alston, Wallace. "The Education of a Pastor-Theologian." In *The Power to Comprehend With All The Saints*. Ed. by Wallace Alston and Cynthia Jarvis, Grand Rapids: Eerdmans.

Auden, W.H. *Collected Poems*. New York: Vintage, 1991.

———. *The Dyer's Hand*. New York: Vintage, 1989.

Barth, Karl. *Church Dogmatics* I/2. Ed. by G.W. Bromiley and T.F. Torrance. Edinburgh: T. & T. Clark, 1963.

———. *Church Dogmatics* III/4. Ed. by G.W. Bromiley and T.F. Torrance, Edinburgh T. & T. Clark, 1961.

———. *Church Dogmatics* IV/1. Ed. G.W. Bromiley and T. F. Torrance, Edinburgh: T. & T. Clark, 1961.

———. *Church Dogmatics* IV/2. Translated by G. W. Bromiley. Edinburgh: T. & T. Clark, 1958.

———. *Church Dogmatics* IV/3/1. Ed. by G.W. Bromiley and T.F. Torrance. Edinburgh: T. & T. Clark, 1961.

———. *Dogmatics in Outline*. Tranlated by G.T. Thomson. New York: Harper & Row, 1959.

———. *Evangelical Theology*. New York: Holt, Rinehart and Winston, 1963.

———. *How I Changed My Mind*. Richmond, Virginia: John Knox, 1966.

———. *The Humanity of God*. Richmond, Virginia: John Knox, 1969.

———. *The Word of God and the Word of Man*. Translated by Douglas Horton. Grand Rapids: Zondervan, 1935.

Berry, Wendell. *The Selected Poems of Wendell Berry*. Berkeley, Counterpoint, 1998..

Bonhoeffer, Dietrich. *Letters and Papers from Prison* in Dietrich Bonhoeffer Works. Vol 8 ed by Eberhard Bethge et al., trans. Isabel Best et al. Minneapolis: Fortress 1997.

———. *Life Together* in Dietrich Bonhoeffer Works. Vol 5. ed. by Geffrey B. Kelly. Translated by Daniel W. Bloesch and James H. Burtness. Minneapolis: Fortress, 1996.

———. "Protestantism Without Reformation: Report on the American Church, 1939" in *A Testament to Freedom*. Ed. by Geffrey B. Kelley and F. Burton Nelson, New York: HarperSanFrancisco, 1995.

Book of Common Prayer (Proposed). Church of England, 1928.

Book of Common Prayer. Protestant Episcopal Church in the United States of America. New York: Oxford University Press, 1928.

Book of Common Worship. The Theology and Worship Ministry Unit for the Presbyterian Church (U.S.A.). Louisville, Kentucky: Westminster/John Knox, 1993.

Boswell, James. *Life of Johnson*. New York: Oxford University Press, 2008.

Bottum, Joseph. *The Christmas Plains*. New York: Image, 2012.

Brown, Clarence. "Introduction" to *Hope Against Hope* by Nadezhda Mandelstam. New York: Modern Library, 1999.

Brown, Robert McAfee. *The Spirit of Protestantism*. New York: Oxford University Press, 1965.

Browning, Robert. *Pippa Passes and Shorter Poems*. Westerville, Ohio: Odyssey Press, 1947.

Buechner, Frederick. *Now and Then*. New York: HarperSanFancisco, 1983.

Busch, Eberhard. "*Lobe den Herrn*" in *Karl Barth 1886–1968 Gedenkfeier*. Zurich: EVZ-Verlag, 1969.

———. *Karl Barth: His Life from Letters and Autobiographical Texts*. Translated by John Bowden. Philadelphia: Fortress, 1976.

Calvin, John. *The Institutes of the Christian Religion*. 2 Vols. Ed. John T. McNeill. Translated by Ford Lewis Battles. Philadelphia: Westminster, 1960.

Capon, Robert. *The Parables of Judgment*. Grand Rapids: Eerdmans, 1993.

Chesterton, G.K. "The House of Christmas" in *As I Was Saying*. Ed. Robert Knille. Grand Rapids: Eerdmans, 1985.

Currie, Thomas W. Jr. *The History of Austin Presbyterian Theological Seminary*. San Antonio: Trinity University Press, 1978.

de Cherge, Father Christian. "Last Testimony." In *First Things*, August-September, 1996.

Dickens, Charles. *Hard Times*. New York: Barnes & Noble Classics, 2004.

Dickinson, Emily. *The Complete Poems*. Boston: Back Bay Books, 1976.

Donne, John. *The Complete Poems of John Donne*. Ed. A.J. Smith.London: Penguin Classics, 1977.

Dostoyevsky, Fyodor. *The Brothers Karamazov*. Translated by Constance Garnett. New York: Barnes and Noble Classics, 2004.

Duncan, David James. *The Brothers K*. New York: Bantam Books, 1992.

Eliot, T.S. *Selected Poems*. New York. Harcourt Brace and Company, 1963.

Frank, Anne. *The Diary of a Young Girl*. Translated by B. M. Mooyaart-Doubleday. New York: Bantam Books, 1993.

Gerson, Michael. "Mark Souder and the Case for Grace," in *Washington Post*. June 4, 2010.

Greene, Graham. *The End of the Affair*. New York: Penguin Books. 1971.

Hardy, Thomas. *The Collected Poems*. London: Wordsworth Editions Ltd.1998.

Hauerwas, Stanley. *Prayers Plainly Spoken*. Eugene, Oregon: Wipf and Stock. 2003.

Herbert, George. *The Temple*. Brewster, Mass.: The Paraclete Press, 2001.

Hopkins, Gerard Manley. *Gerard Manley Hopkins: The Major Works*. Oxford: Oxford University Press, 2009.

Jacobs, Alan. *A Theology of Reading: The Hermeneutics of Love*. Boulder, Colorado: Westview Press, 2001.

———. *Original Sin, A Cultural History*. New York: HarperOne, 2008.

———. *Wayfaring*. Grand Rapids: Eerdmans, 2010.

Jenson, Robert. *Systematic Theology*. 2 vols. New York: Oxford University Press, 2001.

Lasch, Christopher. *The True and Only Heaven*. New York: W.W. Norton & Company, 1991.

Lewis, C.S. *Reflections on the Psalms*. New York: Harcourt, Brace and Company, 1958.

Lischer, Richard. *Open Secrets*. New York: Doubleday, 2001.

Lundin, Roger. *Emily Dickinson and the Art of Belief*. Grand Rapids: Eerdmans 2004.

MacIntyre, Alasdair. *After Virtue*. Notre Dame, Indiana: University of Notre Dame Press, 1984.

Mandelstam, Nadezhda. *Hope Against Hope*. Translated by Max Hayward. New York: Modern Library, 1999.

McGill, Arthur. *Death and Life: An American Theology*. Eugene, Oregon: Wipf and Stock, 2003.

McGinley, Phyllis. *Times Three*. New York: Viking, 1960.

"The Martyrdom of Saint Polycarp," in *Early Christian Fathers*. Translated and edited by Cyril Richardson. Library of Christian Classics, Vol.I. Philadelphia: Westminster, 1953.

Meilaender, Gilbert. *Faith and Faithfulness*. Notre Dame, Indiana: University of Notre Dame Press, 1991.

Migliore, Daniel, ed. *The Lord's Prayer: Perspectives for Reclaiming Christian Prayer*. Grand Rapids: Eerdmans, 1993.

Milosz, Czeslaw. *Milosz's ABC's*. Translated by Madeline Levine. New York Farrar, Straus and Giroux, 2002.

Neuhaus, Richard John. *Freedom for Ministry*. Grand Rapids: Eerdmans, 1992.

Newbigin, Lesslie. *The Gospel in a Pluralist Society*. Grand Rapids: Eerdmans, 1989.

Norris, Kathleen. "Wasted Days" in *The Christian Century*. September 23, 2008.

O'Connor, Flannery. *Flannery O'Connor the Complete Stories*. New York: Farar, Straus and Giroux, 1971.

Park, Clara Claiborne. *Rejoining the Common Reader*. Evanston: Northwestern University Press, 1991.

Parler, Jan. *For the Beauty of the Earth*. Charlotte, NC: Privately Published 2010.

Pascal, Blaise. *Pascal's Pensees*. Introduction by T.S. Eliot. New York: E.P. Dutton & Co., 1958.

Pearson, Hesketh. *The Smith of Smiths*. Pleasantville, New York: Akadine Press, 1999.

Peguy, Charles. *Basic Verities*. Translated by Ann and Julian Green. New York: Pantheon, 1948.

Plantinga, Cornelius. "Deep Wisdom" in *God the Holy Trinity*. Ed. Timothy George. Grand Rapids: Baker Academic, 2006.

Rutledge, Fleming. *The Undoing of Death*. Grand Rapids: Eerdmans, 2005.

Sayers, Dorothy. *Letters to a Diminished Church*. W Publishing, 2004.

Schmemann, Alexander. *The Journals of Father Alexander Schmemann 1973–1983*. Crestwood, New York: St. Vladimir's Press, 2000.

Shakespeare, William. *Hamlet*. New York: Simon & Schuster, 2012.

———. *The Merchant of Venice*. New York: Simon & Schuster, 2009.

Shermer, Michael. "Defying the Doomsayers." A review of *Abundance* by Peter Diamandis and Steven Kotler, in Feb. 22, 2012 edition of *The Wall Street Journal*.

Stroud, Dean. Ed. *Preaching in Hitler's Shadow*. Grand Rapids: Eerdmans, 2013.

Study Catechism. Approved by the General Assembly of the Presbyterian Church (U.S.A.), 1998.

Teachout, Terry. "Freedom and the Role of the Artist." Comments on winning the Bradley Prize, June, 2014; www.bradleyprizes.org.

Teresa of Avila. *Collected Works of Teresa of Avila*. Vol.2, trans. Otilio Rodriguez, Washington, D.C.: ICS Publications, 1980.

Thomas, R.S. *Collected Poems*. London: Phoenix, 2004

Twain, Mark. *Huckleberry Finn*. New York: Bantam Classic, 2003.

Updike, John. *Collected Poems*. New York: Alfred A. Knopf, 2003.

Ware, Kallistos. *The Orthodox Way*. Crestwood, New York: St. Vladimir's Press, 1969.

Weil, Simone. *Gravity and Grace*. New York: Ark Paperbacks, 1987.

———. *Waiting for God*. Translated by Emma Crauford. NewYork: Perennial Classics, 2001.

Williams, William Carlos. *Selected Poems*. New York: New Directions, 1985.

Willimon, William. "Hard Truths" in *The Christian Century*. Feb. 2005, vol.122, no.4.

———. *Pastor, The Theology and Practice of Ordained Ministry*. Nashville: Abingdon, 2002.

———. "Preaching as Demonstration of Resurrection" in *Journal for Preachers*. Easter, 2014.

———. "Salvation" *Currie Lecture*. Austin Presbyterian Theological Seminary 2008.

Wolfe, Humbert. *Humoresque*. London: Ernest Benn, 1926.

Wood, Ralph. *Chesterton: The Nightmare Goodness of God*. Waco: Baylor University Press, 2011.

———. *The Comedy of Redemption*. Notre Dame, Indiana: Notre Dame University Press, 1988.

———. *The Gospel According to Tolkien*. Louisville, Kentucky: Westminster John Knox, 2003.

———. "Obedience to the Unenforceable" in *Flannery O'Connor Bulletin*. 1996–1997.

———. "Orthodoxy at a Hundred" in *First Things*. Nov. 2008.